Contents

Acknowledgements

I would like to thank all those who helped me in the writing of this book.

Bryce Evans, Dr Stephen Kelly, Michael Lavalette, Mike Simons, Cathy Cross, Marika Sherwood, Mike Brocken, Red Saunders, Roger Huddle, Syd Shelton, Peter Hain, Don Letts, Billy Bragg, Dame Cleo Laine, Rosemary Squires, Marty Wilde, Yuri Prasad, Colm Bryce, Ruth Pallesen-Mustikay and all those who took time to answer my endless questions.

This book is also dedicated to the memory of founding SCIF members, Hylda Sims and Karl Dallas.

About the Author

Rick Blackman has been a musician and anti-racist activist since the 1980s and has been a member of Love Music Hate Racism, Unite Against Fascism and Stand Up To Racism. This book is an adaptation of his PhD thesis.

Introduction

This book is a study of three musical anti-racist and anti-fascist organisations of the last 60 years: The Stars Campaign for Interracial Friendship (SCIF), Rock Against Racism (RAR) and Love Music Hate Racism (LMHR). Its purpose is to understand the social, political, economic and musical circumstances in which these three organisations arose and the fascist organisations they opposed in the three different eras in which they existed, SCIF: 1958-1959, RAR: 1976-1981 and LMHR: 2002-2020. It also seeks to explore the influence of subcultures in both the fascist organisations and their anti-fascist opponents and the role music played in each of the movements. The title *Babylon's Burning* comes from a song recorded in 1979 by punk rock band The Ruts, who were heavily involved in the second anti-fascist musical organisation RAR. Babylon is a word which appears frequently in reggae music and is used as a generic term to describe the oppression suffered by the African diaspora.

Cultural opposition to the political right is not unique to post-WWII British society. Such an opposition to the threat of persecution and oppression has a rich history throughout the world. The Edelweiss Pirates were a group of young Germans who were opposed to the Hitler Youth. They used music as one of their tools to organise against the Third Reich and they risked the concentration camp for their troubles. Operating under similar hazardous conditions, after Anschluss in 1938, the Schurlfs in Austria used fashion and music as expressions of their anti-fascism. The jazz loving and besuited Zauszaus did the same in the 1940s, in occupied Paris and under the Vichy government in the south of France. Hispanic-Americans articulated their grievances against American racism in the guise of Pachucos, street-sussed, well-dressed, music-obsessed night-clubbers, their movement culminated in the so-called zoot suit riots of 1943. Nova Canco, the Catalonian expression of cultural and linguistic autonomy, thrived in opposition to Franco in 1950s Spain. The Japanese Yitsakis displayed their displeasure to authoritarian rule in the 1960s by listening to Jazz and wearing 'foreign' Ivy League clothes, as did the Tropicalismo musical movement in Brazil in the 1960s. Most famously, American folk singer Woody Guthrie had the message 'This Machine Kills Fascists' emblazoned on his guitar.

This book in part is an investigation into how subcultures have interacted with both the far right and its opposition throughout the last 70 years. But whilst there is an emphasis on subcultures, there is a recognition from the outset that when discussing these groups, this discussion is about a minority of the teenage population in any of the periods examined. The vast majority of young people went happily about their lives without feeling the need to attach themselves to one particular tribe or another and it seems almost all have come through life relatively unscathed. However, minorities can, at particular times, have a profound effect on majorities, teenage or otherwise. So, whilst acknowledging the differentials, it is the impact that those young people who were active inside subcultures that is of concern in this work, not their size proportionate to the rest of their generation. Likewise, where racist and anti-racist activists are discussed, it is again important to acknowledge that the numbers of people that we are discussing falls short of the total population of the UK therefore the materials and recollections from those who were politically active serve as an indication of racist and anti-racist sentiment, not necessarily as a nationwide consensus.

In Britain, fascist organisations from Mosley in the 1930s through to the present-day Democratic Football Lads Alliance (DFLA) place much emphasis on the recruitment of young people. Much of the violence meted out to people of different ethnicities in the three periods discussed comes from members of teenage subcultures. British youth subcultures were a complex and somewhat idiosyncratic aspect of British life. They had tribalistic loyalties, based on music and sartorial styles and these cultural loyalties on occasion influenced their political perspectives. Teddy boys for instance, were very active in the Notting Hill riots of 1958 and were the perpetrators of some of the worst violence toward black people, a phenomenon repeated in the 1970s with skinheads and again in the new millennium with casuals. Conversely, the opposition to 1970s fascism was focused on a combination of two subcultures, reggae and punk. This symbiotic relationship between subcultures and fascist/anti-fascist movements did not exist in the rest of Europe.[1] Therefore, in order to understand the relationship between British youth and fascism/anti-fascism we have to look partly through the prism of subculture.

It is important to clarify some issues that arise throughout this work. The political organisations discussed in this book are outlined in the glossary at the end. Also included in the glossary is a guide to the musical styles, genres and subcultures that feature throughout. These guides will be expanded upon as each is discussed during the course of the book. For many academics, the quest for a descriptive terminology appropriate for the far right has proved problematic. Received wisdom dictates that the terms Fascist and Nazi apply only to those involved in far right politics prior to the WWII. Those active after the war are prefixed with the word 'neo'. However, this in itself has problems, as some like Oswald Mosley and Colin Jordan were active fascists before and after the war. Their politics did not change so there was nothing 'new' about them post-1945. Many of the fascist organisations that emerged after the war held identical politics to their pre-war ancestors, indeed many individuals in these organisations learnt their trade from those active on the fascist right in the 1930s. However, in order to avoid any confusion in terminology, the term 'fascist' has been used to describe them pre-war and 'neo-fascist' and 'far right' to describe them post-war. Furthermore, unless used contemporaneously, the designation Nazi has been avoided as this relates to a specific form of German fascism in the interwar period.

The history of British fascism is one of short peaks and long troughs. In each period discussed in this book, a pattern emerges, where every variation of British fascism achieved rapid success, electorally or as a street movement, which in turn was followed by an equally rapid demise. Subsequently, there were long periods of internecine fighting, recrimination and rebuilding. Much of the debate relating to British fascism and anti-fascism centres around two things. Firstly, definitions: were the organisations discussed in this work actually fascist? Argument abounds relating to strict definitions of what constitutes a fascist and these arguments will be developed throughout this book. Secondly, if we establish that organisations were indeed fascist, then why was it they did not succeed? Was it the actions of anti-fascist activists (and in this case musical anti-fascist organisations) that caused their demise or were there other factors at play? The argument around the effectiveness of anti-fascist organisations will also be discussed throughout.

Fascism is a European ideology, and although incubated across Europe in the late 19th century, its birth is in Italy, in the years after WWI. The success of fascist governments firstly in Italy in the 1920s, then Germany in the 1930s, means that much of the literature that exists relating to fascism concentrates on these two countries. Herein lies another problem; whilst Italy and Germany may be the clearest examples of fascism in action, other systems of totalitarian rule simultaneously existed, Franco's regime in Spain and Estado Novo in Portugal for example. Debate continues over the nature of the Spanish and Portuguese systems and whether the term fascist can be accurately applied to them. Similarly, some of the authoritarian regimes that grew up in Latin America in the post-war years have also been described as fascist. Although historically, international events and the growth of large fascist parties in Europe gave and continue to give succour to British neo-fascism, this book is not attempting to give a world history of fascism. This research is much more specific. It is the relationship between the growth of particular neo-fascist groups in post-war British society and how political organisations (and in particular, musical organisations) opposed to fascism, responded. But before we begin, it would seem prudent to first attempt some sort of broad definition of what fascism is. One of the leading scholars of fascism is Roger Griffin, who suggests that the essential ingredients of fascism are thus:

1. Opposition to a perceived decadence in society.
2. Palingenesis, the rebirth of nation.
3. Ultra-nationalism.
4. The subsumption of the individual to a highly centralised state.
5. Anti-communism.[2]

I will use these components as a guide to how we interpret far right thinking, but caution needs to be exercised here, as they are by no means an absolute definition. Each fascist organisation, party or government must be placed in its historical time and place. It grows organically from its own political, social, economic and cultural heritage. It would be folly to pass judgment on political organisations using this as a check list: 1/5 not fascist; 3/5 semi-fascist; 4 and over definitely fascist, as many 'traditional' nationalist parties display one or more of these traits.

In his 1932 *Doctrine of Fascism* Benito Mussolini outlines his philosophical conception of fascism but warns of the difficulties of too rigid an interpretation: "This shall not and must not be a robe of Nessus clinging to us for all eternity, for tomorrow is something mysterious and unforeseen. This doctrine shall be a norm to guide political and individual action in our daily life".[3] Fascism, therefore, must be malleable in order to survive and be relevant to both the changing world of Italy in the 1920s/30s and as a universal ideology. The difficulty in defining an opaque philosophy such as fascism was also attempted by German Marxist Clara Zetkin; writing in 1923 she commented: "Fascism possesses a mass character...[that offers on the one hand]...A special appeal to petty-bourgeois layers threatened by the decline of the capitalist order...[and on the other]...An asylum for all the politically homeless, the socially uprooted, the destitute and disillusioned".[4] Fascism's appeal is not singular, nor is its political essence, it appeals across all structural divides. The circumstances in which people become displaced, economically or ideologically, will depend upon the specific crisis being experienced by that person or society, but ultimately Zetkin argues that fascism is a philosophy based on despair and ultimately rooted in middle-class impotency and working-class inertia. A concentration simply on the methods and ideas of fascist thinkers is not enough to fully understand them as a historical force. A more comprehensive understanding of fascism is needed, and this involves using two key components, a critical theory and an interpretive theory. How they grow and why they grow.

There are different interpretations of fascism and peculiarities in each expression of the ideology. These peculiarities relate to the specific cultures and traditions of the countries they evolve in, for instance, the first point of Griffin's guide, decadence inside society. Decadence has been articulated in a variety of different ways. For Mussolini decadence was caused by the end of WWI, a perceived moral degradation caused by Bolshevism and the Russian Revolution. For Hitler and the National Socialist German Workers Party it was the political, economic and cultural influence of Jews that caused the decadence, whereas antisemitism played little part in Franco's thinking. Current far right thinking in Marine Le Pen's

Rassemblement National revolves around Islam as the cause of the perceived decay in modern-day France. The country that concerns us in this work, Britain, has seen fascist explanations for decadence develop from antisemitism in the 1930s, black immigration in the 1950s and Asian immigration in the 1960s and 1970s. This has now been superseded by anti-Muslim rhetoric. So, Griffin's five 'essential ingredients' of fascism are just that, ingredients not a recipe, as what is eventually served to us is a dish dependent on the culture, traditions and cuisine of the countries cooking the meal.

Hopefully these small points, addressed here, will clarify any ambivalence whilst trying to distinguish between the different types of fascists encountered and the right-wing populists with whom they sometimes align. What must be made clear though, is none of these terms are used flippantly and any group or individual given the epithet of fascist will have adhered to, at the very least, the above working definition of what fascism is.

The terminology for the political left also needs a brief explanation. Where possible the term socialist is used to describe a Social Democrat, ie someone who believes in the parliamentary road to socialism, in Great Britain mostly associated with the Labour Party. However, as the revolutionary left also use the term, it is used to describe them as well. Where possible the 'revolutionary left' is defined as such, but complex definitions and pedantic interpretations of Marxism complete with needless sectarian rivalries and splinter groups have been avoided. Instead, two broad strains of communist thinking have been advanced where relevant to this work. For simplicity's sake, they come under two terms of reference: Stalinist and Trotskyist. Where both may identify as Marxist, Leninist or Communist, there was no need to discuss the points of agreement, but where there was disagreement, it was necessary to draw these disagreements out. They centred around two important things. First, Soviet Russia and the Eastern Bloc, were they communist countries or not? Stalinists, ie those in the Communist Party believed that they were. Trotskyists argued they were either deformed communist states or fundamentally not communist at all. Secondly, how is communism achieved? The Stalinists had opted for the same parliamentary road as the Labour Party by 1951 and saw elections and gradual reform as the way to achieve communism. The Trotskyists believed in a working class, revolutionary transformation of society. As the century progressed, these disagreements would prove to be intractable and clarification is necessary now, as the theoretical positions of each left-wing group had a profound effect on their tactics and strategies relating to anti-fascism throughout each period discussed in this book.

Lastly, terminology in reference to race. Race, like racism, is a social construction and we are not, whatever the colour of our skin, from different races. However, prejudice against another person frequently manifests itself on the basis of skin colour so in this work it is thus defined. Therefore, in the discussions on racism, the prevailing generalisations have been used in order to group together people from similar countries and cultures. 'Afro-Caribbean' and 'West Indian' have been employed as a generic term for all the people from the multifaceted islands of Trinidad, Jamaica, Barbados and so on. Likewise, 'Asian' has been adopted to describe Indians, Pakistanis, Bangladeshis and anyone originating from the so-called Indian subcontinent, irrespective of their culture or religion. Lastly, the word 'black' is at times used to describe all of the above and the oft-forgotten men and women of African heritage who also resided in the United Kingdom during the period discussed.

Chapter One

The Origins of the Notting Hill Riots of 1958

After WWII dramatic changes occurred in British society. Although the National Government and especially Winston Churchill's rhetoric throughout the conflict had been to rid the world of fascism and to fight for freedom and democracy, the post-war reality was different. The Yalta and Potsdam conferences carved out the map of Europe into spheres of political and economic influence between the victors. Britain's attitude to empire also ran contrary to its grand statements of liberty for all, with one exception. The fight for independence that had escalated under Gandhi's tutelage and the subcontinent's enormous sacrifice during the war had left India pregnant with political expectation.[1] The 'jewel in the crown' was to demand self-determination and demand it very quickly. India and Pakistan won independence in 1947. However, this was not the case elsewhere in the British Empire. Although many colonies had burgeoning national liberation movements, no other country would see itself free from British rule for some ten years.[2] Continued colonial rule was in contradiction to the *Atlantic Charter;* this agreement between Great Britain and the USA was to be the blueprint for post-WWII independence and stated that "all peoples have a right to self-determination".[3]

The war had left large parts of Britain in ruins and the rebuilding of its cities at the end would necessitate a high demand for labour. Initially soldiers were requisitioned, and prisoners of war were used as labourers to help this process. Also, there were over 120,000 Poles who had stayed in Britain at the war's end.[4] This pool of labour was to prove insufficient and the government had to look further afield for fresh supplies. On 22 June 1948 the *Empire Windrush* docked from Jamaica and a new chapter in British society began. The small existing black populations in London, Liverpool and Bristol would not only grow, but this first influx of 492 West Indians was the beginning of a real and permanent change in British society. Many of the men who arrived on *Windrush* had served in the forces and been posted to Britain during WWII. Indeed, for the duration of the conflict, tens of thousands of Africans, West Indians and Asians had spent some time living in the UK, assisting with the war effort. In the year leading up to the D-Day landings over 100,000 black Americans were stationed in the UK plus an estimated 8,000 Caribbean troops.[5] The experience of the African American troops was markedly different to the Jim Crow or de facto segregation they had grown up with in the United States. Many testaments from black GI's state that there was little or no prejudice exhibited toward them from English people.[6] For the war's duration at least, there seemed limited hostility toward people of any colour who were willing to fight the Nazis. After the war in 1948 the Labour government passed the Nationality Act and granted United Kingdom citizenship to all people, of all colours from the colonies and ex-colonies. British passports were issued and the right to come and live in Britain was granted for life. Although at first, the flow was slow, Caribbean migration began to increase in the following years:

> In October 1948, the *Orbita* brought 180 into Liverpool, and three months later, 39 Jamaicans, 15 of them women, arrived in Liverpool…next summer, the *Georgic* brought 253 West Indians, 45 of them women. A few hundred came in 1950, about 1,000 in 1951, about 2,000 in 1952 and again in 1953. Larger numbers arrived in the next four years, including many wives and children of men who had settled here: 24,000 in

1954; 26,000 in 1956; 22,000 in 1957; 16,000 in 1958. Ten years after the *Empire Windrush* there were in Britain about 125,000 West Indians who had come over since the end of the war.[7]

During this time an active recruitment process had been initiated from the UK for industrial labour. For example, London Transport had by April 1956 sent several representatives to Barbados offering not just careers, but loans to pay for passage to England. These loans were to be deducted from wages after people had started work as bus drivers and conductors. This process would continue into the 1960s, expanding into Trinidad and Jamaica. The British Hotels and Restaurants Association also recruited from the West Indies and Conservative Minister for Health, Enoch Powell, sought Caribbean workers to clean the hospital corridors and nurse in the hospital wards of the newly founded National Health Service. Alongside this, similar recruitment had begun in the Indian subcontinent where by 1958 around 55,000 Indians and Pakistanis had arrived in Britain and would grow in the following decades as the graph below demonstrates.[8]

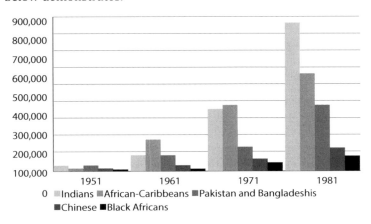

Estimated size of Britain's visible minority populations: 1951-1981.[9]

There were many reasons why people came to the United Kingdom. In the first instance, because they had been asked to do so, but also to better their lives. Those from the Indian subcontinent had seen their whole world turned upside down at the end of empire as the legacy of British imperialism—partition and sectarian violence—had seen millions die on the streets of India and millions more displaced. Faced with flood and famine, turmoil and tumult and without homes or hope, armed with a British passport and the offer of gainful employment, Britain seemed too good an opportunity to turn down.

Without any form of social security under British rule, many West Indians had historically seen emigration to the US as an economic solution to their financial woes. America was the world's most powerful economy, it had jobs, it had opportunity. It also had the music and the clothes that were so popular and influential to the development of indigenous Caribbean culture in the post-war years.[10] Although as subjects of the Queen and with many Afro-Caribbeans considering England as the 'mother country', America was the greater attraction. However, this main thrust of pre-war migration was to change post-war. Four things contributed: firstly, the positive experience during WWII of thousands of young West Indian men and women who had gone to Britain to assist in the war effort. Secondly, Britain's drive for labour to fuel their post-war economic boom. Thirdly, the 1948 Nationality Act which gave British citizenship for life to all colonial subjects and lastly the US McCarran-Walker Act of 1952 that restricted Caribbean entry into America.

Upon arrival into the UK, irrespective of their qualifications and what employment they had been promised, many of the jobs that black people were offered were menial and unskilled. As Fryer explains:

> Of the men who came here, a mere 13 percent had no skills, of the women only 5 percent. In fact, one in four of the men and half of the women were non-manual workers, and almost half the men (46 percent) and over a quarter of the women

(27 percent) were skilled manual workers.[11]

Many of these young men and women were employed in occupations they were overqualified to do; moreover, their remuneration for this labour did not have parity with their white co-workers. This, though, was only the beginning of their disappointment. They received a less than welcoming reception from their workmates. Many white workers were opposed to the employment of black workers at all, white was promoted over black irrespective of experience or qualification and demands for quotas to keep black labour to a minimum rang out from the factory floors. The usual recourse to justice for the working class, the trade union movement, was also a hostile environment for black labour. One example of this was the welcome that greeted new arrivals on the buses:

> In 1955 Wolverhampton bus drivers banned overtime 'as a protest against the increasing numbers of coloured workers employed'. The Transport and General Workers Union (TGWU) insisted that no more than 52 of the city's 900 bus workers should be black. A branch secretary said they were not operating a colour bar, but 'don't intend to have platform staff made up to its full strength by coloured people only'. West Bromwich bus workers staged one-day strikes in 1955 against the employment of a solitary Indian conductor, and a TGWU official said: 'I do not think there is any racial antagonism behind this'. The Bristol Omnibus Company refused to take on black crews until a boycott of its buses by black people forced a change of policy.[12]

The craft unions fared no better, as one black clerical worker sardonically explained: "*Union*: 'Get a job and we will give you membership.' *Employer*: 'Join the union and we will get you a job'".[13] Although the General Council of the Trades Union Congress (TUC) had a policy that denounced discrimination, at local branch level:

There was a gap, sometimes a wide one, between policy at top level and the attitudes at other levels. While the 'high command' of a trade union passes resolutions deploring colour prejudice, the local branches may operate colour quotas.[14]

This wasn't random and sporadic discrimination, the racism went right to the heart of the British establishment as Ron Ramdin's research shows: "The Conservative Government were determined to keep blacks and Asians out of the civil service".[15] When and if the day's work was done, a place to rest your head was to prove even more difficult to find.

No Blacks, No Dogs, No Irish

The level of open hostility to the new immigrants fitted into a prejudice that had been honed over decades. The Huguenots, German émigrés and Jews had all suffered. The Irish, Britain's first casualty of empire, had been systematically discriminated against for centuries: the skin colour this time was different, but the prejudice remained the same. With the enormous mobilisation of black troops stationed in Britain for the war's duration, it would be reasonable to expect a certain familiarity of the British with other races within living memory. However, the opposite appears to be true. According to Fryer half the British population had never met a black person and those that had had not formed any lasting friendships. Over 66 percent held a 'low opinion' of black people and when pressed, half of that 66 percent were 'extremely hostile'.[16] Furthermore many saw black people as:

Heathens who practised head-hunting, cannibalism, infanticide, polygamy and black magic. They saw them as uncivilized backward people, inherently inferior to Europeans, living in primitive huts 'in the bush', wearing few clothes, eating strange foods and suffering from unpleasant diseases. They saw them as ignorant and illiterate, speaking strange languages and lacking proper education. They believed that black men had stronger sexual urges than white men, were less inhibited and could give greater satisfaction to their sexual partners.[17]

Confines of space do not allow a full discussion of the reasons for this racism; however, suffice to say that the inhumane treatment of black people during the slave system followed by the racialised ideological justification for slavery and imperialism had permeated its way into every corner of British society.

Socially, a 'colour bar' was in operation all over the country. What this meant in reality was not just discrimination in employment and housing but an inequity in restaurants, hotels, dance halls, bars and pubs. Sometimes an open refusal into establishments would be in operation, where there would be signs prohibiting entrance to 'coloured people'. If they did make it into a pub to buy a drink and were unmolested, black people could stand at a bar, be ignored for the whole evening and not served.[18] Historian Robert Beckford and Senior Pentecostal Bishop Joe Aldridge explain that this racism wasn't just reserved for pubs, it even went as far as the church. Black members of the Baptist, Anglican and Methodist congregations described: 'Testimony after testimony of black church people... [who]...weren't made to feel welcome' and Bishop Aldrich recalled white ministers approaching black worshipers after service saying: "We'd prefer it if you didn't come back here".[19]

Slum housing was often the only option available to the new arrivals. Countless numbers of West Indians tell the tale of arriving at a property that they had been assured was available, only to be informed that it had been let when the colour of their skin became apparent. However, the living conditions of working-class white families were not of a superior nature. Indeed, the area that most concerns us in this chapter, North Kensington, was notorious for some of the worst housing in the capital. Portland Road, one of the main thoroughfares that runs through the district, was classified as unfit for human habitation as early as 1886 when social reformer Charles Booth created his colour-coded poverty map of the capital.[20] He concluded:

> The area to the west was black: as deep and dark a type as anywhere in London...[inhabited by] the lowest class which consists of some occasional labourers, street sellers, loafers, criminals and semi-criminals. Their life is the life of savages, with vicissitudes of extreme hardship and their only luxury is drink.[21]

Then, as now, one end of Portland Road remains firmly yellow and the other black.[22] Post-war tenants were bullied, exploited and harassed by ruthless landlords; however, there was some protection afforded them by legislation. This all changed with the passing of the Rent Act in 1957. Prime Minister Harold Macmillan's Conservative government removed the statutory restrictions on the rents of privately let accommodation which had been operative since the Great War. The government argued that by abolishing rent controls landlords would be encouraged to maintain, improve and invest in private rented property and thereby increase its availability and standard. In reality what the 1957 Act did was to enable unscrupulous and racketeering landlords like the notorious Peter Rachman to run amok in the area. Such landlords were now able to charge whatever rent they wanted, in whatever squalid condition. They proceeded to evict (often with menaces) the existing white tenants from their homes and install the recent émigrés from the West Indies in their place. Now with no statutory protection from the law and often unable to secure rented property elsewhere, the black community were given little choice but to accept the slums offered by Rachman and his like. For the already prejudiced white community, convinced 'their' jobs were being taken away, the eviction tactic adopted by Rachman and others was further fuel on the fire. Now, so they thought, their homes were not safe either. It was these small flames that the groups of fascists around Oswald Mosley and Colin Jordan were to fan in 1958 and 1959.

British Fascism

Although political groups in England espousing extreme right-wing views can be traced back to late Victorian and Edwardian society with groups like the British Brothers League and the Immigration Reform Association, British fascism, or a proto-fascism, emerged from the devastation of WWI in its first guise as the Britons Society, a nationalist, anti-immigration and fiercely antisemitic organisation. Formed in 1918 they began the dissemination of their ideas through a publishing house that continued its operations as the *Britons Publishing Society* up until the 1970s. Every fascist group used this publishing house; from the British Union of Fascists (BUF) to the National Front (NF).[23] By 1923, another far right group; British Fascisti (BF), had emerged. The BF was the first UK party to openly call themselves fascist and partly modelled the organisation on Mussolini's National Fascist Party. The BF may have been the first, but they were not alone for long, as other groups of right wing extremists soon operated up and down the country.[24] As we shall see, the history of the British far right is littered with tiny groups, organisations and factions all vying for hegemony and all infected with internecine rivalries that, combined with the external activities of anti-fascists, precipitate their demise.[25]

In 1922, Oswald Mosley was elected to parliament as the youngest MP in the house, at the age of 21. Initially a member of the Conservative Party, he crossed the floor to join the Labour Party, then joined the Independent Labour Party (ILP) where he served as a cabinet minister in Ramsey MacDonald's government. Shortly after this he left the ILP to form his own organisation, the New Party, which drifted further and further toward the right. After meeting Mussolini in 1932 Mosley fully

Oswald Mosley, London, 1930s. © Getty Images

embraced fascism as a political ideology, folded the New Party and formed the BUF in October 1932.

Operating outside of parliament was Arnold Leese. Leese had been a veterinary surgeon who had served in India and West Africa, and whose conversion to fascism would overshadow his only other contribution to society: *A Treatise on the One-Humped Camel in Health and in Disease.* Leese should always be thus remembered, as the parasite responsible for causing infections in camel's eyes (*Thelazia Leesei*) is named after him. Joining the British Fascists in 1924, Leese soon became disillusioned with them for not being sufficiently fascist and left. He then proceeded to create the Fascist League (FL) and by 1930 he had become leader of the Imperial Fascist League (IFL). A fanatical antisemite, after reading the apocryphal *Protocols of the Elders of Zion,* (which profoundly influenced Hitler) Leese developed a prototype for fascist activity that was revisited in the 1950s. Leese saw the IFL as a training ground in antisemitism and as an active organisation for spreading fascist ideas. This was to be done by IFL 'legions' split into two separate cells: 'active and passive'. The passive were the graduate associations: aristocrats, university alumni and professionals. They disseminated information, wrote the IFL newspaper, *The Fascist,* and produced many pamphlets. They also engaged in fundraising. The active cells were working class, hardened 'street fighters' used as muscle to protect the passive cells and terrorise both the Jewish community and sections of the left. Of course, this organisational model was not Leese's own creation, as Mussolini had initiated such a tactic in Italy and Hitler had operated along similar lines in the Weimar Republic.

Of the two men organising in London at the time, Mosley was a shrewder political operator and by 1933 the IFL had been eclipsed by the BUF, much to Leese's chagrin. Thus, the headlines for 1930s British fascism are taken by the BUF. Mosley was supported by press baron Lord Rothermere who owned the *Daily Mail* and the *Daily Mirror* newspapers. There were headlines such as: 'Hurrah for the Blackshirts' (*Daily Mail*) and 'Give the Blackshirts a Helping Hand' (*Daily Mirror*), although the subsequent withdrawal of Rothermere's support in 1935 was a setback for Mosley.[26]

> The ending of Rothermere's support and the turn to political antisemitism were crucial to the future history of the BUF. Dropped by the one section of the establishment which supported it and adopting policies that ensured that public opinion would become increasingly hostile, Mosley destroyed whatever small likelihood the BUF had of becoming an effective force in British politics.[27]

Whilst this certainly did not help the BUF, it removes the agency of those who organised the opposition to the blackshirts:

the constant arguments had *with* them, the agitation and propaganda *about* them, and the bravery of those who physically were *against* them. Two grandstand events planned in the pre-war decade for Mosley and the BUF both backfired.

The first was a mass rally at Olympia in 1934. At this event some 10,000 people attended; however, among those 10,000 there were many anti-fascists and the meeting descended into disruption and violence and caused a series of negative reports

Arnold Leese, 1930s

in the national media which led to the withdrawal of support from Lord Rothermere. The second event, two years later, was to provocatively march through a predominantly Jewish area of East London.

Despite a massive police presence essentially enabling Mosley's march the BUF did not pass. They were routed. They were stopped in their tracks in an area of Whitechapel by a united front of local people, Jews, trade unionists, communists and socialists. The Battle of Cable Street on 4 October 1936, although not the final page in Mosley's political life, nor the story of British fascism, marked the end of that particular chapter. With the outbreak of WWII, the BUF was proscribed and the ragtag collection of British Nazis were gathered up and interned under Defence Regulation 18b, which suspended *Habeas Corpus;* many would remain in prison until the war's end.

The 43 Group

The horrors of WWII, the estimated 58 million dead, the Holocaust and Europe left in ruins did nothing to dampen the spirit of the British far right. Thurlow estimates that there were some 24 different fascist groups of varying shapes and sizes at the war's end.[28]

Mosley was released to house arrest in 1943, although he was unable to undertake any activity until 1945. Only 16 weeks after VJ day (15 August 1945), Mosley addressed his first post-war rally to an audience of 600.[29] Ever the opportunist and political operator Mosley began to slowly rebuild his movement and political profile. No longer calling himself or his organisation fascist, he set about building a new party, the Union Movement (UM).

> Mosley himself had set aside an estimated £400,000 out of his large fortune, plus he anticipated those industrialists and aristocrats who had funded him before the war would do so again. Some 250 wealthy members of *The Right Club*

had stayed intact and underground throughout the war and saw the Blackshirts as their main defence against Jews and Communists.[30]

Whilst the war was raging in Europe, a group of disgruntled Tories, anti-Semites and fascists had formed the semi-clandestine coterie *The Right Club* whose motto was *Perish Judah!* The group had a dual-purpose: a) to exert pressure on the government to sue for peace as swiftly as possible and b) to consolidate British fascism into a central organisation.

A key member was A K Chesterton, one-time editor of BUF newspaper *The Blackshirt* who later went on to co-form the National Front. Another familiar face was Arnold Leese who despite his calls for the extermination of Jews as far back as 1935 was now, post-war, a holocaust denier. Leese published a journal called *Gothic Ripples,* another virulent antisemitic diatribe which contained a regular column *Nigger Notes.*[31] There were remnants of pre-war antisemitism in London and fascist meetings proliferated during the late 1940s. The Israel-Palestine conflict and the stationing and killing of British troops still not returned from WWII fanned these racist flames. Headlines in *The Fascist* cried: 'Our boys being murdered by Jewish terrorists in Palestine'.[32]

A new wave of far right groups appeared and hundreds of fascist meetings occurred each month up and down the country, although the epicentre was in London.[33] In opposition to these new parties and Mosley's UM in particular, was a new anti-fascist group, the 43 Group. The 43 Group was a combative organisation of Jewish ex-servicemen and women who had served in WWII. When they returned from fighting in Europe after the liberation of the concentration camps, they were shocked to find that fascist meetings were still taking place in London.

The group formed in response to these fascist meetings (estimated by leading 43 Group member Morris Beckman at an average of 15 per week), physically broke them up and were in constant opposition to any activities of the UM.[34] Unable to gain purchase in the wider political area and worried at the constant threat from the 43 Group, Mosley attempted to coalesce the disparate neo-fascists into one party. He concocted a six-point plan:

1. The smaller fascist cells should be absorbed into larger ones.
2. These new larger groups would in turn merge, ceasing all rivalry.
3. Their meetings would all follow the same programme 'Britain for the British'.
4. Book clubs and discussion groups would be welded into a national organisation for education for the upper and middle class.
5. All parts of the organisation would be drawn together to emerge as the Union Movement.
6. A massive publicity campaign would culminate in large rallies at the end of 1947.[35]

Mosley's planned mass meetings did not occur until 1948 and then were all disrupted by the 43 Group and proved to be a flop. This lack of success in UM and the resolute opposition of the 43 Group led to fratricidal rivalries inside the organisation. Some individuals left and denounced the UM, some drifted away and some defected to Leese's IFL.

Despite repeated requests from the Jewish community, the Labour government had allowed Mosley to organise his highly provocative meetings. The British Board of Jewish Deputies, whilst opposing Mosley, acquiesced to the government and their opposition was only in a form of words. Without the open defiance from the 43 Group it is possible that Mosley's influence could have grown. Counter demonstrations accompanied the UM almost everywhere they went and what support they had garnered from local people had waned and by 1950 the fascists again retired into the shadows.

The 1958 Notting Hill Riots

From 1951 to 1964 the Conservative Party was in government. Immigration ambled on throughout most of the 1950s and the reception to it, on the whole, was lukewarm. By the summer of 1958 the temperature was rising. Opposition to immigration arose in Nottingham and nascent prejudices over job insecurities and interracial relationships erupted into confrontation and two weeks of sustained rioting.[36] Tensions on the streets of west London were also starting to spill over into violence. Throughout July assaults against black people increased. At the end of that month a group of teddy boys attacked a (black owned) café in Askew Road, Shepherds Bush (just a mile west of Notting Hill), seriously injuring the owner and causing £250 worth of damage.[37] Sporadic and violent incidents occurred throughout the month, but on 24 August 1958 two separate and vicious attacks occurred, hospitalising several Caribbean men in Shepherds Bush and Notting Hill and resulting in a police chase and the arrest of a group of white men. There had been rioting of a racial, or to be precise, racist nature before in 20th century British history: anti-German rioting prior to the WWI, anti-black riots in Bristol, Liverpool and Cardiff in 1919, antisemitic riots throughout the 1930s, anti-Italian riots during WWII. There had also been minor disturbances against the newly arrived Caribbean communities in the late 40s and early 50s in Camden, Birmingham and Deptford, but the events about to unfold in Notting Hill were different in scale and focus as the whole nation's media concentrated their glare upon the streets of west London.

Whether there were any genuine grievances and difficulties over the incidents that occurred in the area prior to the riots is almost impossible to decipher. The level of invective and unadulterated racism from the locals who voiced concerns leading up to the riots and the absence of any objective police reporting makes any analysis difficult. The animosity toward the Caribbean community is clearly demonstrated by the countless letters to the editors each week in local newspapers. Many could be used as examples but are best illustrated by the following from the *Kensington News* which, although lengthy, is worth quoting in full:

> Sir- It is quite apparent that your correspondent "Red Robins" in your last week's issue of *Kensington News* must live in a very elite part of Kensington when he suggests that white folk should be more patient and tolerant, believe me, we have no option. It is most deplorable that these immigrants are allowed to squeeze into our homes and flats, our authorities turning a blind eye to overcrowding, this being mainly the cause of vice.
>
> First of all I would like to emphasis I am neither a supporter or sympathiser of Sir Oswald Mosley or the White Defence League. I was full of pity when they arrived, but my pity now goes to the white folk. They have turned the place into a slum. Hot Dogs being sold all through the night in our streets, to satisfy the coloured folk who frequent the drinking dens. These places are open from the early evening to 6am. The activity is intolerable, and we seldom get a decent night's sleep.
>
> They have acquired the most expensive cars, and yet were seeking assistance when they first arrived. These cars are being driven at the most erratic speeds all through the night, they obviously get much amusement with their screeching brakes. The neighbourhood has sadly deteriorated, and yet our rates go up and up. The district is inundated with prostitutes, and we have many brothels in our houses, cars and taxis drawing up all night.
>
> We have no black colour bar, it is a white colour bar and we are slowly being purged out of our homes, by their unseemly behaviour, thus paving the way for more immigrants. This is the most-evil part of London, Soho being a comparatively peaceful neighbourhood.
>
> I have nothing against the coloured workers, who are

doing an honourable job, but I do complain bitterly of the street corner louts, who almost compel pedestrians to walk on the roads. They are asleep until mid-day, then, keeping the workers awake most of the night, brawling with prostitutes. I am still looking for the words of sympathy for the white residents, who very soon will have to change their lives, by doing night work and sleep by day.[38]

This was indicative of the comments voiced by many locals at the time and this letter leaves no stone unturned in identifying what the author determines as the problems in the borough of Kensington, post *Windrush*. The overwhelming response to any difficulties facing white locals was that immigration was the problem and the perception was of 'another' taking what little there was from an indigenous community. The housing in North Kensington, declared unfit for human habitation by government in 1886, had seen little done to improve it throughout the following decades. WWII bomb damage had exacerbated an already untenable situation and overcrowding in the limited housing that was available was rife and scarcity of employment was also an issue. Concerns over prostitution and lawlessness appear again and again in letters to the local newspapers at the time. Local councils had been left with the responsibility of dealing with an influx of people without the resources from central government to adequately cope. Writing in 1964, journalist Paul Foot observed:

In that crucial decade of commonwealth immigration, [1954-1964] the Conservative Government had no policy about meeting them at the port of arrival; no policy about accommodation; no policy about schooling their children.[39]

Furthermore:

Local councils had no estimate from the central government of the numbers coming into their area, no guidance from

Health or Education Ministries on the possibilities of different health and sanitation standards or on the difficulties of teaching children who could not speak English. Had every councillor been a humanist of soaring imagination, pledged unequivocally to assist his brothers from abroad, the problems would still have been insurmountable without some assistance or guidance from the centre.[40]

Clearly there were problems, but who was responsible for the situation and how was it to be overcome?

Edwardian Dandies

Another group of 'outsiders' much debated and much derided at the time were also to be held responsible for the events about to unfold in Notting Hill Gate. Edwardian dandies or teddy boys as they became known, were disproportionately blamed for many of the ills that occurred in British society in the 1950s and have been the focus of the 1958 Notting Hill riots ever since. Such was the entrenchment into common parlance of 'teddy boys' as a form of abuse that, in denigrating John Osborne and his play *Look Back in Anger,* one literary reviewer dismissed him as an 'intellectual teddy boy'.[41] But who were the teddy boys and where did they come from?

No urban street style or subculture truly comes from one singular thing, but the origins of the clothing that gives teddy boys their name can be pinpointed to one item of men's attire. In sartorial protest at the ration book austerity of post-war London, Saville Row tailors in the late 1940s began experimenting with suits that harked back to more flamboyant times, those of Edward VII's reign from 1901-1910.

The cut of the cloth was different: [The] "jacket is generously skirted and button-four with a very short lapel and squarely cut fronts. Jacket pockets are slanted and are offset by narrow trousers (narrow all the way, not pegged topped) and double-breasted waistcoat".[42]

Teddy Boys, 1954.
© Getty Images

Below, Teddy Girls 1955.
Ken Russell. © Topfoto

Young affluent men, especially army officers, adopted the look and it also became fashionable in and around Oxbridge universities. It was introduced to the world in 1950 and the Edwardian style as it became known, evolved, and as it was adopted by working class youth, it was adapted with other styles. Pre-dating the rock 'n' roll it has since been associated with, teddy boys and girls existed, in fact, fully five years before rock 'n' roll arrived in the UK in 1955. The working-class expression of this middle-class fashion emanated from Elephant and Castle, south east London, an area noted for its deprivation, then as now.

As it grew it was adapted with other styles, notably, the hugely popular western television shows of the time. 'Bootlace ties' from the westerns accompanied very-tight 'drainpipe' trousers, crepe-wedged shoes, known as 'brothel creepers' often in lurid pinks and sky-blues, and this was topped off by an elaborate greased-back layered hair-style, known as a 'ducks-arse'. The female equivalent, the teddy girls, were often androgynous and dressed in similar clothes to their male counterparts. Their rebellion was rolled up jeans, flat shoes and drape jackets, a stark contrast to the heels, pencil skirts and closely-defined waistlines of dresses inspired by Christian Dior's highly influential 'New Look'.

Teddy boys were also influenced in elements of their dress style by the spiv. Small time criminals that became notorious during WWII, spivs were later personified in the British consciousness in the form of Private Walker from the TV show *Dad's Army* and George Cole's character in the *St Trinians'* films. Spivs dealt in illicit black-market goods that were in short supply because of wartime and post-war rationing. They were flamboyant and ostentatious dressers at a time when the watchwords for fashion were 'make do and mend'. But along with this sartorial legacy, teds also inherited an association in the public perception with the petty crime spivs were notorious for. Whether there was any foundation to this accusation or not, the whole subculture became tainted by it. Sociologist Dick

Hebdige described this relationship, their style as "a focus for an illicit delinquent identity".[43] Teds and criminality became synonymous with each other. Headlines involving coshes, bicycle chains, razors and flick-knives were commonplace. Violence was the predominant factor associated with teds as this excerpt from the *Brighton Herald* demonstrates:

> Strong action is expected by police and dance hall managements to prevent any repetition of the gang fight started at the weekend by 'Teddy Boys' from London in which three innocent bystanders received nasty injuries. The three victims, all local men, were slashed it is believed with shoe-maker's knives, sharpened to a razor edge. Every person seeking admission to the Regent dance hall tonight will be scrutinised by the ballroom manager, Mr Lionel Stewart. 'I don't have to bar everybody that looks like a teddy boy, but I shall sort them out and those with big rings on just won't get in'.[44]

As the decade progressed, this association with violence was cemented into the nation's consciousness when American films *Blackboard Jungle* and *Rock Around the Clock* were shown in Britain in 1955 and 1956. Cinema seats were ripped out and young people flouted convention and danced with each other in the aisles of cinemas up and down the land.

In *Folk Devils and Moral Panics* Stanley Cohen describes how 'teenage delinquency' in post-war Britain became the moral panic of the day and teddy boys, the disaffected youth of the 1950s, were crowned the folk devils. Despite the fact that many sociologists and indeed Cohen himself may have distanced themselves from aspects of this book, much of what was written in this seminal text still has resonance. The media, eager to sensationalise the smallest and most insignificant of events, perpetuated a myth, a panic over teenage delinquency with lurid tales of promiscuity, criminality and above all violence. Cohen explains that whilst it was clear that the government and media thought there was a problem with teenagers, less obvious was the cause, or the remedy:

> Each society possesses a set of ideas about what causes deviation—is it due, say, to sickness or to wilful perversity? —and a set of images of who constitutes the typical deviant— is he an innocent lad being led astray, or is he a psychopathic thug?—and these conceptions shape what is done about the behaviour.[45]

What caused the teddy boy phenomenon: nature or nurture? Written off by society because of this ted-equals-violence equation, Cohen argues that this became a self-fulfilling prophesy. MP for Scarborough and Whitby, Sir Alexander Spearman speaking at Conservative Party conference in his hometown in 1958, blamed a crime wave:

> On these so-called teddy boys, because they never had the stick...[He advocated that on conviction]...they should be fined tremendously heavily and, if unable to pay, be made to work and work and work until they can pay off the fine.[46]

Sir William Robson-Brown, Conservative MP for Esher, Surrey predicted that: "The teddy boy of today is likely to be the irresponsible shop steward of tomorrow".[47] Nationally, the Conservative Party proposed teddy boy jails designed to: "De-teddy the teddy boys as a way to solve the problems of British youth", to take the stuffing out of the teddies, so to speak.[48] However farcical this may seem today, this was the moral panic of the time. The problem of teenage delinquency was currency and was heavily reported in the local and national press. Cohen again:

> The media have long operated as agents of moral indignation in their own right: even if they are not self-consciously engaged in crusading or muckraking, their very reporting of certain 'facts' can be sufficient to generate concern, anxiety, indignation or panic.[49]

War on Teddy Boys, Sunday Dispatch, 1958

When it came to the reportage of the Notting Hill riots and the involvement of teddy boys, the media travelled down what would become a familiar path: "The real causes of [the riot] appear to be principally in the boredom and frustration experienced by our teddy boys... Coloured people are simply a convenient and often defenceless target for aggression".[50] If for just one moment, we substitute the words *teddy boys* and *coloured people* for *mods* and *Clacton* an uncanny similarity unfolds. A bank holiday weekend, a group of teenagers who are bored and a lack of facilities. This could be exactly what Cohen was referring to when he reflected years later in his description of the first mods versus rockers confrontations in Clacton on Easter bank holiday in 1964. Cohen then goes on to describe the use of emotive language for dramatic effect in the reporting of the Whitson bank holiday 'riots' in Hastings later that summer, what he called 'over-reporting':

> The regular use of phrases such as 'riot, 'orgy of destruction', 'battle', 'attack', 'siege', 'beat up the town' and 'screaming mob' left an image of a besieged town from which innocent holidaymakers were fleeing to escape a marauding mob.[51]

Again, change the word *holidaymakers* for *coloureds* and a pattern emerges with how disturbances are presented by the media. Nuanced and evocative reporting sets the stage, all that changes are the actors. From a sociological perspective there are similarities between the perceptions of both teddy boys and the 'coloured' community in what Cohen calls *volatility*: "Successful moral panics owe their appeal to their ability to find points of resonance with wider anxieties".[52] The inference is that teddy boys were symptomatic of a wider malaise in society: "It's not only this but...it's been building up over the years...it will get worse if nothing's done". This is precisely the same language used by the media when discussing Caribbean immigration.

Whatever similarities there may be between the overall media commentary of the Notting Hill riots and the mod versus rocker skirmishes in Clacton and Hastings and whether or not boredom might have played its part in the bank holiday events, this should not diminish the real and violent racist attacks that occurred in west London in August 1958. Nor should it cloud the response from the government. Desperate to assuage any accusation of 'racialism' endemic in British society or accept that the appalling conditions people were living in had a part to play, the government and the national media needed to find another reason for the disturbances in 1958. Fortunately, 'deviance' in the guise of the teddy boy was at hand. However inaccurate and overblown some of the reports were though, the fact remains that teddy boys *were* active in and around the riots of 1958. Television, newspaper and police reports all carry stories and photographs of gangs of teds armed and looking for trouble. Files from the Metropolitan Police during the summer of 1958 show disproportionately higher arrests of the ted to the non-ted variety. Their involvement takes George Melly's statement; "what starts as revolt finishes as style" and turned it on its head, in this instance fashion had morphed into rebellion.[53]

The Union Movement and the White Defence League

Whatever difficulties teddy boys were having as teenagers, and whatever problems were being faced by West Indians integrating into their new society, these issues were exploited and exacerbated by organised fascists who began operating in Notting Hill in the mid-1950s. Although never disappearing completely, the various grouplets of far right activists had been dormant in the wider political arena since their defeat by the 43 Group at the end of the 1940s. Whilst Mosley had spent much of his time in prison learning German which he thought would be useful at the war's end, when the war did finally come to a conclusion, he tactically distanced himself from Hitler and using the term 'fascism' and by the beginning of the next decade his antisemitism was not having the resonance it once had. Alongside Mosley, other familiar faces reappeared and began organising in west London but this time around the issues of immigration and the crumbling of empire.

Arnold Leese based his post-war operations in Notting Hill. Leese was mentor to a younger equally fanatical neo-fascist called Colin Jordan, who had earned his stripes as Leese's foot soldier in the 1940s. Splitting from the League of Empire

White Defence League Headquarters, Princedale Road, Notting Hill, 1959

Loyalists (LEL), a far right pressure group formed in 1954 to 'defend the empire', Jordan formed The White Defence League (WDL) in September 1958. The WDL were rabid in their racial hatred and swiftly began a sustained agitation and propaganda campaign to 'Keep Britain White'.[54] Leese died in 1956 and left his house to Colin Jordan. 74 Princedale Road, W11 was often referred to as Arnold Leese House and could not have been more ideally situated as a centre of operations for the WDL: it was right in the middle of Notting Hill. From there they distributed their newspaper *Black and White News*. Posters, leaflets and graffiti carrying the message *Keep Britain White* began appearing all over W11 and their headquarters brazenly displayed their name and logo.[55] Colin Jordan explained their philosophy:

> The objects of the White Defence League are to keep Britain the white man's country that it has always been, to preserve the white civilisation which is the product of our race and to preserve our northern European blood which in our opinion is our greatest national treasure... We believe in the bold and vital step of stopping all coloured immigration into Britain and repatriating with all humane consideration the coloured immigrants who are already here.[56]

The tactics of British fascists in the 1930s and 1940s had been to recruit from the aristocracy via Oxbridge and Whitehall for funds and political influence, the middle-class using reading groups to develop speakers and leadership and from the working-class for its street fighting forces.[57] Throughout those 20 years there had been vicious and systematic attacks against Jews from the BUF and the UM. Young working-class men were recruited to form terror gangs to intimidate and beat up Jews, trade unionists and left-wingers. Incidents of violence were commonplace and no-go areas and unofficial curfews for Jews existed in parts of London.[58] Organised gangs of these street fighters or 'biff boys' as they were known in the 1930s were replaced by Mosley and Jordan's teddy boys of the 1950s.[59] UM meetings addressed by radicalised university graduates proliferated, and as the summer of 1958 progressed, violent incidents against black people began being reported to the police.[60] The savagery of some of these attacks has been lost in time. There were beatings, razor attacks, stabbings, the windows of black families smashed on a constant basis with the tenants left cowering in fear. A black man was attacked in a pub in North Kensington and battered with metal dustbin lids and broken bottles, another was shot in the leg. Petrol bombs were thrown through house windows with pregnant women inside. Gangs of white teenagers roamed the streets of west London with knives, iron bars, sticks and razors, slashing and attacking black people at will. A particularly ugly development was the regular late Saturday night attempts by white drivers to run down black people in their cars; this was described by white locals as a 'sport'.[61]

What has now been accepted as the opening of the riots began on the night of Saturday 30 August 1958. After a fracas with her black husband the previous night, Majbritt Morrison, a young white Swedish woman, was confronted by a group of white locals unhappy with her marriage to a Jamaican, who was allegedly also her pimp. She had stones and bottles thrown at her and was attacked with an iron bar. Soon after a 400-strong crowd of white men, many of them teddy boys, gathered and began attacking houses occupied by West Indians including a blues party with a sound system run by Count Suckle.[62] Sensing an opportunity, the following day the UM organised an impromptu open-air meeting amid the aftermath of the attacks. A reporter from the *Kensington Post* was there:

> In the middle of a mob of screaming, jeering youths and adults, a speaker from the Union Movement was urging his excited audience to 'get rid of them' (the coloured people). Groups of policemen stood at strategic points carefully watching the meeting...suddenly hundreds of leaflets were thrown over the crowd. A fierce cry went in the air and the mob rushed off in the direction of Latimer Road shouting 'kill the niggers'.[63]

Police eyewitness reports were withheld by the Metropolitan Police in documents not released until 2002 when they were obtained by *The Guardian*:

> The disturbances were overwhelmingly triggered by 300 to 400-strong 'Keep Britain White' mobs, many of them teddy boys armed with iron bars, butcher's knives and weighted leather belts, who went 'nigger-hunting' among the West Indian residents of Notting Hill and Notting Dale. The first night left five black men lying unconscious on the pavements of Notting Hill.[64]

Another censored police witness PC Richard Bedford provided graphic evidence of the motives of the gangs of youth, some several thousand strong, at times who roamed the streets of Notting Hill, breaking into homes and attacking any West Indian they could find. He said he had seen a mob of 300 to 400 white people in Bramley Road shouting: "We will kill all black bastards. Why don't you send them home"?[65] PC Ian McQueen on the same night said he was told: "Mind your own business, coppers. Keep out of it. We will settle these niggers our way. We'll murder the bastards".[66] The files also revealed that senior police officers at the time had assured the then Home Secretary Rab Butler that there was little or no racial motivation behind the disturbances despite testimony from individual police officers to the contrary.

The 3 September 1958 edition of *The Times* reported: "A big crowd of youths chanting 'Down with the Niggers' assembled in Lancaster Road and a youth leading one group held up a banner with the slogan 'Deport all Niggers'."[67] This group of young men, the report continued, had been selling *Action,* the Union Movement's newspaper and prior to their paper sale had attended a highly charged meeting addressed by Oswald Mosley. The whole of W11 was a war zone, Labour MP Tony Benn later recalled in his diaries: [Seeing] "the debris and the corrugated iron up behind the windows of the prefabs where the coloured families lived... the use of petrol bombs and iron bars and razors is appalling...there is a large area where it is not safe for people to be out".[68] That there were organised fascists groups orchestrating the violence is corroborated by journalist Mervyn Jones: "The gangs [using the Kensington Park Hotel as their rallying centre] have a plan of campaign...I saw obvious messengers on fast motorcycles. Gangs arrive in cars from other parts of London".[69]

What was the official response to the violence? Eager to present itself to the Commonwealth as 'enlightened conservatives' the Conservative government was not moved to an immediate knee-jerk reaction and Rab Butler stated: "No change would be forced on the government's immigration policies by extremists".[70] However, Tory backbencher Cyril Osborne spoke for many in his party when he declared in the Commons: "It is time someone spoke for this country and for the white man who lives here and the idleness, sickness and crime that coloured people brought to the country".[71] Echoing this were Conservative and Labour MPs from Nottingham who jointly said: "No more black people should be allowed in the country and that new deportation laws should be passed".[72] Tony Benn urged Labour leader Hugh Gaitskill to make an intervention, but none was forthcoming. Initially, the silence from the Labour Party leadership was deafening.[73]

Not so quiet was North Kensington Labour MP George Rogers who firmly laid the blame for the riots on the black population and called for 'tighter immigration controls'. Rogers blamed West Indians for provoking the 'response' of locals by failing to adapt to the British way of life. He demanded an end to unrestricted immigration, the deportation of anti-social elements and the re-housing of immigrants to stop ghettoes forming. Leading British neo-fascist Jeffery Hamm joked: "I welcome Mr Rogers conversion, and look forward to his application for membership".[74] Rogers' words were echoed by then TUC general secretary Vincent Tewson: "The government must introduce legislation quickly to end the tremendous influx of coloured people from the Commonwealth...white people have been tolerant...now their tempers are up...there should be gates in their land of origin and here through which people must pass".[75] Later that first week of September 1958, at the Friends Meeting House in Euston, a huge meeting was addressed by Jamaican First Minister Norman Manley; he urged black people to stand up for their rights. Also speaking from the top table (or trying to) was George Rogers. His contribution proved somewhat difficult though, as every time "the Labour MP attempted to speak he was booed, hissed and heckled" by the audience.[76] Rogers and Tewson were pandering to the outpouring of racism in the aftermath of the riots. A nationwide Gallup poll conducted on 3 and 4 September found that 55 percent wanted restrictions on 'coloured' immigration; 71 percent disapproved of 'marriages between white and coloured people'; 54 percent wanted people born in Britain to have preference on housing lists and 61 percent said they would move house 'if coloured people came to live in great numbers' in their district. This was despite the fact that only 49 percent of those polled had ever known a non-white person.[77]

The West Indian community had begun organising against the level of racism and violence during the riots. On the bank holiday Monday, a well-known meeting place called *Totobags Cafe* at 9 Blenheim Crescent became the headquarters of Caribbean defence. A large group of men, including many Jamaicans who had travelled over from Brixton, south London, to give solidarity, assembled inside awaiting the inevitable attack. Baron Baker, in the building at the time and one of the first to be arrested remembered:

> During the day we made our preparations for the attack and I can quite clearly remember I was standing on the second floor, with the lights out in Blenheim Crescent, when I saw, look out and see from Kensington Park Road to Portobello Road, a massive lot of people out there and I distinctly remember what they say, 'let's burn the niggers, let's lynch the niggers' and from those spoken words, I said 'start bomb them' then we see the Molotov cocktails coming out from number nine Blenheim Crescent.[78]

The disturbances continued night after night until they finally began to peter out on 5 September 1958. In total 108 people were arrested. Later in the year at the Old Bailey, Judge Salmon handed down exemplary sentences of four years and a £500 fine to each of the nine white youths who openly admitted they had gone 'nigger hunting'. Asked by the judge why they had been involved in the violence, this explanation for their actions was offered by one: "I hate niggers".[79] The National Labour Party, another small neo-Nazi group operating in Notting Hill at the time, organised a petition opposing the 'severity' of the sentences, collecting 10,000 local signatures in just one week.[80] Sitting alongside the defence in court was Oswald Mosley who provided funds for the teds on trial. Mosley was trying to subvert this subculture of white working-class youth to become a tool to be used by the UM. He would try to exploit their disaffection and champion their cause whilst cynically attempting to use their violent potential for political gain. "They're fine fellows some of these so-called teds up in

Notting Hill...", Mosley said, whilst trying to get their sentences remitted on the grounds of their "good previous character".[81] Both Mosley and Jordan increased their activity in Notting Hill after the riots. Whilst all around west London groups and organisations were forming, trying to find ways of avoiding further violence and an escalation of antipathy, Mosley and Jordan sought to exacerbate the tensions in the area. As he had done in the 30s and the 40s, Mosley was building for another grand event. 1959 was to be an election year and he was to stand in North Kensington. But before he could even begin to campaign for that election an organisation was set up to oppose him and Colin Jordan, one that would become the most high-profile anti-racist/fascist organisation in the country.

Chapter Two
The Stars Campaign for Interracial Friendship

The Musicians Union (MU) had been ground-breaking in its response to racism. In 1947 it passed a resolution at its annual conference, declaring that it would oppose the colour bar wherever it appeared. The union was one of the first British organisations to demand a boycott of South Africa and its Apartheid regime. MU initiatives were integral to opposing racism in dance halls and after a sustained campaign the colour bar was lifted in *Mecca* ballrooms in Nottingham, Birmingham, Streatham and Sheffield on 16 October 1958.

After the August bank-holiday violence in Notting Hill, the reaction from musicians was swift. Aside from the predictable statements later issued by the established political parties in the national and local media, the first responses to the riots came from musicians.

There were two weekly musical newspapers in Britain at the time, the *New Musical Express* (NME) which was orientated toward the teenage pop and rock 'n' roll market and *Melody Maker* (MM), a more earnest publication that concentrated on folk, blues and jazz. The following appeal appeared on the front page of *Melody Maker* on 6 September 1958, just a day after the trouble had finally subsided:

> At a time when reason has given way to violence in parts of
> Britain, we, the people of all races in the world of entertainment,

appeal to the public to reject racial discrimination in any shape of form. Violence will settle nothing: it will only cause suffering to innocent people and create fresh grievances. We appeal to our audiences everywhere to join us in opposing any and every aspect of colour prejudice wherever it may appear.[1]

This statement was initially signed by 27 celebrities: Larry Adler, Chris Barber, Pearl Carr, Alma Cogan, Johnny Dankworth, Lonnie Donegan, Charlie Drake, Ray Ellington, Tubby Hayes, Ted Heath (band leader not Tory MP), Teddy Johnson, Cleo Laine, Humphrey Littleton, Matt Monro, Mick Mulligan, Otilie Patterson, Marion Ryan, Ronnie Scott, Harry Secombe, Peter Sellers, Tommy Steele, Eric Sykes, Dickie Valentine, Frankie Vaughan, Kent Walton, David Whitfield and Marty Wilde. It also became a leaflet that was distributed in Soho jazz clubs and around the Notting Hill area.

In the same edition of *Melody Maker*, music critic and independent record producer Denis Preston demanded that: "Something is needed, roughly on the lines of America's National Association for the Advancement for Colored People to articulate the concerns of the black population".[2] Agreeing with Preston, was folk singer Fred Dallas, who also used the name Karl Dallas when working as a journalist. He wrote that SCIF:

...wants to form a committee of big-name entertainers and get out a statement protesting against mob violence and prejudice, then the permanent organisation can follow. Already a body exists called the British-Caribbean Welfare Service. Maybe it can assist in the birth of Britain's NAACP. I am confident the Musicians Union and a great many jazz players and listeners would support such a movement.[3]

By the following week *Melody Maker* declared:

Letters, telephone messages, even telegrams and personal callers offering support have come into this office from all directions since last Friday. They confirm that in the jazz world there is a lot of racial tolerance and at present, indignation about the whipped-up outbursts of anti-colour feeling waiting to be tapped.[4]

A two-page article written by Frank Sinatra also appeared in that week's edition of *Melody Maker* under the title: 'Frank Sinatra Says Jazz Has No Colour Bar'. Fred Dallas had teamed up with saxophonist John Dankworth and singer Cleo Laine

'WHAT THE STARS SAY' ABOUT RACIAL HATRED

Daily Worker Reporter

A BROADSHEET to promote inter-racial friendship which is backed by some of the most famous names in show business is being distributed in North Kensington, London.

Larry Adler, Winifred Atwell, Eamonn Andrews, Max Bygraves, Tony Hancock, Sir Laurence Olivier and Peter Sellers are among those backing this move by the Stars Campaign for Inter-Racial Friendship.

"What the Stars Say" is the title of their publication which they are distributing in the Notting Hill area to counteract the flood of propaganda being issued there by the racialist bodies.

SINATRA CALL

"You can't hate and be happy!" says an article by Frank Sinatra, which leads the paper.

This stars' organisation was formed last year at the time of the riots in Nottingham and Notting Hill. In a declaration issued yesterday its members call "very urgently on all men and women who respect their

FRANK SINATRA
You can't hate and be happy.

Frank Sinatra writes article for SCIF newsletter. Reported in the Daily Worker.
© *Marx Memorial Library & Workers' School, London*

and with the addition of industry friends Winifred Atwell, Ken Colyer, Max Jones, George Melly, Russell Quaye and Hylda Sims they formed the Stars Campaign for Interracial Friendship (SCIF). At its initial meeting early in September 1958, the decision was made to appoint a chairman, they opted for the most high-profile member in the group and actor Lawrence Olivier took the job, with Johnny Dankworth as vice-chair. Fred Dallas told this writer that Olivier was happy to be the chairman on condition he played absolutely no part in SCIF's activities.[5] The organisation was loose, but they decided its strategy would be to organise around the single issue of racism and use the 'celebrity' of its members to promote racial harmony. Author Eric Hobsbawm was later to say: "The purpose of SCIF... was to articulate through the combined presence of music and culture, *and* left activists and writers, a cultural policy of racial inclusion and social solidarity at a time of crisis".[6]

SCIF decided that a statement in opposition to the racism behind the riots was needed. An appeal in an eight-page illustrated broadsheet *What the Stars Say* was produced and handed around jazz clubs in the West End and the Notting Hill area. It was SCIF's mission statement; the campaign [it said] intended to promote:

> The ideals of racial tolerance and harmony through the example of those who earn their living in the world of art and entertainment, and in the associated realms of journalism, writing and the productive side of show business. Its aims are to promote understanding between races and banish ignorance about racial characteristics; to combat instances of social prejudice by verbal and written protests; to set an example to the general public through members' personal race relations; and to use all available means to publicise their abhorrence of racial discrimination.[7]

SCIF organised itself quickly, before any established parties or organisations and local newspaper the *Kensington Post*

SCIF organising meeting. Amongst those present are Lonnie Donegan, Cleo Laine, Johnny Dankworth and E.R Braithwaite.

carried a headline on 3 October 1959 announcing that SCIF was the: "Only unofficial body to publicly condemn the riot…[and]… had held several meetings at Johnny Dankworth's premises in Denmark Street, the home of Tin Pan Alley".[8] Hylda Sims remembers:

> There were a few meetings at Johnny Dankworth's office, I think it was in Tin Pan Alley. It was here that I first met Johnny and Cleo, also Francis Newton which was Eric Hobsbawm's jazz name. I remember MacInnes, Colin MacInnes being there and after these meetings he would go leafleting around Notting Hill. From here we organised activities and some gigs.[9]

The *Kensington Post* reported that SCIF intended to hold these concerts in London with guest appearances from national celebrities. The first gig at Soho's Skiffle Cellar was recalled by SCIF founder Fred Dallas: "It was a fundraiser in Soho, on a weekday night where we assembled and were blown away by this very tall white kid who sounded like an old delta bluesman, but he had the most amazing voice…it was Long John Baldry".[10] Hylda Sims again:

We did a fundraiser, somewhere around Leicester Square in a big club with a stage, [most likely this was Ken Colyer's *Studio 51* in Great Newport Street] it was mine and Russell's [Quaye] group The City Ramblers; we also did another couple of gigs around Soho.[11]

SCIF then began organising gigs and seeking support from any others politically opposed to the racism prevalent at the time.

The CPGB

Whilst SCIF was an independent organisation, it relied on a network of friends and sympathetic associates to help organise activities and propaganda, but the political and cultural support SCIF received was sporadic. Although SCIF supporters were also members of their relevant unions there was no 'official' support for SCIF from the MU or the TUC, neither was there such support from the Labour Party or any other organisations on the political left, such as the Communist Party of Great Britain (CPGB). The CPGB had an ambiguous position regarding popular culture. There was enthusiastic support for British folk music and the CPGB had been influenced by Edwardian folklorists Cecil Sharp and Vaughan Williams who had been keen to seek out and cement into the popular consciousness a traditional British heritage and indigenous 'national' culture as separate from its European counterparts. Sharp and Williams had set up the English Folk-Dance Society in 1911.[12] The CPGB created a similar organisation in the 1930s with folk music, but with one difference, class replaced nation. Central to this initiative was the Workers Music Association (WMA), established in 1936 to provide cultural support to the labour movement.[13]

Championed by social historians such E P Thompson and Christopher Hill, the CPGB developed a theory that there was a buried history of working-class culture that needed cultural archaeologists to unearth the musical aspects. The CPGB and WMA sought to find this music and classify it as the true cultural representation of the British working class. However, what started as an attempt to rescue a lost or forgotten art form ended up as a relentless search for 'proletarian authenticity' which had four unintended consequences. The first was to reject (or at best marginalise) the music of any other nation, notably America. Arguably the·most original and important cultural musical forms to emanate from the 20th century were jazz and the blues, both were relegated to the side-lines in the WMA.[14] Secondly, in keeping with the 'popular front' theories of the 1930s the CPGB developed, intentionally or otherwise, a 'progressive nationalism' that attempted to establish a unique 'Britishness' to folk music, irrespective of class and in contradiction to its original 'authentic and proletarian' position. Thirdly there was technophobia. The romantic and retrospective philosophy of 'traditional' folk music rejected the modern 1950s folk idiom, partly in its form and wholly in its execution.[15] Lastly, the unequivocal insistence of the CPGB for a pure folk music, one which rejected other popular forms of music (in the 1950s, skiffle), alienated huge layers of teenage musicians and music fans and lost a potentially massive audience for the CPGB because of their insistence on a specific proletarian culture or *prolekult*.[16]

In the post-WWII period, the British establishment was re-evaluating its position in the world vis-á-vis its decaying empire. It now was a supporting and subservient junior partner to the new superpower—the United States—which was locked in a cold war battle with the Soviet Union. The CPGB faced with a choice of allying themselves to one power or the other, opted for the latter and to an extent this is understandable. As the only example of a successful workers' revolution in history, it was the Soviet Union's prerogative to instruct and guide the global communist movement on their tactics and strategy. Although some on the left, loosely based around Trotsky, had broken ranks and rejected Moscow's diktats, the CPGB, despite occasional misgivings, acquiesced to Stalin's Comintern for over 30 years.[17]

With some justification the CPGB in the 1950s saw the massive increase of American films, music and consumer products into the UK not as a cultural exchange but as American cultural imperialism, they were not alone. The remnants of the "over sexed, over paid and over here" antipathy toward American GI's from WWII lingered in post-war Britain. Whilst many welcomed launderettes, supermarkets and the birthplace of British rock 'n' roll, the coffee house, others saw these changes as an erosion of a 'British way of life'. Designed to save jobs for British musicians, the MU put in place policies that prohibited American musicians from performing in the UK. It operated a 'one in-one out' policy that enabled American musicians to perform in Britain on the proviso that there was a reciprocal process in the United States. However, in the 1950s, the traffic was only flowing one way and whilst there was an unsated hunger to watch American musicians in the UK, bookings for British bands to tour stateside were few and far between. Of course, this was to radically reverse with the advent of The Beatles.[18]

SCIF lacked the money and the support that unions and organised political organisations could have given, but in many ways, this was a blessing as they had some level of autonomy and were not bogged down by the theoretical musings of the central committee of the Communist Party. Consequently, they organised independently. The first high profile SCIF event was a Christmas party for children of all races picked from three local schools on 23 December 1958 in Holland Park School, London W8.[19] Over 250 children attended from the West Indian, Irish, African and English communities and music was provided by SCIF members. The event was also attended by the Mayor and London County Council vice-chair, the local press covered the festivities and according to the *Kensington News,* the day was a great success.[20] The food and drink was provided by the US embassy—somewhat surprisingly considering their attitude to non-segregated lunches in their own country at the time—and the BBC televised the party, the recording of which has sadly been lost.

SCIF as an active organisation

SCIF's first permanent initiative was to create a club to promote interracial mixing and openly oppose the colour bar. *The Harmony Club* opened its doors in Blenheim Crescent on 19 January 1959. Josephine Douglas, SCIF member, actress and co-host of Britain's first pop-chart television show *Six-Five Special* hosted the club alongside actor Harvey Hall. SCIF's simple yet ambitious aim for the club was articulated by Jo Douglas: 'To bring racial harmony to the Notting Hill Gate area'.[21] Also present on the opening night were jazz singer Rosemary Squires and Caribbean folklorist and singer Edric Connor. Rosemary Squires recalls the evening:

> I was asked by one of the presenters of the show *Six-Five Special*, a popular lady called Jo Douglas, to visit a young people's youth club, a multi-racial club, I suppose as a morale booster, which I gladly did. This is where the photo of me was taken and the other person was another singer of the day, a very nice gentleman, named Edric Connor.[22]

A special message of support was sent from Paul Robeson and was read out at the opening. The *Kensington Post* reported on the night:

> White and coloured children hammered on the door of St Marks Church Hall Notting Hill on Monday evening. But they had to stay outside to listen to the beat of the bongo drums and the rhythm of the top-class jazz for it was invitation only at the opening session of the Harmony Club. Inside the hall was packed tight with singing, stamping and jiving teenagers of all races.
>
> There was only one colour problem at the club—started by the Stars Campaign for Interracial Friendship—and that was the possibility of getting wet paint on clothes. Right up to the last moment the youngsters in the working party

had been busy cleaning up the church hall and putting on new bright paint. Over the weekend television personality Josephine Douglas helped with the work. Very soon 'Joe' was an old friend of the boys and girls. This helped to make the show a very formal affair.

The juke-box is already part of the club's equipment, but there was no need to put on records. Music was provided on stage by Jonnie Dankworth, Rosemary Squires and coloured singers Edric Connor, Frank Holder and 'Cuddly' Dudley Heslop. Before the youngsters pushed back the chairs for jiving, TV actor Harvey Hall, the chairman spoke about the club. He said: "You can use a lot of high-sounding words. But all it comes down to is getting to know each other better".[23]

The club promised to open twice a week on Mondays and Fridays and Johnny Dankworth, Cleo Laine, Humphrey Littleton and Dickie Valentine, amongst others, would attend and perform. Not only was this club open to all irrespective of race, it positively encouraged: "Young people of all races together in a non-political, non-sectarian social club".[24] Black and white people would meet each other, talk to each other and most importantly dance with each other. Furthermore, chairman Harvey Hall told the *Kensington Post*:

> There will be weekly meetings and the youngsters will have a say in the running of the club. And they will be asked to bring their friends in. But this will not be a select club, we do want to bring the rougher element in, teddy boys will be welcomed.[25]

Jo Douglas claimed: "This club isn't a deep thing. It's essentially a social club. We want young people of different races, nationalities and creeds to get together and enjoy themselves".[26] Looking into the future, Hall hoped that this club: "May lead to a chain of Harmony Clubs bringing white and coloured people together all over London and in other parts of the country".[27]

The Kensington News, 26 December 1958.[28]

The *Harmony Club* was not alone in its endeavours to ease racial tensions, as community clubs and integration groups began appearing in the area, but because of the celebrity status of SCIF members and the sheer amount of stars it recruited, it was guaranteed to draw the biggest headlines, but this was calculated, it was part of the SCIF's strategy from the start.

It is difficult to comprehend the climate at this time and understand how provocative the setting up of an interracial club must have been to some white people, notwithstanding the neo-fascist presence in the area. The calls for repatriation rang from every corner in the streets around the *Harmony Club.* It was a brave decision both physically and politically to make Blenheim Crescent the club's home as the street had been literally at the centre of the racial violence only months before. According to Trevor Grundy's *Memoir of a Fascist Childhood:* "Several hundred teds [had] joined the Notting Hill branch of the [Union] movement".[29] So the very people responsible for the racist violence were sought by SCIF to frequent their racially inclusive club. It would of course have been pointless setting up an interracial club where there was no racial diversity, superfluous to ease tension where none existed, so Notting Hill was the only logical place the club could locate; this does not however, negate the courage of those who made it happen. Indeed, both black and white activists received death threat letters from neo-fascist groups on a regular basis and several arson threats were made to burn the hall that housed the club to the ground.[30]

The importance of London as a place is also relevant here, as music historian Sara Cohen explains: "There is a dynamic interrelationship between music and place: it suggests that music plays a very particular and sensual role in the production of place partly through its peculiar embodiment of movement and collectivity".[31] Why did SCIF occur in London, why did it not happen in Nottingham? There had been riots there and there

STARS BACK HARMONY CLUB

The Harmony Club—a venue to promote inter-racial friendship —opened at St. Mark's Church Hall, Notting Hill Gate, on Monday. Pictured (above) are Rosemary Squires, Edric Connor and Josephine Douglas at the opening.

The Harmony Club, opening night. Daily Worker 1959. © Marx Memorial Library & Workers' School, London

was also Caribbean migration and Nottingham also had a small jazz and skiffle scene. Of course, London geographically is a much bigger city, but in terms of creating the dynamic that Cohen talks about, bigger does not necessarily mean better as it can create problems in travel, cost, communication and even finding out that there are others who share your interests. This helps to explain why Soho became so important for the music scene and SCIF in London. It was a gravitational pull to the centre of the city, where everyone from the outskirts could meet and all the clubs were within walking distance. Soho did not create a 'scene' and a 'scene' did not create Soho, but the two were interdependent. Peterson and Bennett explained what a scene was/is:

> A focused social activity that takes place in a delimited space and over a specific span of time in which clusters of producers, musicians, and fans realise their common musical taste, collectively distinguishing themselves by using music and other cultural signs often appropriated from other places but recombined and developed in ways that come to represent the local scene. The focused activity we are interested in here, of course, centres on a particular style of music, but such music scenes characteristically involve other diverse lifestyle elements as well. These usually include a distinctive style of dancing, a particular range of psychoactive drugs, style of dress, politics and the like.[32]

The Soho jazz scene fulfils each of these criteria, and the detachment of the jazz scene from wider 'square' society may have had political implications and an input into the identification the musicians had with other 'outside' groups like West Indian immigrants. Place becomes important also when we look at the specificity of the riots. They did not and could not have happened in Soho, as the area is too small to accommodate any sizeable migration, but it did have a scene. Notting Hill could cope with immigration, but it did not have a jazz scene where musicians could congregate. That Soho was the home of London jazz may also partly explain later criticisms of the activities of SCIF as representing gesture politics: what is now colloquially called 'parachuting in' activists not native to an area. Whilst a valid criticism, this cannot be levelled at all SCIF members, notably Colin MacInnes who lived and worked tirelessly in and around Notting Hill throughout the period and according to Hobsbawm: "Went about the area, a favourite stamping ground of his, posting [SCIF] news-sheets through letter boxes".[33] Poet and art dealer Victor Musgrove, who was a close friend of MacInnes at the time, recalled him driving round Notting Hill posting *What The Stars Say* through people's doors and being convinced that this had prevented further rioting.[34]

Resistance to Racism

SCIF was not the only organisation operating in W11; in the borough there were other initiatives organised by a variety of groups, the largest being The Coloured Peoples Progressive Association (CPPA) founded by activist Frances Ezzrecco. Alongside this, the Association for the Advancement of Coloured People (AACP) was formed by Amy Ashwood Garvey, co-founder of the Universal Negro Improvement Association in America, one-time director of the Black Star Line and first wife of Marcus Garvey. The Peoples' National Movement (PNM), The Africa League (AL), the African-Asian Congress (AAC), St Peter's Coloured Peoples' Group (SCPG), the West Indian Gazette (WIG) and the Indian Workers Association (IWA) all had parts to play. The local council employed a West Indian welfare worker 'as a first step to reducing inter-racial tension'.[35] The Mayor of Kensington promised a 'Goodwill Week' sometime in the summer of 1959 where a variety of music, food, costume and culture would be celebrated, although this failed to materialise. A demonstration for interracial fellowship was also organised by the Movement for Colonial Freedom in Trafalgar Square. SCIF was either active in, or actually on, many of the events organised by the above groups.

Here we have to take some time to understand why SCIF or at least some of its members were able to be immersed in local Caribbean organisations in Notting Hill. This is largely explained by the input of one woman, Claudia Jones. Born a Trinidadian in 1915, her family moved to New York when she was nine years old. At age of 21 she joined the Young Communist League of America and 12 years later she was on the National Executive of the American Communist Party (CPUSA). Politically active at the height of the McCarthyite witch-hunts, after several sojourns to the state penitentiary she was deported from the United States in 1955 and chose England as her new home. A seasoned political campaigner, Claudia took no time in becoming active in her adopted London. Gravitating toward the CPGB, here she met Eric Hobsbawm, CPGB member, academic, historian and SCIF member. Years later Hobsbawm had this to say about Jones:

> While it lasted, it [SCIF] enjoyed the invaluable help of the remarkably able and admirable Claudia Jones, a US Communist Party functionary born in the West Indies and expelled as a 'non-citizen' from the USA in the witch-hunt days, who did her best, with indifferent success, to bring some Party efficiency and some political structure into the Caribbean immigration in West London and to get adequate backing for her efforts from the British CPGB. An impressive woman.[36]

Her relationship with the CPGB was to prove fraught. Claudia Jones struggled with the political work of the party in relation to racism. The CPGB had issued a 'Charter of Rights for Coloured Workers of Britain' in 1955. There were four main points to the charter:

1. Racial discrimination should be a penal offence
2. Government restrictions and discrimination against coloured workers should be opposed
3. There must be equality in employment, wages and conditions

4. Coloured workers should join appropriate trade unions
on equal terms to white workers.[37]

The CPGB produced 150,000 leaflets and pamphlets to this effect; they proclaimed, 'No Colour Bar for Britain'. Also, by 1956 a West Indies Committee of the Communist Party had been set up. However, anti-racist work did not always appear to be prioritised by the rest of the party and even leading CPGB members like Eric Hobsbawm seem to have been involved in anti-racist work almost by accident, via music rather than political principal:

> With the American civil rights movements and the influx of coloured immigrants to Britain, racism became a far more central theme on the left than it had been. Through jazz I found myself associated with an early anti-racist campaign [SCIF] in Britain after the so-called Notting Hill race riots of 1958.[38]

The Communist Party's charter of rights struggled to find practical application. In the Kentish Town by-election in the winter of 1958, the Conservative, Labour and Communist candidates met secretly beforehand and agreed to keep race out of the forthcoming election. Unfortunately, a fourth candidate, publican William Webster didn't and stood as an independent on a 'Keep Kentish Town White' platform. "Even if the coloured people were acceptable biologically, there is neither work nor accommodation for them in this area", Webster declared during the hustings.[39] He enjoyed a free and unopposed campaign of racism and repatriation and polled 479 votes of the 6,500 cast.[40]

For Claudia Jones the attitude of the CPGB, however well intentioned, fell short of the task at hand. Indeed, fellow West Indian CPGB member Billy Strachan commented: "The party itself did not know what racism was".[41] The analysis of the CPGB toward black people residing in Britain in the 1950s was framed by two things: 1) the so-called colonial struggles—these were national movements of indigenous peoples in

Africa and Asia organising against British imperial rule and; 2) an economic determinism that saw class conflict as the singular division in society. The CPGB did not identify how the oppression suffered by black and Asian people distorts their class position and how this discrimination works as an ancillary to both the imperial and economic systems that the CPGB had identified. For a Marxist organisation such as the CPGB, this was a profound misreading of Marx. They had the 'base' without 'superstructure'. In reality, this "...led to a promotion of 'colour blindness' amongst CPGB members where appeals to fraternal notions of class disregarded the actual experiences of racism felt by black workers and undermined practical actions to combat racism at shop-floor level".[42] In their weekly publication *World News* the CPGB commented that, as black and Asian workers had only come to the UK to escape the poverty caused by imperialism: "The real solution to the problem [of race relations] is to free the colonies and end imperialist exploitation, so that the colonial workers can freely build up their own countries and reap the benefits of the wealth which they produce".[43] Evan Smith points out in his *Science & Society* article:

> This statement lends to the notion, pervasive in the 1950s, that black immigrants were the 'problem'. By favouring struggles in the colonies, the CPGB avoided making any serious suggestions for tackling the problems faced by those immigrants in Britain.[44]

Furthermore, as Marika Sherwood has observed: "In doing so [the CPGB] confounded the issues of racial discrimination and the effects of imperialism".[45] Much of Claudia Jones' input at this time was to work inside the various black groups that existed in London and to concentrate on two in particular: The AACP and the CPPA. Afro-Caribbean groups both, they were engaged in political work at a local and national level especially around attempts to enact legislation in parliament which outlawed racial discrimination. Jones campaigned tirelessly against racism: in housing; education and employment, addressed demonstrations, peace rallies and the Trade Union Congress. However, she shall always be remembered for two massive contributions to anti-racism and black political history in the UK. In April 1958 Jones set up the *West Indian Gazette and Afro-Asian Caribbean News* (WIG). This was the first wholly black newspaper in Britain. She saw the paper as:

A catalyst, quickening the awareness, socially and politically, of West Indians, Afro-Asians and their friends. Its editorial stand is for a united, independent West Indies, full economic, social and political equality and respect for human dignity for West Indians and Afro-Asians in Britain, and for peace and friendship between all Commonwealth and world peoples.[46]

Arguing a consistent line against racism, the newspaper was an important political forum, but it also served a cultural need as well, as it was a focus for displaced people feeling homesick and seeking solace, inside their own community, in an otherwise hostile environment. Towering over all her other achievements, though, was the creation of Notting Hill Carnival. Organised specifically to make a cultural and political statement that black people were here to stay in England, Carnival was Jones and her associates' attempt to use this Caribbean tradition as a tool of political defiance and cultural seduction. As an early member of SCIF Claudia Jones had already seen this combination utilised with the *Harmony Club* and SCIF gigs/ events in Soho. Carnival in England, like the prototype from Trinidad, was to be a celebration of the Afro-Caribbean: food, dress, music and dance. Understanding the delicate nature of the political situation vis-à-vis white and black residents of Nottingham and Notting Hill just months after the riots, the front page of the carnival brochure fanfared the event but also carried an important political message: "Part of the proceeds [from the sale] of this brochure are to assist the payments of

The First Notting Hill Carnival at Kings Cross Town Hall, 1959. © Getty Images

fines of coloured and white youths involved in the Notting Hill events".[47] This was political pragmatism, whatever Jones and the other carnival organisers may have thought about the teddy boys' violent rampage and their open racism, carnival was to be an ointment that eased the pain. Despite the fact that the first carnival was held in freezing cold January, despite the fact it was held indoors in St Pancras town hall and despite it being organised inside only 12 weeks it was a huge success. They repeated this success the following year and it has now grown into the largest free event and carnival in Europe.

Meanwhile, the *Harmony Club* despite its best intentions lasted only six weeks and ceased activities on 9 March 1959 after an acrimonious split between Jo Douglas and blues musician Alexis Korner over the running of the club. Douglas had said on national TV that the club had been a failure due to the "'un-clubbable' nature of the dead-end kids who were its members'"[48] A furious Alexis Korner was 'indignant' saying: "He wished to entirely disassociate himself from Jo Douglas' comments".[49] Furthermore Korner argued: "The trouble was the club was too successful, we were limited to 50 and got hundreds" and added that he: "had already made preliminary moves to open a new club for young people of all races in the area".[50] Asked if it would be a successor to the *Harmony Club* Korner replied: "No, I hope it will be an antidote".[51] Commenting in 1964 on why even the most sincere of the community and race relations projects failed, journalist Paul Foot suggested:

> The main stumbling block to success in such ventures is the 'tea and buns' approach. All too often, a local authority or church group decides to sponsor a multi-racial committee and provides a hall for the purpose. There is an opening party. Invitations are sent out to all known West Indians or to all the 'Singh's on the electoral roll. The Mayor attends, together with other civic dignitaries, as do a band of West Indian students and a few middle-class Indians. There are a couple of speeches, a few cups of tea, everyone applauds and goes home, and soon afterwards the project collapses.[52]

Writing in 1959 sociologist Ruth Glass observed: "While the [SCIF] campaign had a rather energetic 'newsworthy' start...since then it has been rather quiet".[53] Another journalist commentating on SCIF's campaign and similar 'friendship' endeavours accused them of 'gesture politics and short-term solutions'.[54] Reflecting years later Eric Hobsbawm concluded:

> Stars Campaign for Interracial Friendship [was] not so much a real political operation...[it was] an example of the modern media operation which, like others of its kind, fizzled out after a few months of rather successful publicity. It did indeed mobilize the 'stars', mainly of jazz—most of the big British names were there, Johnny Dankworth and Cleo Laine,

Humphrey Lyttelton and Chris Barber, as well as some pop stars—but its strength lay in the operators who could get stories into the press and programmes on to television and produced newsworthy ideas such as the televised interracial children's Christmas party of 1958.[55]

Nevertheless, there were still further attempts to find a winning club formula. Korner went on to set up a new venue in the Paddington area for an older, paying clientele. The City Ramblers Skiffle Group played regular SCIF gigs in Leicester Square alongside Cleo Laine. A new weekly SCIF club was established at *The Skiffle Cellar* 49 Greek Street, Soho. Humphrey Littleton, jazz trumpeter, music journalist and SCIF member wrote the following piece entitled 'Integration in Soho' in his column in *Melody Maker* on 28 March 1959:

The regular SCIF parties held in Russell Quaye's 'The Cellar Club' in Soho are becoming a standard event in the London jazz calendar. SCIF—The Stars Campaign for Interracial Friendship—holds these informal parties as a medium through which people of all races can meet each other in a relaxed social atmosphere. The music is suitable heterodox, ranging from 'spasm' through Caribbean folk song to modern jam session. Though the first party in February was a tentative affair, launched on a modest scale without much trumpeting from the rooftops, the old reliable grapevine went into operation and brought a continuous stream of guest musicians on to the bandstand during the evening....

As the evening progressed and the rum and coca cola flowed the two groups became inextricably entangled and at the climax of the evening, we all set off round the room in a spontaneous procession, followed by a winding, kaleidoscopic crocodile of dancers. The SCIF parties are rapidly establishing the right atmosphere for a similar outbreak of spontaneous combustion. When it happens Soho and its precincts may witness a 'racial disturbance' of an altogether happy and festive nature. Being of a generous and expansive frame of mind, we might even wind our joyful way to Notting Hill and serenade Sir Oswald Mosley in his electoral headquarters.[56]

The *Harmony Club* and the *Skiffle Cellar* were examples of how SCIF used music and dancing as a political tool against racism and the far right. However tame these events may now seem by modern standards, for 1959 it was ground-breaking. The colour bar was being openly challenged and music was at the heart of it. These small interracial dances proved that integration could work. But some in Westminster were uneasy with any racial mixing at all. Winston Churchill, who had his own personal file entitled *Immigration of Coloured Workers to Britain* brought up the 'problem' of 'coloured' immigration again and again at cabinet meetings and had argued that the campaign slogan for the 1955 General Election should be 'Keep England White'.[57]

Two secret civil service committees had been set up and were enthusiastically supported by Churchill after his 1951 general election victory. The first committee, the *Working Party on Coloured People Seeking Employment in the United Kingdom* was engaged in subterfuge to establish false narratives about black immigrants who had allegedly come to Britain to draw unemployment benefit.[58] The second committee, the Immigration and Repatriation Commonwealth and Coloured Colonials Home Office Working Party, chaired by Conservative MP and Under-Secretary of State K B Paice, sought evidence that 'coloured immigrants' had undesirable biological characteristics that made them incompatible with white English people.[59] The information collated from these two committees would become 'evidence' used to push through a forthcoming bill which became the Immigration Act of 1962, whose obfuscation finally enabled a way for the government to facilitate white Commonwealth immigration whilst impeding those who were black.[60]

The White Defence League

The WDL had intensified their demonstrations and meetings around Notting Hill after the riots. *Keep Britain White* leaflets, posters and graffiti were everywhere, to such a degree that the weekly documentary programme produced by the BBC, *Panorama*, ran a feature on them on Monday 13 April 1959. Leader Colin Jordan explained the WDL focus:

> Naturally we shall try and smooth the repatriation with every humane consideration. We appreciate of course that there are bound to be inconveniences and discomforts, but against that we have to say, the ultimate future of our nation, and if mass coloured immigration continues as it is doing now it will inevitably lead to a coffee coloured half-breed Britain of the future and we are going to fight to stop that.[61]

The second part of the programme was centred on SCIF and had interviews with four of its leading members to counteract Jordan. Band leader, saxophonist and vice-chairman of SCIF Johnny Dankworth explained what the organisation was all about:

> Well, the objectives of the campaign are largely to counteract any cranky organisations which try to preach the gospel of a master race anywhere, such organisations such as Mr whats-a-names [Colin Jordan] seem laughable on the face of it but they aren't really laughable because Adolf Hitler started a similar organisation about 20 or 25 years ago which caused the deaths of millions and millions of people and the sufferings of millions more.[62]

Asked why he had become involved in SCIF, musician Lonnie Donegan replied: "In my little span of life I've come across such a sea of bigotries and prejudices that I get so fed up with now that I have to do something about it".[63] *Panorama* then interviewed jazz singer Cleo Laine:

> *Panorama*: Now it was put to me earlier by the spokesman for the White Defence League that coloured people ought to be repatriated from this country to their country of origin. Now where were you born for instance?
> *Cleo Laine*: Southall, Middlesex, or [affects accent] 'Sarfall' Middlesex
> *Panorama*: So, in fact you are a Londoner, you're an Englishman? [*sic*]
> *Cleo Laine*: Yes
> *Panorama:* Where would you be, if you had to be repatriated, where would that be to?
> *Cleo Laine*: Southall, Middlesex [laughs].[64]

SCIF member and author of *To Sir With Love,* E R Braithwaite, was asked if the sort of language used by the WDL discouraged or upset him he replied:

> Not for a moment, you see it indicates to me the strength of British democracy that Mr Jordan or his associates can say this sort of thing and they are free to say it. It also indicates to me that democracy means something to the British people; they can contain this sort of thing, just as a healthy body can contain a boil or a pimple if it becomes painful then they'll take steps to deal with it.[65]

That SCIF had been given such a large part in *Panorama,* the BBC's flagship political magazine programme is an indication of just what they had achieved in such a short time. Their tactics of using their celebrity to highlight injustice and expose racism and fascism had been very successful. It is worth emphasising here just how important this coverage was and how far-reaching SCIF's profile became. BBC1 was the *only* nationwide broadcaster in the UK in 1959. Its solitary competitor ITV had been operational for only four years and was still regional in its output. The UK population was around 51 million in the late 1950s, and of that number it was estimated:

[That] the adult television public numbered about 19.5 million, and that viewers spent on average nearly 40 percent of each evening watching television. Those who had a choice of programmes spent one-third of the time devoted to television watching BBC programmes.[66]

By any standards these are massive viewing figures. SCIF was appearing in the BBC's most important current affairs programme guaranteeing it an audience of millions. But the high-profile TV work did not stop there. *Six-Five Special* was Britain's first teenage rock 'n' roll program; it ran for two years from 1957. Broadcast at five minutes past six on a Saturday night, its intention was to capture the new teenage market before they went out dancing or to the cinema. Its audience was around eight million people each week. *Six-Five Special's* presenters were Jo Douglas and Pete Murray, both of whom were in SCIF. The cast of the programme reads like the membership list of SCIF: Jim Dale, Johnny Dankworth, Tubby Hayes, Ted Heath, Rosemary Squires, Ronnie Scott, Humphrey Littleton, Terry Dene, Lonnie Donegan, Cleo Laine, Joan Regan, Jimmy Lloyd, Marty Wilde, Tommy Steele and many other members.

SCIF recruited these musicians and other celebrities to be the public face of anti-racism. The logic was simple: teenagers loved rock 'n' roll; they watched shows like *Six-Five Special*; they identified with the stars on the shows, learnt of their membership of SCIF and this would influence their opinions on race. This is not to say that *Six-Five Special* was overtly political as it was not, but the stars from the show were open about their SCIF membership in the weekly music newspapers and organised gigs and fundraisers separate to the show. The intention was to make racism unattractive and unpopular by suggestion. However, one edition screened immediately after the riots contained a film made by SCIF member and hugely popular singer Marty Wilde which did directly address the violence and the racism of the riots:

> I remember [the] racial problem in our country...my manager Larry Parnes felt that I might help to calm down the situation if I appealed to the younger people to refrain from violence, as my status as a pop star could influence a potentially dangerous situation on our streets. A film was made with me appealing for calm, and for the younger element to cool down.[67]

Six-Five Special stopped broadcasting in early 1959, when producer Jack Good jumped ship from the BBC and went over to ITV to produce a new show *Oh Boy!* but many of its stars and SCIF members went with him. The presenter on *Oh Boy!* was Tony Hall, who was also in SCIF. One of the resident performers on the show was Cuddly Dudley, Britain's first black rock 'n' roller and an active SCIF member.

SCIF's recruitment of Frank Sinatra and Paul Robeson was also a reflection of how far-reaching its influence was. Following Sinatra's Oscar winning performance in *From Here to Eternity* in 1953 and his new musical relationship with Nelson Riddle, both his film and musical career had undergone a renaissance that established him as one of the world's most famous celebrities. Sinatra's two articles for SCIF therefore had a massive impact. Paul Robeson (who alongside Claudia Jones was another victim of Senator Joseph McCarthy's witch-hunts) was residing in Britain in 1958. Robeson, a Shakespearean actor and singer was arguably the world's most popular African American artist at that time. Robeson played a part in a variety of SCIF activities. The fame of SCIF's members ensured their contributions carried a weight far more influential than SCIF's diminutive size.

The first to issue a statement opposing the racism of the riots, the first to become politically active against that racism, the first to organise social events opposing the colour-bar, SCIF had inside a matter of months launched the UK's only high-profile campaign against racism and fascism. Their initiative had seen it recruit world celebrities. It had seen the BBC beam the SCIF Christmas party into homes all over the country. Every Saturday night millions of young people watched SCIF singers, musicians, actors and comedians on prime-time music programmes. Within six months of the riots SCIF was in every living room advocating an anti-fascist and anti-racist opposition to the WDL and Oswald Mosley on *Panorama*. No other organisation anywhere in the country, be it political or cultural, had managed to obtain the platform opposing violence and racism that SCIF achieved.

1959 General Election

After the riots, as they had done in the 1930s and 1940s, the fascists coalesced. Historically, an increase in fascist activity had always meant an escalation in antisemitic attacks, but throughout the summer of 1959 there were reports of increased violence against black people and another shooting. On 17 May 1959, a 32-year-old carpenter, Kelso Cochrane from Antigua, was walking home from hospital, his arm in a sling, when he was set upon by a gang of white youths. Cochrane was fatally stabbed during the incident. Eye-witness statements said they heard repeated racist abuse directed at Cochrane and though he had no money on him the police insisted it was a robbery and no racial motive existed. For black people in North Kensington a sense of déjà vu prevailed. As we have seen, Scotland Yard had gone to great lengths to refute racism as a cause of the 1958 riots, saying: "There had not really been a racial element...but was the work of 'ruffians, both coloured and white, hell-bent on hooliganism'."[68] The cartoon below from *The Daily Worker* sums up the feeling of those convinced racism played a key part in Cochrane's murder and the riots.

Thousands of people, black and white, lined the route of Cochrane's funeral to show respect. The denial of racism in his murder on top of the efforts of the police to deny any prejudice in the previous summer's riots was a defining moment in

" HAVEN'T GOT A CLUE ! "

Daily Worker, 27 May 1959 © Marx Memorial Library & Workers' School, London.

post-war British history and sullied relations between the black community and the Metropolitan police for the decades to follow and it is arguable whether they ever recovered. Years later Peter Dawson, a Union Movement member at the time, admitted it was one of Mosley's party that had killed Cochrane in a racially motivated attack.[69]

Immediately following the death of Cochrane, SCIF issued another publication again called *What The Stars Say*: "which they [were] distributing in the Notting Hill area to counteract the flood of propaganda being issued there by the racialist bodies".[70] The lead article was another anti-racist polemic written by Frank Sinatra specifically for SCIF; it was entitled *You Can't Hate and be Happy*. On the front page an entreaty called:

> ...very urgently on all men and women who respect their fellow human creatures, uncompromisingly to denounce all instances of racial intolerance they may meet with... [furthermore] that every man and woman living in our country shall be judged entirely by his or her personal qualities and not by the racial group into which each of us happens to be born.[71]

Making their own personal and political point, black women Cleo Laine and Lena Horne appeared in photographs with their white husbands Johnny Dankworth and Lennie Hayton, happy together and in defiant opposition to Mosley's call for a prohibition on mixed marriages. In another article the broadsheet carried information from: "an international panel of scientists appointed by the United Nations which has found that racial discrimination has no scientific foundation in biological fact and that the range of mental capacities in all races is the same".[72] Other contributions came from Lonnie Donegan who said: "The worst kind of bigotry of all is racial prejudice".[73] Fellow SCIF member Tommy Steele declared: "Louis Armstrong, Count Basie, Duke Ellington, Paul Robeson, Joe Louis... show me better whites than these".[74] Folk singer and SCIF founding member Fred Dallas explained that: "We recruited Lonnie and Tommy as we knew the teddy boys listened to them and rock 'n' roll came from black America so we thought we could challenge the racism by using the stars they liked".[75]

In counteracting the racism of the WDL and UM, SCIF were becoming politically sophisticated. They employed a combination of methods to undermine the racist arguments they faced. They used the populism of teenage celebrity (Donegan and Steele) to send a message to young people, they used actors Lawrence Olivier and Paul Robeson to add a 'cultured' credibility to their anti-racist cause. Physical evidence that racially mixed marriages *do* work was presented using Cleo Laine and Lena Horne and their white husbands. An international perspective was given from a world superstar Frank Sinatra and finally, empirical facts were presented by scientists to reject the racial superiority theories from the neo-fascists. This broadsheet was posted through local letter boxes and handed out in the streets and clubs of Notting Hill, Soho and the West End of London.

For Colin Jordan and the WDL, Cochrane's death was proof that the 'evils of the coloured invasion' will only lead to trouble. That neo-fascists were responsible for this tragedy he overlooked. The activities of the far right continued in and around the area. Immediately after the murder, Mosley held several highly provocative Union Movement meetings on the exact spot where Cochrane was slain. The general election in October 1959 saw Mosley standing in the North Kensington ward. Determined to capitalise on the tragic death of a young black man and the antagonisms of white people toward the black community, Mosley used all the experience he had gathered in the 30s and 40s to gain political traction from racial unease. He situated his campaign office in Kensington Park Road, opposite the local synagogue, which subsequently became regularly daubed with swastikas. For a small organisation the sheer scale of the campaign is impressive. There was an enormous effort involving hundreds of meetings, indoor and out; demonstrations; marches; leafleting; paper sales and sustained canvassing. Mosley's campaign, called by some at the time 'the ugly election' was dripping with racism. Mosley repeatedly announced he was in Notting Hill 'to call a spade a spade'.[76] Insinuations that black people were uncivilised and ate cat food were commonplace and at his street corner meetings Mosley used the local teddy boy 'joke': 'Lassie for dogs Kit-e-Kat for wogs'.[77] In his *Memoir* Trevor Grundy recalled Mosley: "Shouting ranting and raving that West Indian men captured English girls and kept them locked up in flats, where the girls were repeatedly raped".[78] Mosley's election campaign leaflet below exemplifies this

MOSLEY SPEAKS

Martin Street
Bramley Road
Tuesday 22nd September
If wet Oxford Gardens School

Sutton Way
Dalgarno Gardens
Wednesday 23rd September
If wet Barlby Road School

Edenham Street
Golborne Road
Thursday 24th September
If wet Wornington Road School

St. Marks Place
Blenheim Crescent
Friday, 25th September
If wet Lancaster Road School
All Above Meetings at 7.30 p.m.

Cambridge Gardens
Portobello Road
Saturday, 26th September
If wet Bevington Road School
at 3 p.m.

Some of Mosleys general election public meetings in Notting Hill. The Kensington Post 1959.

MOSLEY WITH THE PEOPLE, FOR THE PEOPLE
Let Him Do The Job For You

1 **Fight to end coloured immigration,** and to send all the coloured people back with fares paid to a fair deal at home in Jamaica. Stop at once the brothels, vice-clubs and all-night parties in North Kensington. Mosley will ask the question in Parliament. Peoples Watch Committees in North Kensington will give him the facts. This exposure will make ministers instruct the police to act.

2 **Fight to get a good house or flat for every family at rents the people can afford.** This can be done when the housing problem is treated as seriously as a war, and the cost of building houses is brought down by a national plan in the same way as the cost of munitions in war. Immediate action in Parliament will at once wake up Government, councils and landlords to repair existing houses.

3 **Begin to build the new Britain in a world at peace,** which will be made possible by the Union of Europe.

Remember — Mosley has said throughout that the way to solve the coloured problem is by votes not violence. There has been much less violence since Mosley came to North Kensington, because the people can now get their rights by the vote.

NOW IS YOUR OPPORTUNITY TO END

COLOURED IMMIGRATION BY

VOTING MOSLEY X.

Remember too — that a vote for any of the other parties will mean FIVE coloured men will be here after ten years for every ONE here today (see back page) unless you stop it now.

This is your last chance to save the Britain we know and love, and the future of our children.

How it can be done — See Page 2. Mosley's constructive policy on British, Commonwealth, European and World Problems — The proof that Mosley will not let you down — See Page 3. What the best judges say Mosley can do — See Page 4.

NORTH KENSINGTON PARLIAMENTARY ELECTION POLLING DAY THURSDAY OCTOBER 8th
VOTE

REMEMBER THE BALLOT IS SECRET

Mosley 1959 election leaflet. [79]

concentration on race, as three out of the five sections of the leaflet discuss opposition to black immigration. Furthermore, although Mosley tried to distance himself from the fascism of the 1930s, this leaflet adhered to almost all of the points from the working definition of fascism that was established in the Introduction.[80]

Despite the intense activity, the outcome from the election was disappointing for the neo-fascists and the UM lost their deposit. Mosley polled only 8.1 percent with 2811 votes.[81] This was his penultimate crusade before he finally admitted defeat after faring even worse in the 1966 election and became an immigrant himself as he retired to France for the remainder of his life. Colin Jordan will feature again in Chapter Three as the British far right reappear in a new guise.

Legacy

SCIF was a reactive anti-racist, anti-fascist organisation. Whilst racism certainly did not go away after Mosley's defeat in 1959, the fascist parties that fed off that racism were undermined by the reaction to Kelso Cochrane's death and the thousands of hours work put in to counteract their racism by SCIF and many other organisations and individuals. With the UM and WDL in retreat, SCIF's raison d'être diminished: "SCIF was a short lived thing that didn't really become a campaign as such, it just ran its course" recalled founding member Hylda Sims.[82] The last mention of SCIF was a small advert for a gig in south east London, tucked away in the corner of page seven in *Melody Maker* on 14 November 1959 entitled 'Jazz stars to play for SCIF funds':

> A jazz ball in aid of the Stars Campaign for Interracial Friendship will be held at Dulwich Baths on December 14th. Giving their services free will be Johnny Dankworth, The Lennie Best Quartet, Norman Days Jazzmen, Kenny Robinsons Jazz Band and blues singer guitarist Alex Korner.[83]

For the jazz and blues world the importance, nay reverence, of black musicians had always informed their politics.[84] In 1950s pop music and rock 'n' roll this corollary was not always there, as audiences in the UK often heard black American songs for the first time through white performers doing cover versions making this black to white link 'once removed'. The first mass subculture for British teenagers was the teddy boy and although it adopted a musical expression, it was primarily a sartorial manifestation of alienation, dissatisfaction and post-war hangover. By 1960 it was beginning to wane, certainly in London, and in its place a new subculture was forming. Modernists, who SCIF member Colin MacInnes discusses so eloquently in *Absolute Beginners,* were not the same as the teddy boys. Like MacInnes, mods celebrated black culture, they lived black culture. They shared the same clothes, the same clubs, the same drugs and the same music as their West Indian neighbours. Part of the job that was done by SCIF in its short life, championing black culture, was taken up by this new set of teenagers in London. It was also passionately promoted by a new wave of musicians with an incomparable fanbase to that of the jazz and skiffle players in SCIF. The Beatles, The Rolling Stones, The Kinks, The Animals *et al* all were blues and R&B fanatics, constantly name checking the black sources of their inspiration and bringing black American artists over to the UK to tour with them in large arenas.

Most importantly, an organised black response to racism had been awoken. There was also much that had happened during this time in the wider world to challenge at least some of the racist misconceptions that the '58 generation had ingested: the Sharpeville Massacre in South Africa and the struggle against Apartheid, the March on Washington and the ongoing civil rights movement in America. Britain was also slowly coming to terms with its diminishing role as a world player. As SCIF member Eric Hobsbawm outlined in his work *The Age of Empire,* no imperialism or colonial power can last forever. Paradoxically, the war that Britain had fought to save its empire proved to be the catalyst for its demise.

It is clear that there was no *single* event, person or organisation that can be held responsible for the 1958 riots nor the amelioration that would slowly develop in the decades that followed them. The cause and the remedy were both multi-faceted. There is an ancient Chinese proverb that states: "The longest journey starts with the smallest step". Indeed, the journey that began in Notting Hill has yet to reach its destination. However, the myriad organisations that were born to fight discrimination and oppression in the late 1950s and began to push anti-racism onto the political agenda in the 1960s have their origins in the events in west London that summer of 1958.

SCIF sought to use the celebrity of its members to make anti-racism respectable, even cool in 1950s Britain. That some of its members were journalists in the music press ensured that in the year after the riots SCIF was never far from the news. Denis Preston, Fred Dallas, Max Jones and Humphrey Littleton all used their columns in the *Melody Maker* and the *New Musical Express* to promote anti-racist events and argue a political line out of step with large parts of society. For a small organisation SCIF punched well above its weight. The most obvious legacy of SCIF and the 1958 riots is the Notting Hill Carnival. Many later on claimed parental rights of Carnival but the correlation between the inaugural albeit indoor Carnival in St Pancras town hall and the North Kensington troubles seems irrefutable. Claudia Jones, one of SCIF's leading members, and a Trinidadian by birth, saw through her involvement with SCIF the power of music and its potential to disarm racist ideas. The first Carnival is held in January 1959, just five months after the riots and Claudia Jones' statement that with Carnival: "[we] wash the taste of Notting Hill and Nottingham out of our mouths" suggests that her title of 'the mother of Carnival' is befitting.[85] The environment for Afro-Caribbean and Asian communities residing in the UK at the end of the 1950s was challenging to say the least, and Harold Macmillan's assertion: "You've never had it so good" for black people lacked empirical evidence.[86] But Mosley's nose had been bloodied in the electoral defeat of 1959 and the support for Jordan's WDL had been undermined by Kelso Cochrane's death and the wave of revulsion that followed it. What was the future for British neo-fascism and how would they rebuild? For everyone else the new decade promised much; Britain was visibly changing. The 1960s saw an incremental increase in the visibilty of black people in everyday life and the now hackneyed comment of the 'fifties being in black and white and the sixties in colour' would ring true.

Economically the new decade would be 'forged in the white heat of new technology'.[87] Politically, 1964 would see the end of 13 years of Conservative rule. In terms of youth culture, the teddy boys, destined forever to be associated with the racism and violence of the Notting Hill riots, were to be usurped by mods who openly embraced black culture. By the end of the 1960s skinheads, Britain's first truly multi-racial youth subculture, was to evolve from mods and, the other subcultural expression of the late 1960s, the hippies, flagrantly professed their love for all races in humanity, a mere nine years after teddy boys did the opposite in 1958. But all this was to come. To close this chapter, and to sum up the tumultuous events at the close of the decade, sociologist and author Ruth Glass's words written in 1959 are particularly poignant:

About 50 years from now, future historians in Asia, in Africa and perhaps in England—writing about Europe in the nineteen fifties...[will] presumably devote a chapter to the coloured minority group in this country. They will say that although this group was small, it was an important, indeed an essential one. For its arrival and growth gave British society an opportunity of recognising its own blind spots, and also looking beyond its own nose to a widening horizon of human integrity. They will point out that the relations between white and coloured people in this country were a test of Britain's ability to fulfil the demands for progressive rationality in social organisation, so urgently imposed in the latter part of the 20th century. And the future historians will add that Britain had every chance of passing this test, because at that period her domestic problems were rather slight by comparison to those of many other areas of the world. All this can be anticipated. But it is still uncertain how the chapter will end.[88]

Chapter Three
1960 to 1976: Culture and Society

Oswald Mosley's defeat in the 1959 British election signalled the beginning of the wilderness years for the far right in Britain. They undertook a period of reflection on their previous 40 years of success and failure. For the rest of society, the new decade promised much. Paul Addison argues that from the end of WWII a model of political co-operation existed in Britain that lasted up until Margaret Thatcher's election victory in 1979.[1] This post-war consensus encouraged by Labour, accepted by the Liberal party and tolerated by the Tories was reflected in a wide variety of policies that began with the Labour Party's general election victory in 1945. Full employment was an aspiration almost achieved. There was trade union consultation on government policy, the National Health Service was created alongside the expansion of education, a comprehensive housing programme, a number of welfare programmes and the consensus also included the nationalisation of many industries.[2]

The 1950s saw a gradual move away from a war economy footing and toward a modern liberal society. Rationing was ended in 1954, conscription was phased out beginning in 1957.[3] There were landmark court cases such as the Wildeblood trial in 1954.[4] This case, as infamous as Oscar Wilde's in 1895, resulted in The Wolfenden Report, published in 1957 by the Departmental Committee on Homosexual Offences and Prostitution.[5] The report concluded that homosexuality should be legalised and urged that public statutes should avoid attempts to legislate on matters of private morality. Two high profile murder trials, those of Derek Bentley in 1952 and Ruth Ellis in 1955 had seen large public demonstrations against the death penalty outside the Old Bailey and the prisons where both Bentley and Ellis were eventually executed.[6] These cases were instrumental in the 1957 Homicide Act that introduced provocation and diminished responsibility as grounds for mitigation in murder trials. Barely had the new decade begun when the case of the *Crown versus Penguin Books* opened on 21 October 1960.[7] When the full unexpurgated version of D H Lawrence's *Lady Chatterley's Lover* was published the year before, it set in motion a vehicle that would end in collision with the British state and its antiquated obscenity laws. *Penguin's* victory heralded what Phillip Larkin was later to quip:

> Sexual intercourse began in 1963 (which was rather late for me), between the end of the "Chatterley" ban and the Beatles' first LP. [8]

Dominic Sandbrook, a revisionist historian not noted for his sympathy toward the progressive elements of the 1960s, was even moved to state that the trial was: "a simple clash between the repressive old Establishment on the one hand, and the youthful forces of progress and enlightenment on the other".[9]

The 1960s were to revolutionise many aspects of British social life: the introduction of the birth control pill in 1961, the Race Relations Acts of 1965 and 1968, the Sexual Offences Act 1967 (which de-criminalised homosexuality) and the Abortion Act 1967 which allowed limited access to terminations for women in England, Scotland and Wales. The Windrush years had seen a fledgling multicultural society establish itself in many of the UK's major cities. Black people began tentative steps toward employment across all industries.[10] Engagement in everyday activities and the involvement in cultural life that had begun with the demise of the so-called colour bar meant that although racism had not by any stretch of the imagination disappeared, Britain was changing.

For post-war teenagers, identifiable as a separate group, with spending power of their own, the world would be different than that which their parents inhabited. The near-full employment throughout the period meant a financial independence only dreamt of by their parents.[11] Nothing demonstrated this job security and economic confidence more than the rapidly changing world of music and youth fashion.[12] By 1960 skiffle and trad jazz had wilted, and the teddy boys, so central to the racism and the riots in Nottingham and Notting Hill in 1958, had been superseded by a new subculture, modernists.

Modernism

The advent of bebop in the United States heralded a break from swing. For some jazz players, swing had become a white emasculation of jazz and they felt the need to re-establish it in the African American tradition. The new bebop musicians were younger and hungrier. John Coltrane, Miles Davis and Dizzy Gillespie were all in their twenties during the formative years of this new genre and this younger generation wanted a radical shake up of what they saw as a tired and outdated musical expression. Conversely, traditional jazz or trad was incredibly popular in 1950s Britain. Trad musicians and fans as the name would suggest sought tradition, a yearning to recreate Dixieland jazz from New Orleans, a music that was made in the years following WWI. Some went to perilous lengths to find 'the sound'.[13] By definition trad jazz was backward looking, whereas modernists were looking forwards, they wanted a music that spoke for their generation, not their grandparents'.[14]

Alongside their discomfort with the music, mods also sought an aesthetic departure from trad. A pattern had already been established in British youth subcultures whereby an unofficial uniform accompanied the music teenagers were listening to, as already discussed with teddy boys. For trad fans, anti-fashion was the fashion and loose, ill-fitting clothing was their act of defiance against the 'squares' in suits. Whilst there was no singular look, nor a retail altar under which they could worship, there were two items of attire that gave the men in the group their identity and this was catered for by ex-military surplus stores. Royal Navy submariners' sweaters and duffle coats became *de rigueur* for the trad subculture and beards, though not essential, were often sported. For women, there was a less defined style, though knitwear was popular, worn with full skirts or trousers. Many wore their hair in the 'Italian cut', short, but sculpted and influenced by actresses such as Sophia Loren. Nevertheless, for trad fans, their emphasis was on the authenticity of the music; style was not the main concern.[15] Women immersed in the new modernist subculture also bucked the trend for catwalk fashion. They wore clothes that erred toward androgyny; shoes without heels, shift dresses that hid the figure, twin sets, trousers and skirts below the knee, even as hem lines began to rise as the 60s progressed. The 'bob' in all its myriad styles was the go-to haircut.

Male modernists in the UK not only saw modern jazz as the musical expression of their forward-looking ethos, but they also took their sobriquet from the genre and their wardrobe from its musicians. Albums featuring artists such as Lou Donaldson, Lee Morgan, Miles Davis and Jimmy Smith had photographs of these artists on the cover.[16] They were wearing clothes almost unobtainable in 1950s Britain: "The jazz culture was an Ivy League culture. Chet Baker and all those people wore Ivy League from the early 1950s. They were your idols, so you wanted to wear what they wore".[17]

Ivy League clothing was itself an unofficial uniform for white middle-class collegiate kids attending the most prestigious universities in America.[18] The style had developed over many decades, borrowing items of clothing from around the world: the button-down collared shirt from British polo players, the slip-on loafer shoe from Norway, a little bit of Italy, a little bit of France, but always sharp and worn with immaculate three button suits with short lapels and narrow trousers from Brooks Brothers in New York.[19] African-American jazz musicians had usurped this style and claimed it as their own. Oppressed and marginalised inside American society, they wore the clothing of the privileged white elite as a political statement. The now universal acceptance into common parlance of the word 'man' also began its life as a defiant political stance by black jazz players. Denied the courtesy of adulthood, black men were regularly demeaned and called 'boy' by white society, as Martin Luther King pointed out in his now famous *Letter from Birmingham Jail*:

> [We are] humiliated day in and day out by nagging signs reading "white" and "colored"; when your first name becomes "nigger," your middle name becomes "boy" (however old you are) and your last name becomes "John", and your wife and mother are never given the respected title "Mrs."; when you are harried by day and haunted by night by the fact that you are a Negro.[20]

In opposition to this infantilism, jazz musicians began calling each other 'man'. Modernists in the UK adapted the walk and adopted the talk from across the Atlantic. Richard Barnes, author of *Mods,* art school friend and flatmate in the early 60s of The Who's guitarist and songwriter Pete Townshend recalls Peter Meaden, face around Soho in 1964 and later manager of The Who:

> He was English but talked like an American radio disc jockey, really fast and slick. He called everybody 'baby!' 'Hey, how are you Peter baby, too much, what's happening, great, keep cool. Can you dig it? Barney baby, s'nice to see you again, OK baby? [21]

Modernists in London, 1962. L to R: Tommy Balderson, Bernadette O'Day, Georgie Hunt, Jean Hanlon, Mickey Modern. © Mickey Modern

Tony Foley, a 1963 modernist and his scooter. © Tony Foley

Meaden lived, ate, drank, and when the pills wore off, slept mod. For Meaden, mods were: "Living on the pulse of the city... neat, sharp and cool, an all-white Soho negro of the night".[22] This was a departure from previous British subcultures, an explicit identification with black American people, their music and clothes. As Dick Hebdige observed in *Subculture, The Meaning of Style:* "The mod was the first all-British white negro" of Norman Mailer's essay, *The White Negro*.[23] Likewise, in *Generation X,* Deverson and Hamblett's ground-breaking study of British subculture, one young mod interviewed expressed his feelings thus: "At the moment we're worshipping the spades...they can dance and sing".[24] SCIF member Colin MacInnes' novels from this period, *City of Spades*, *Mr Love & Justice* and *Absolute Beginners* are littered with references to, and in adulation of, all aspects of black culture.[25]

However, mods were also picking up on a style much closer to home. When the Empress Windrush docked in Tilbury in 1948, West Indian immigrants began disembarking and unloading their luggage, but with their clothes and photographs of home, they had also packed their culture. Successive generations arriving in the United Kingdom throughout the following 50 years would bring with them up-to-date Caribbean styles and sounds. A new musical phenomenon had been percolating around Orange Street in Kingston, Jamaica and by the late 1950s, on the streets of Brixton and Notting Hill, this fresh sound was beginning to filter through. It became known as ska.[26]

Evolving out of calypso, mento, jazz and American rhythm & blues, ska was distinctive for its 'off beat' rhythm and walking bass lines and was heavily used by the 'sound systems' starting to become popular in Jamaica. Living in London at the time, original mod Amber Humphreys recalled:

> [We]...referred to the sound as *Blue Beat* and it was what we danced to in the Limbo club in Wardour Mews, the Candy Lounge in Gerrard Street and of course the Roaring Twenties and it was on all the juke boxes in Soho bars like Etchers in

Frith Street [Soho] and the Lorelei and the Coffee Pot.[27]

Clubs that catered for a Caribbean clientele now began to see a young white working-class audience absorbing first the musical and then the sartorial styles:

> The Flamingo was partly responsible for bringing in the West Indian influence. The Bluebeat hats, like bowler hats but with a very short brim and called 'Pork Pie' hats, were first worn by West Indians in the Roaring Twenties club. But the same West Indians frequented the Flamingo and All-nighter as well, and the mods picked up the style from them. Dances like 'The Dog' and 'The Ska' were also copied from the West Indian dancers at the Flamingo.[28]

The Roaring Twenties was one of the most successful of the early 1960s Soho clubs. Although the colour bar had been officially broken, the prejudice that lay behind it remained resolute. We have already briefly met Count Suckle in Chapter One when one of his 'blues parties' was attacked in Notting Hill in 1958. Suckle was the resident disc jockey at the Roaring Twenties:

> I opened the Twenties on the 4th of July, a Wednesday night [1962], American Independence. But the club wasn't opened for black people, it was owned by Jewish people and it only catered for Jewish kids. I was the only black guy there because I was the leading DJ at the time, and they wanted a popular `front` figure to pull in the crowds so I was hired.[29]

Jeff Dexter, DJ, original mod 'face' at the time, and now an advisor on all things from that period recalls:

> After a while Suckle's young black followers began to seek admittance to the Twenties which resulted in Suckle putting his foot down and threatening to quit if the management

did not change its 'no admittance' policy towards blacks. When they gave way and West Indians were allowed into the Twenties, it became a predominantly `black` club.[30]

One does not want to overstate this interracial mixing and claim that black and white sharing of nightclubs was a wholesale negation of racism in British or at least London society in the 1960s. But mod was different to what had been witnessed in the 1950s with teddy boys, skiffle or trad. Although the language used by some of these young people may not be acceptable in 2021, this subterranean subculture was a *total* celebration of black culture, in language, clothes and music and although modernism would remain singularly white for reasons explained later, mods were Britain's first foray into a multicultural society. Nonetheless, it needs to be restated that this should not lead to the conclusion that Britain was flowering into an open multicultural paradise where no prejudice existed. Indeed, on 27 September 1963 the *Daily Mirror* announced that the Institute of Race Relations had begun

Colin Jordan with Françoise Dior after their marriage in 1963 © Getty Images

a five-year investigation into race hate.[31] This investigation was to begin ironically in Birmingham, West Midlands, its purpose to avoid precisely the violence occurring in Birmingham, Alabama. However, investigations aside, instances of violent organised racism as were witnessed in Notting Hill in 1958 had not thus far recurred on any similar scale. Why? What were the reasons for this? What was happening to the far right in Britain throughout this period?

The Far Right

The internecine rivalry, which impeded the growth of fascist groups in the 1930s, 1940s and 1950s was never far from the surface of the 1960s groups either. Tactical disagreements, political heritage arguments and power struggles accompanied the far right throughout the decade. A further problem was the leadership of these groups. Thurlow states: "The most important contrast with the [1960s and the] interwar period was that there was nobody who possessed the moral authority, the intellectual power or political experience of Sir Oswald Mosley".[32]

With Mosley playing less of a role in British politics after the 1959 general election, there began a battle for leadership that would last until the end of the decade. Colin Jordan's White Defence League, also pivotal in the 1958 riots, had dissolved by 1960.[33] Aside from his liaisons with Mosley, Jordan had developed close links with another far right group, The National Labour Party (NLP), and its founders John Bean and a disgraced ex-Conservative candidate, Andrew Fountaine.[34] Two other names from the NLP will feature in later events: John Tyndall and Martin Webster.

After the murder of Kelso Cochrane, the NLP and the WDL had organised a 'Stop the Coloured Invasion' rally in Trafalgar Square in May 1959 with banners proclaiming *Keep Britain White;* this drew a crowd of 3,000 and many of its supporters were openly wearing fascist insignia. In February 1960 the two organisations merged. After rejecting the name, the Racial

White Defence League demonstration, Trafalgar Square, 1959. © Getty Images

Nationalist Party, the group became the British National Party (BNP). Its maxim was 'For Race and Nation' and they pledged to oppose the 'international Jewish-controlled money-lending system' in their founding policy statement.[35] At their height in 1967 the BNP could claim 1,000 members and until the formation of the National Front, they were the biggest far right group in Britain throughout the decade.[36] Arnold Leese was the inspiration for this new generation of neo-Nazis. They rejected the tactics of pre-war fascists A K Chesterton and Oswald Mosley in trying to build an electorally respectable party and many had been unhappy when the Nazi symbolism had been discarded. Indeed, Tyndall and Jordan split from Webster over precisely this issue and on 20 April 1962, what would have been Hitler's 73rd birthday, they formed the National Socialist Movement (NSM). Tyndall and Jordan (by now 'Führer' in the World Union of National Socialists) argued that German fascist traditions were more important than British ones. The BNP, Bean, Fountaine and Webster stated that 'anti-coloured immigration' should be the focus of fascist activity.[37] The 1962 Commonwealth Immigration Act had become, as predicted by Claudia Jones, a colour bar bill that restricted immigration for potential migrants from Asia, Africa and the Caribbean and the focus of the far right during this period concentrated on this bill's journey through parliament alongside their traditional antisemitism.

On 4 July 1962 in Trafalgar Square, Reverend Bill Sargent stood alone, a defiant solitary demonstrator as Colin Jordan began speaking from a platform addressing a rally entitled 'Free Britain from Jewish Control'. Sargent was wearing a yellow star cloth badge, as worn by Jewish prisoners in Nazi concentration camps. He was soon joined by another 40 or so people and this group soon became known as the Yellow Star Movement (YSM).[38] It was an 'informal' organisation with no official members or structure, but its supporters were ready to be utilised should a fascist threat occur. Their tactics centred around mobilising support for demonstrations and the 'jump the pitch' tactic used by the 43 Group in the 1940s. Essentially this meant, once a fascist group was known to be conducting a meeting or rally, the YSM would arrive prior to said fascist organisation and set up stall to prevent any other group from doing so. This 'first come, first served' principal was enshrined in British law in relation to political meetings. The other focus of the YSM was around lobbying to make incitement to racial hatred a crime and to this end they collected over 440,000 signatures on a petition to parliament.[39] Small fascist meetings began to grow in London in the early 1960s and arguments over the tactics to combat these meetings developed and a split occurred within the YSM. The more militant of the activists left to form the 62 Group. This organisation included some ex-members of the 43 Group, and like their forerunner concentrated on physically opposing and breaking up far right meetings. They had an elaborate network of spotters, friends and supporters and Jewish traders at local markets:

> Ridley Road [Hackney] and the surrounding area was a traditional spot for fascist street meetings. The 'quick call out' system meant that whilst the fascists were gathering prior to their meeting and before the Met deployed their forces, we could often surprise them. At best we reckoned we could get 60-80 comrades to Ridley Road within 20-30 minutes of the call from the market. Where we had prior knowledge of a fascist street meeting, it was often cancelled.[40]

Tactics to break up fascist meetings involved the use of 'the wedge', again borrowed from the 43 Group, whereby a tightly knit group of men would force their way into a crowd or meeting and begin to heckle or physically fight fascist supporters and break the meeting up. As one member recalled:

> The tactics varied from (1) quietly infiltrating the fascist supporters until we had enough there—then do them, to (2) meet a quarter of a mile away until we had sufficient numbers, then a running wedge straight in—and do them.[41]

Both the YSM and the 62 Group concentrated their focus on the Union Movement, but there were also attacks on the NSM. One such raid on the NSM headquarters broke up their printing press and confiscated the NSM membership list; they also found evidence which they submitted to the police, of a series of arson attacks on synagogues and Jewish property that led to the arrest and conviction of John Tyndall.[42] In early 1963 there was even a nod to SCIF as the YSM held a jazz and folk festival against fascism and racism in Kensington town hall. There are countless stories of individual and collective opposition from YSM and 62 Group members to Mosley and Jordan wherever they appeared. Like the 43 Group before them their tactics made it very difficult for fascists to meet; disruption, violence and the threat of violence made meetings and public rallies almost impossible and as Testa concludes: "By 1963 the UM and NSM were utterly demoralised and finally withdrew from street politics".[43] With the immediate fascist threat diminished, the YSM and the 62 Group dissolved.

However, events toward the end of 1964 seemed to bear out what the BNP had been arguing and three election results were an indication that immigration was beginning to have an effect on voting patterns in inner-city areas. The first was Peter Griffith's Conservative Party campaign and election victory in Smethwick. The campaign was run on a highly racialised basis and the Conservative Party slogan for the election was: 'If you desire a coloured for a neighbour, vote Labour'.[44] However, written on walls and billboards across the constituency were the words 'If you want a nigger for a neighbour, vote Labour'![45] Griffiths did nothing to counter this racism, indeed the differences in words were considered only semantics. The Labour candidate, Patrick Walker, lost with a 7.2 percent swing to the Tories.[46]

The second was the loss of veteran Labour MP Fenner Brockway's seat in Slough and the third, in Leyton, east London. The 1965 by-election in Leyton had arisen when the constituency's long-serving Labour Member of Parliament, Reginald Sorensen, was made a life peer on 15 December 1964. Patrick Walker, the Labour candidate, defeated only months before in Smethwick, experienced a highly racialised campaign with Colin Jordan following him around with a man in a monkey suit eating bananas and a black and white minstrel declaring Walker a 'race mixer' who wanted to make Britain black.[47] Walker lost again, bringing the Labour majority in the House of Commons down to just two seats. All three of these electoral defeats were safe Labour seats, all three had a sizeable influx of black or Asian immigrants and all three were lost to opponents campaigning on an openly anti-immigration platform.

Whilst the Labour Party had won the 1964 election with a slender majority of four, the leadership blamed this loss of safe seats on 'liberal ethnic policies' and with an eye on an inevitable snap election in the near future, drafted a white paper that not only pandered to the racism of the 1962 act but went further and proposed limiting [black] immigration to only 8,500 in times of 'labour shortages'.[48]

Whilst clearly having an effect on local elections and the government response, the tactics adopted by the far right caused a rift between John Tyndall and Colin Jordan as Jordan became increasingly involved in electoral publicity stunts, individual acts of terrorism and bizarre personal situations.[49] Tyndall would split from Jordan and begin his journey of reconciliation back to Bean and Webster.[50] Once an open and vituperative anti-Semite, Tyndall was now beginning to temper his outbursts and become more measured and reasonable in tone as he presented his argument in more rational terms.[51]

Rivers of Blood

Labour leader Harold Wilson won the 1966 general election with a 96 seat majority and aside from occasional stunts and violent attacks on both the left and minorities, the far right, numerically too small for any significant intervention, withered on the margins of British political life. This was to change after a speech given by Enoch Powell in Birmingham in 1968. Enoch Powell was a Conservative MP in the shadow cabinet and had been Minister for Health in Harold Macmillan's government in 1960. Whilst in post he had overseen the recruitment and emigration of Caribbean and Asian labour into the UK to fill labour shortages. By 1968 Powell was expressing doubts about large scale immigration and was also in opposition to Labour

Government's Race Relations Act of 1968 which superseded the Race Relations Act of 1965 and made discrimination on the grounds of race a *criminal* offence. The 1968 Act also created the Community Relations Commission to promote harmonious community relations.

On 20 April 1968, Powell delivered what has become one of the most infamous and incendiary speeches in British history. The 'Rivers of Blood' speech as it has become known, not only opposed the immigration Powell had helped create, but laid the blame for any inter-racial difficulties, be they social, political or economic, with the migrant population. Furthermore, any attempt by parliament to legally address the racism suffered by Britain's black and Asian population, or any measures taken to ameliorate their situation must be opposed. For Powell, the victims of substandard housing, discrimination in employment, the violence, the colour bar, in short the immigration that he was partly responsible for, were white and British:

> The discrimination and the deprivation, the sense of alarm and of resentment, lies not with the immigrant population but with those among whom they have come and are still coming. This is why to enact legislation of the kind before parliament at this moment is to risk throwing a match on to gunpowder.[52]

Powell was immediately suspended from the shadow front bench of the Conservative party, but his speech was a clarion call to those unhappy with Britain's immigration policies over the previous 20 years. Reports of attacks against black families increased following the speech.[53] Fryer describes the murder of one Jamaican man in Smethwick, the near murder of a schoolboy in North Kensington and burning crosses erected outside homes in Leamington Spa, Rugby, Coventry, Ilford, Plaistow and Cricklewood.[54]

The local newspaper near to where Powell had given his speech, the *Shropshire Star,* was deluged in the weeks after the speech with postcards and letters of support for Powell.[55]

Local demonstrations in the Midlands were organised against immigration and on 23 April 1968 over 1,000 London dockers struck in protest at Powell's sacking and marched from the east end of London to the Palace of Westminster carrying placards. The following day 600 dockers at St Katharine Docks voted to strike and numerous smaller factories across the country followed. Hundreds of Smithfield meat porters, also on strike, marched to Westminster and handed Powell a 92-page petition supporting him.[56] The Gallup Organisation took an opinion poll at the end of April and found that 74 percent of those surveyed agreed with what Powell had said in his speech and 69 percent felt Conservative Party leader Edward Heath was wrong to sack Powell.[57]

Whilst Powell was opposing the legislation that would prohibit discrimination in Britain, the Labour Government, equally concerned about public hostility to immigration: "steamrolled through Parliament in three days of 'emergency

Dockers march in support of Enoch Powell, 1968. © SWP Archive

debate' the 1968 Commonwealth Immigration Act [which had] the 'sole purpose of restricting entry into Britain of Kenyan Asians holding British passports'."[58] This act was deliberately designed to halt the flow of black and Asian immigrants into Britain whilst being careful not to impede the movement of white Commonwealth citizens.[59] This was not Labour pandering to racism, this was a total capitulation. Writing concomitantly, journalist Paul Foot observed: "One of the most constant rules in the history of immigration control is that those demanding controls are encouraged, not silenced, by concessions".[60] Foot's comments would prove to be prescient.

For the far right, the Rivers of Blood speech could not have been better timed and enabled the neo-fascists to finally look outwards after years of marginalisation in British politics. The previous year an attempt to overcome factional divisions inside the various groups on the far right had been successful and they had coalesced into one organisation, what Thurlow has called the grand synthesis:

> The formation of the National Front in 1967 was the most significant event on the radical right and fascist fringe of British politics since internment [in 1939]. It represented the culmination of a process whereby the various strands of revisionist neo-Nazi and racial populist politics came together in an attempt to form a national mass party, which although anti-Mosley, had distinct roots in the BUF of the later 1930s.[61]

In essence, the National Front (NF) represented a merger between the LEL and the BNP, but it managed to draw around it random individuals, disaffected Tories and groups of other festering malcontents. The Racial Preservation Society (RPS) was one such group. A loose confederation of anti-immigration organisations littered around the country, the RPS funded a number of publications that periodically appeared during the years 1965-1969 (Thurlow estimates this to number over two million leaflets, pamphlets, posters and books).[62] Whilst not being openly fascist the RPS was militantly anti-immigration and possessed significant financial backing. The RPS had been approached by John Tyndall in 1966 with a request to merge with his Greater Britain Movement and the BNP. They initially rejected the request as the group had no desire to surrender its separate existence; however, with the formation of the National Front the following year Martin Walker claims a significant proportion of the 2,500 members that the NF claimed came from a split in the RPS.[63] Despite the split the RPS remained intact as an organisation and the relationship between them and Tyndall would continue until the 1980s.

It would be a mistake however, to assume that the newly formed National Front was not without its problems. This first phase of the NF was plagued by political chasms that arguably were never resolved. At its inception the leadership of the NF was immediately riven by arguments between Chesterton (from the LEL), Fountaine (from the Conservative Party) and Beauclair (from the RPS). Personal grudges, inefficient administration, ideological differences and disputes over disciplinary powers ensured a climate of mutual suspicion and hostility that would see Chesterton depart within three years.[64]

As the decade wore on Tyndall continued his shift in speaking style from splenetic vitriol into 'reasoned oratory'.[65] But this was not an epiphany; the Race Relations Act of 1968 had outlawed language and activities deemed to provoke racial disharmony.[66] Tyndall had already begun to use euphemisms and coded language to hide his Nazi sentiments, seek political respectability and to garner support for his organisation as early as 1964. This was partly to delineate between himself and Webster, whose gutter antisemitism would soon graduate to a virulent anti-black racism. However, they were reconciled inside the NF after Tyndall was allowed to join in 1968. The far right seized upon the opportunity afforded them by Powell's Rivers of Blood speech and were to grow exponentially in the coming years.

Original skinheads, Northampton, 1969 © Norman Rogers

Skinheads

By 1966 mods were no longer the prominent subculture in British society. Dancing to Tamla Motown in sharp suits, fuelled by a high dose of amphetamines, was to be replaced by two new developments that had not just sartorial, but political repercussions as well: skinheads and hippies.[67] Like most subcultures it is difficult to say with exact precision where the first hippy or skinhead was seen; however, by late 1967 to early 1968 something was reverberating on the streets of London. Initially the first group had a variety of names: peanuts, lemons and boiled-eggs amongst many others. But on 3 September 1969, the *Daily Mirror* in an article headlined 'No Love from Johnny' finally gave them a name that would resonate: skinheads.[68]

The skinhead subculture came from three sources, firstly, the so-called 'hard mods'. They were gangs of working-class teenagers, clothes-obsessed still, but lacking the business acumen to obtain them. They were centred around council estates where territorial disputes and turf wars abounded.[69] As Marshall argues: "Most importantly for the skinhead cult... [was]...the rise in numbers of the gang mods who stalked the urban jungles of Britain's towns and cities".[70] Parts of London had still not fully recovered from the war. Bomb sites were not uncommon in inner city areas, unemployment was beginning to rise and a sense of 'lost community' and a 'forgotten working class' used so much in recent years to explain the Brexit vote and the rise of UKIP, can be seen 50 years ago with the advent of skinheads. Nick Knight writes:

> Sociologists, describing the original skinhead movement of the late 60s called...[the] nostalgic aspect of skinhead culture an attempt to 'symbolically recover' the sense of cohesiveness and community of the old working-class slum. Hence, they argued, the preoccupation of the skinheads with territory and turf...with local allegiances...the exaggerated tribalism, the bull-headed racism...[and] the dogged male chauvinism.[71]

In his essay *Resistance Through Rituals,* Jefferson draws a similar conclusion, and although talking about teds ten years prior, his comments are equally valid when examining skinheads: "Thus, the group life and intense loyalty of the teds can be seen as a reaffirmation of traditional slum working-class values and a strong sense of territory".[72]

The second aspect of the development of skinhead was football. Whilst always being a bulwark of working-class entertainment, attendance had dwindled at British games after WWII. England's victory in the 1966 World Cup gave the ailing sport a much-needed injection of publicity and the sport entered into the popular culture vernacular. Alongside sartorially conscious football stars like George Best, Bobby Moore and Jimmy Greaves, fashion began to enter a world hitherto bereft of style. The football terrace took on a new role, becoming a catwalk for working-class male fashion as the latest styles and trends from London were projected courtesy of thousands of 'away day' fans the length and breadth of the country. As original skinhead Nigel Mann recalls: "The first time I ever saw a skinhead was when Chelsea came to play Leicester in 1968. Tons of them showed up. I was absolutely fascinated by their dress, their style".[73] Fellow 1960s skinhead James Ferguson concurs: "That was the first time I saw skinheads as well...They were wearing mainly Levi's jeans. They were kind of mod but a bit grubby looking. They had on donkey jackets and boots, not Dr Marten boots, but any kind of boots".[74] Football became increasingly important as an expression of working-class fashion, authenticity and masculinity.

The third component of what became the skinhead comes from Jamaica. As already discussed, the slow breakdown of the colour bar had begun after the Notting Hill riots. The myriad Afro-Caribbean groups politically active at the end of the 1950s had been instrumental in pressing for legislation to outlaw discrimination. Organisations like SCIF had seen the potential power of music to challenge discrimination and Claudia Jones' first indoor Carnival at Kings Cross in 1959 had, by 1965, become the outdoor summer Carnival that we know today in Notting Hill. The influence of Jamaican style and music with mods in London has also been discussed; this influence became more pronounced when the first wave of skinheads appear. Indeed, of this first wave, there are noticeable numbers of black skinheads. The reasons for this need to be explored.

In 1948 the passengers from the West Indies on the *Empire Windrush* were overwhelmingly male. Successive boats after *Windrush* had similar cohorts. On the whole, the first arrivals were men, young and single. Fryer breaks down the figures. In January 1949 onboard the ship *Rena del Pacifico* 39 of the 54 Jamaicans were men and out of 299 on the *Georgic* that summer, only 45 were female. Not until the years 1954-1958 did sizeable numbers of women arrive:[75]

For five years, despite the demand for their services, there was only a trickle of West Indians into Britain...larger numbers arrived in the next four years, including many wives and children of men who had settled here.[76]

As young Caribbean women emigrated to England and young black men met young white women, relationships began to forge, and children were born. Although there were no specific questions in the Census relating to ethnicity until 1991, we can see from the following table that the 'visible minority' population slowly rose.[77]

Census year	Indians	Pakistanis and Bangladeshis	Chinese	African-Caribbeans	Black Africans	Total
1991	840,255	639,390	156,938	678,365	212,362	2,527,310
1981	855,025	360,023,	120,123	545,744	79,649	1,960,564
1971	304,370	127,565	60,000	360,000	40,000	927,935
1961	81,400	81,400	29,600	171,800	19,800	384,000
1951	30,800	30,800	12,000	15,300	5,600	94,500

Estimated size of Britain's visible minority populations, 1951-1991.[78]

Part of this study is an analysis of British subcultures, of which the participants were primarily teenagers. The first subculture that appeared in Britain is the teddy boy, making its debut around 1950-1951. Any black male or female, even if they felt inclined toward participating in this subculture, would have had to have been born at the very latest in 1937 in order to meet the teenage pre-requisites for the first wave of teds. Of those arriving from the West Indies, post-Windrush, few were under the age of 20.[79]

Whilst we saw some black cultural involvement in the British music scene at the end of the 50s with artists like Cuddly Duddly Heslop, Cleo Laine and Winifred Atwell, no such black or Asian involvement was witnessed in teddy boy subculture. This was unsurprising as much of the racist violence meted out by indigenous British youth in the 1950s came from teddy boys.[80] As we have already discussed, mods were different and open to ideas and influences from around the world and enthusiastically embraced West Indian and African American style, music and culture. However, almost without exception there are no members of the mod subculture that are black British.[81] The reasons for this are threefold, firstly, the age of participants. If we look at the entire three phases of mod, 1957-60, 1960-1963 and 1963-1966, in order to be of the earliest age where one is able to partake of night clubs (albeit illegally), 15-17 years old, one would have to be born in 1942 for the first wave of mod and 1951 for the last; these dates are before large-scale immigration began. Thus, a black presence in mod would have been difficult in age terms alone. Secondly, culture: most young black people in the UK at this time had not grown up in Britain and would not have necessarily been familiar enough with the cultural nuances of the country to gravitate toward a subculture that rejected them. Thirdly, the evidence suggests that rather than black immigrants gravitating toward the modernist subculture, the reverse actually happened and young white men and women began to inhabit the world created by black people living in the UK.

Therefore, what made the initial racial make-up of skinheads so different is the timing of the subculture. To be black and 16 in 1968, one would have been born in 1952, precisely the time substantive immigration began. These black children had been schooled in the same British education system, watched the same television programmes, listened to the same radio stations, played with the same children as their white counterparts. They were socialised into British society, its values, norms and mores, notwithstanding the strong cultural reference of the country their parents originated from. These black teenagers had a lived experience that was different to their elder relatives who had witnessed Britain solely as immigrants. The new generation was born in Britain and consequently felt they had some investment in the country, even though this may not have been reciprocated by wider society. This explains the difference in the ethnology of original skinheads. In order to feel able to participate in any youth culture with your fellow teenagers, white or black, one would have to fully experience and understand the prevailing cultural life of the country you grew up in before you decided to subvert it.[82]

The music played an important part. Rocksteady was a progression from ska; it was slightly slower and more melodic.[83] It was a new musical form from Jamaica that skinheads and black British teenagers could claim as authentically theirs. But this music was not readily available on the BBC or commercial radio stations; it had to be sought out in the clubs of Brixton and south east London that the early skinheads and young British blacks went to. It was here amongst the styles of slightly older 'rude boys' from Jamaica that the final link was forged into the skinhead's identity.[84] Jamaican music and style was woven into skinhead culture at its onset; Knight suggests that even razor partings in the hair 'was copied from the West Indians who used it as part of their own hairstyles'.[85]

Sartorially, as with all fashions, the contemporary and the historic merged. Much of the early skinhead wardrobe came from mods, then was adapted. However, quickly a look developed that was unique and identifiably skinhead: suits, Tonic/mohair, Ben Sherman/Jaytex/Brutus button-down shirts, union or grandad (collarless) shirts, Levi's, Lee or Wrangler jeans, Levi Sta-Prest trousers, sleeveless knitted jumpers, topped off with Harrington wind cheater jackets, Crombie overcoats and the most prized possession, a sheepskin coat for the winter. Footwear was loafers, brogues and boots.[86] Young female skinheads whilst not having cropped hair, did evolve a distinctive 'feather cut' hairstyle of their own and this became synonymous with the subculture. Like teddy girls before them they often wore the same clothes as their male counterparts and button-down shirts, trousers, jeans and Fred Perry's were frequently worn, though for Saturday nights, dress suits with three-quarter length jackets and above the knee skirts were worn.

All subcultures change and mutate and skinhead was no different. For some the article in the *Daily Mirror* was the signal to depart, others just grew up, but for those left, the movement went in several directions: "Smart suits were put away for nights on the town and fighting was done in shirts and jeans.

Original skinhead girls, Northampton, 1969. Norman Rogers

Similarly, expensive shoes were replaced by boots, all the better for cracking heads".[87] Fighting, football and skinheads became synonymous with each other. Violence became the raison d'être for being a skinhead. Student bashing, hippy bashing, greaser bashing and the development of political violence in 'queer' and 'Paki' bashing were rife.

Richard Allen captures this lifestyle in 1970 with his fictional portrayal *Skinhead.* This book went on to sell a million copies and was later used in secondary schools from London to Sydney as an educational guide. The book is awash with 'realistic portrayals' of life as a skinhead and is peppered with racism throughout: "Spades or wogs didn't count. They were impositions on the face of a London that should always be white, Cockney, true British".[88]

Aside from the turf wars that gang life entails, the football violence and random fighting with other skinhead 'crews', the latter racist/homophobic violence was something not seen since the Notting Hill riots ten years earlier. The sociological explanation for this racism and homophobia is beyond the remit of this book, however, as already pointed out, racism had been endemic inside British society for centuries as an ideological justification for empire and slavery. Indeed so-called 'scientific racism', developed ironically during the Enlightenment, had sought to legitimise racism by creating a substratum of the human race as a means to subjugate it. Sensationalist reporting in the media, opportunist campaigning by all three major political parties and a lack of planned infrastructure to accommodate the new black arrivals had all exacerbated the nascent racism inside Britain.

Homophobic attacks increased with the passing of the 1967 Sexual Offences Act which de-criminalised homosexuality. Skinheads engaged in a culture that celebrated violence, traditional working-class stereotypes and over-exaggerated masculinity; this often manifested itself in violent attacks. This violence, homophobia and racism was exploited by the NF as the 1970s began and this will be explored shortly. One last point needs to be stated however; not all skinheads were happy with this violence and prejudice. Some developed the subculture and by 1971 'suedeheads' had evolved out of skinhead, they rejected the boots, grew their hair slightly longer and returned to a smarter approach to clothing. Suits reappear, belts replace braces, brogues replace boots and music and style become the focus over fighting.

The *Ivy Shop* in Richmond (specialising in collegiate American clothing) was pivotal in this evolution. A further development was 'Smooths', themselves an adjunct of suedeheads, they sported longer 'Feather-cut' hair, Rupert the Bear (check) trousers and 'Norwegians'—clumpy basket weave shoes, which look difficult enough to walk in, let alone fight in. In contrast, skinhead fashion moved even further toward overt masculinity and violence and white butchers' aprons (splattered with blood) became fashionable on the terraces for a while.[89] The suedeheads and smooths orientated themselves around fashion and music, notably in the south of England. For those less concerned with dancing and looking sharp and more preoccupied with football and fighting there was a massive growth of the skinhead subculture nationwide and it was during this period that the skinhead image was cemented, as football violence reached hitherto unprecedented levels during the years 1970-1972.[90] The music became estranged from skinheads too, as the growth of the Black Power movement alongside the ongoing civil war in Jamaica and the rise of Rastafarianism saw rocksteady superseded and reggae become an increasingly dominant *and* politicised music. This cultural and political shift in Jamaica, the rise of skinhead racism, violence and focus on football ultimately leads to both the demise of skinheads and their relationship with Caribbean culture.

Concomitant with the rise and fall of the skinhead was the hippy. In almost every way hippies were the polar opposite of skinheads. They were, broadly speaking, on the left politically, advocates of peace, against violence and seemingly unconcerned about fashion. It was predominantly a middle-class phenomenon, though this is not to say that there were not working-class hippies, rather, there were no middle-class skinheads.[91]

Some hippies were not just part of a subculture, they were part of the counterculture. Some, the so-called 'weekend hippies' did 'normal' jobs during the week and 'freaked out' on a Saturday night and some embraced the philosophy completely and absconded from society and set up communes in the countryside. But as with skinheads, so with hippies, not all were political. Those often called 'heads' were primarily concerned with getting off theirs and drugs were their main focus.[92]

Although taking its lead from America, the underground psychedelic movement in Britain grew out of mod and centred around two clubs in London in the second half of the 1960s, the UFO and Middle Earth. UFO house band Pink Floyd was the most venerated of the new psychedelic bands emerging in 1967. Alongside Jimi Hendrix and Soft Machine, they were the doyens of this burgeoning movement.

Like all youth subcultures, there were clothes, music, drugs and attitudes that accompanied the psychedelic and later hippy movement and they were the antithesis to skinheads in Britain at the time. Much of the political left: the feminist movement, gay liberationists, anti-war activists and counter culturalists, whilst sharing some of the ideals of hippies, were not necessarily enamoured of them and, although it is an important part of British subculture and certainly plays a pivotal role in the evolution of British music and fashion for the next five years, it does not feature in this story. Although it must be noted that many of the activists who were to become the new generation of political activists in the 1970s were forged in the counterculture and the British left of the late 60s, so here there must be a brief discussion on how the left developed in this period.[93]

The Revolutionary Left

The 1960s saw a change in the organised left in Britain and the reasons for this were multiple. The American influence was important: firstly, the civil rights movement, Malcolm X and the Black Panther Party had an impact on how the struggle against racism was conducted here. Secondly, the growth of the American women's movement saw similar feminist groups created in the UK. The 1969 Stonewall riots in New York marked the start of the modern gay rights movement worldwide and the university activism personified by the Students for a Democratic Society (SDS) was also mirrored in the UK.

The world became increasingly smaller and activities in other continents increasingly significant as coverage of events across the planet were beamed into living rooms, by the end of the 60s often in colour.[94] The events of May 68 in Paris alongside the fight to end imperialist rule in Africa had seen a new generation of people engage in political activity.

However, nothing was to prove more politically important for the left, than the campaign to oppose the war in Vietnam. The American anti-war movement, built on the back of the civil rights movement and the burgeoning 'New Left', grew exponentially with the escalation of the war. In Britain the anti-war movement was primarily, though not exclusively, made up of young people, many of them were attending university.

The opening of a series of higher education institutions in the 1960s saw a rapid expansion in student numbers in British universities.[95] Not all became involved in left-wing political activity, but those who did were not automatically recruited to the historic home of the British radical left, the Communist Party. Trotskyist and Maoist organisations such as the International Marxist Group (IMG), the International Socialists (IS) and the Workers Revolutionary Party (WRP) were to be the beneficiaries of this growth in radical politics. Stalin's purges, the repressive nature of the Soviet regime and the tanks rolling into Hungary in 1956 and Czechoslovakia in 1968 saw support for communist parties dwindle around the world. In terms of domestic policy, the CPGB had renounced its pre-WWII revolutionary rhetoric in 1951 with the publication of the *British Road to Socialism,* essentially a programme of gradual parliamentary reform.[96]

Evan Smith suggests: "There was a perception among the younger radicals that...traditional organisations [CPGB] were too culturally conservative".[97] The emphasis on reform and working within the existing parliamentary and trade union structures would also have implications for the CPGB over issues of race as it failed to 'connect' with the growing anger of black youth on the receiving end of police and state racism as the decade unfolded.[98] Many of the people who would become involved in the fight against the NF in the 1970s learnt their Marxism not from the CPGB, but student seminars, Grosvenor Square and Paris in 1968. The countercultural experience of the 1960s would feature heavily in the opposition to neo-fascism in the 1970s and form the basis of wholly different tactics and strategies. But as the 1960s drew to a close, the euphoria and the promise of change that rang so clearly throughout the decade ended with the shock defeat of Harold Wilson in the 1970 general election.

The National Front

When Conservative leader Edward Heath entered government in 1970, unemployment was at 600,000 or 2 percent of the working population.[99] Within two years this had doubled to 1,273,000 and aside from a dip the following year in 1973, it was to rise steadily throughout the decade.[100] Inflation stood at 7.08 percent and manufacturing costs were rising alarmingly.[101] The situation was considerably worsened by the OPEC crisis of 1973. Oil prices quadrupled from $3 to $12 per barrel and long queues at petrol stations were witnessed around the country. Demanding a pay rise that addressed spiralling inflation and their falling standard of living, the National Union of Mineworkers (NUM) had introduced an overtime ban in late 1973. Heath's government reacted by imposing a three-day working week, frequent electricity 'black-outs' occurred, pubs were forced to close, and television companies were instructed to cease transmission at 10.30pm in order to conserve electricity. The overtime ban quickly affected production, but on 5 February 1974 the NUM went on all out strike with dramatic effect.

In response, Heath called a snap general election, asking the country 'who governs Britain, the unions or the government?'[102] This election was to prove the beginning of the end for Heath and resulted in a hung parliament. With no workable majority for either party in parliament, a second election was called later that year in October and on the second time of asking, the electorate answered Heath's question. The Labour Party won the election with a small majority. When in office, Labour resided over an economy in crisis. Inflation and unemployment continued to rise. The failure of Keynesianism to offer a national solution to a world economic problem saw Labour adopt a monetarist policy to rescue the flailing economy. Chancellor Denis Healy asked the International Monetary Fund for the largest loan in its history and despite his promise to the electorate of 'squeezing the rich till the pips squeak', Healy offered tax cuts to the wealthiest in society, dropping the upper tax rates from 70 percent to 65 percent.[103] Public spending was cut from 46 to 40 percent of Gross Domestic Product (GDP) a loss of some three billion pounds. The balance of payments deficit rose from £923 million to £3,565 million and GDP per-head slipped in the world rankings, from ninth in 1961 to eighteenth in 1976.[104] Whilst inflation was running at 33 percent, Healy imposed pay freezes across the board for public sector workers in the form of the bitterly hated Social Contract.[105] Many traditional Labour voters felt a sense of betrayal and despite the continued trade union consultation with Harold Wilson and then James Callaghan's governments, lampooned at the time as 'beer and sandwiches', workers' living standards fell dramatically.

As established in the introduction, Griffin states that there are certain pre-requisites that need to be in place to enable the fascist parties to thrive during a period of crisis: the need for salvation or rebirth, a perceived decadence and the growth of ultra-nationalism. These pre-requisites were evident in Britain during the 1970s and facilitated a resurgent fascism in the shape of the National Front.[106] Britain was a fading military force, a decaying imperial power, rapidly losing its industrial base with high unemployment and its economy in ruins. 'Decadence' was running rife and now with its very culture in peril at the hands of 'savages' from the Caribbean, Africa and Asia, an 'existential crisis' was ripe for palingenetic salvation. As Enoch Powell's 'Rivers of Blood' speech had offered the National Front a way into the main arena of political discourse in 1968, two important events occurred in the early 1970s that would again change Britain's ethnic complexion and be of significant benefit to the fortunes of the National Front, boost its profile and swell the ranks of its membership.

The first involved Asians fleeing persecution, in Uganda, the second in Malawi. After a successfully orchestrated and British-backed coup in Uganda in 1971, Idi Amin overthrew its first premier Obote and within months of usurping power,

National Front demonstration, Yorkshire, 1975. (Photograph: Wikimedia Commons)

ordered the expulsion of the 60,000 Asians living there. They had 90 days to leave the country.[107] By the end of August 1972, 30,000 Asian refugees had arrived in the UK.[108] The NF immediately picketed Downing Street, Manchester and Heathrow airports and were central in organising a strike by Smithfield meat porters against their arrival. Under the banner 'Stop the Asian Invasion' the NF began a sustained campaign against the refugees and their membership increased by 50 percent between October 1972 and July 1973 and may even have reached 17,500.[109]

The political environment at the time in terms of race and immigration was febrile. The Commonwealth Immigrants Act, rushed through parliament in an emergency debate in 1968, had as its sole purpose the restriction of entry into the UK of Kenyan Asians, forced to flee Africa in circumstances almost identical to those experienced by Ugandans. The act provided no restrictions on white colonials. Enoch Powell had not been dormant since his dismissal from the shadow cabinet in 1968; he had been undertaking what Fryer describes as 'unremitting agitation' for yet another bill which became the 1971 Immigration Act and when enacted in 1973, ended virtually all 'primary' immigration, a thinly veiled euphemism for black people.[110] Centre-ground MPs began to adopt an increasingly bellicose and racial tone in their speeches. Calls for repatriation rang out and imperial loss was lamented. Conservative MP John Stokes remarked: "Great Britain had [not] won [WWII] only to hand over parts of our territory to alien races".[111] Speaking on behalf of the Monday Club Immigration Committee against accepting Ugandan refugees, Conservative MP Ronald Bell said: "They were either born in India or have retained close connection with India...they have no connection with Britain either by blood or residence".[112] Pandering to this racism, Labour chief whip and MP for Bermondsey Bob Mellish declared: "This nation has done all it should have done. Its record is one of great honour and integrity, but I say *enough is enough*".[113]

A Labour council in Leicester placed advertisements in Ugandan newspapers warning those attempting to escape Idi Amin's rule that: 'Leicester was already full'.[114] In the racially charged West Bromwich by-election of 1973 Martin Webster secured 16 percent of the vote just under 5,000 votes.[115] Questioned on his campaign and in particular the posters the NF used Webster told the BBC:

> The reason why we publish a poster saying 'The National Front is a Racialist Front' is because we are a racialist front. You must understand what that means. It means that we support the concept of the nation as the means whereby our society is to be organised and we believe the only rational basis for having nations is some kind of a degree of ethnic homogeneity.[116]

The local council elections in Blackburn in 1973, conducted in a similar vein, saw the NF candidates winning between 18 and 23 percent of the vote.[117] In the February general election of 1974, the NF fielded 54 candidates and received a total of 75,000 votes; in the October election they had 90 candidates and received 113,000 votes.[118] Attacks increased against black and Asian people and left-wing meetings across the country.

The NF had created an 'Honour Guard' loosely based on Mosley's 'I Squad', supposedly a self-defence unit but in reality, an offensive and violent street gang. Large fascist meetings proliferated in 1974 across the country in Canterbury, Glasgow, Islington, Oxford, Newbury, Hastings and a massive meeting in Leicester.[119] In response, Anti-Fascist Committees (AFCs) began to appear. A South Tyneside AFC was formed in 1972 with the support of the local Trades Council and Claimants Union. A Manchester AFC was up and running the following year.

At the end of 1973 the Trotskyist International Socialists (IS) group produced a pamphlet which proposed united action to physically oppose the NF wherever they appeared and this initiative was supported by the IMG and the National Union of Students (NUS). The result of this joint campaign and the first major confrontation between fascists and anti-fascists was at Red Lion Square in central London on 15 June 1974, when the NF converged for a meeting after a march. A call to oppose the fascists came from the anti-racist organisation Liberation.[120]

The demonstration was supported by the IMG, IS and the CPGB alongside various trade unions and assorted anti-fascists. In the violence that erupted as the fascists arrived, student Kevin Gately was killed by a 'blow to the head with a blunt instrument', possibly a policeman's truncheon, in circumstances remarkably similar to the death of Blair Peach five years later. This type of confrontation was to become commonplace on the streets of Britain over the next few years as the NF sought to exploit disquiet over renewed Asian immigration into the UK and stage highly provocative marches around the country.

But all was not well inside the ranks of the National Front. There had already been a change of political direction in September 1972 when that month's issue of the NF magazine *Spearhead* had called on its readers to 'prepare for propaganda work among the trade unions'.[121] However, the NF campaign to recruit trade unionists in the industrial heartlands was put on hold until 1974 when the announcement came from the government that the UK had accepted the refugees from Uganda. This shift away from the industrial working-class toward racial populism in the years 1974-1976 would form part of a developing argument over the future direction of the NF and its orientation and signalled a return to inner-party feuding. Should their emphasis be toward building a street fighting working-class army and the trade unions or should they seek parliamentary respectability and electoral success? John Tyndall, who had taken the former position, was ousted as leader and replaced by erstwhile Young Conservative Association (YCA) member and 'populist' John Kingsley Read. This acrimonious leadership battle resulted in a court case, which Read lost. Tyndall was reinstated as leader and, in the spring of 1976, Read left the National Front to form the National Party (NP) taking some 2,000 members or one quarter of the NF membership with him.[122] Irrespective of the split, both parties continued to build and grow, both undoubtedly assisted by a racist media campaign accompanying the third wave of Asian refugees forced to flee another ex-British African colony, Malawi.

In May 1976 when Malawi Asians began to arrive in England, many newspapers, both tabloid and broadsheet, did their utmost to exacerbate the increasing hostility by recycling their favourite memes about the country being overrun by a vast influx of foreigners.[123] The *Sun* claimed that refugees were being housed in £600 a week four-star hotels (they were not), the *Daily Express* claimed the initial 4,000 migrants would turn into 145,000 (they did not) and the *Mirror* condemned what it called a 'New Flood of Asians into Britain' (it was not).

When the Malawians arrived at Gatwick airport the NF were there to greet them chanting, 'Don't unpack, you must go back'.[124] Few paused to check the actual numbers involved. Among the entire Asian population of Malawi there were no more than 6,000 British passport holders. But numbers were not the point, the NF's intention was to fan the flames of the racism inside British society and to stoke up opposition to immigration.The NF and NP made substantial gains in local elections during 1976. They got 38 percent in Blackburn, in Leicester they received 18 and a half percent, and in a Lewisham council by-election of July that year they won over 44 percent of the vote, beating the Labour candidate with 43 percent.[125]

With this electoral 'success' opposition to the NF began to grow. In May and June of 1976 protests against the increasingly strident neo-fascists became larger and more frequent as demonstrations occurred in Birmingham, Portsmouth, Southall, east London, Brixton, Rotherham, Newcastle and Leeds. In July 15,000 people joined a march called by the Indian Workers Association against racism, in central London. Four thousand people protested against the fascists in Blackburn in September. The following month a NF conference was picketed by 250 people, and a weekly confrontation between NF paper sellers and members of the IS began in Brick Lane and continued throughout the year. In November 1976, 25,000 joined a TUC march against racism, and another 1,000 demonstrated in London in support of the Asian immigrants fleeing to Britain from Malawi.[126] It is in this environment that the catalyst for the formation of Rock Against Racism occurred.

Chapter Four
Rock Against Racism

On 5 August 1976, at a concert in Birmingham, rock guitarist Eric Clapton delivered a drunken tirade directed at members of his audience on the parlous state of race relations in Britain at the time. The content of Clapton's comments that night have been discussed many times over the years, but it is worth looking in full at what he said that night in order to understand the reaction to it:

> Do we have any foreigners in the audience tonight? If so, please put up your hands. Wogs I mean, I'm looking at you. Where are you? I'm sorry but some fucking wog... Arab grabbed my wife's bum, you know? Surely got to be said, yeah this is what all the fucking foreigners and wogs over here are like, just disgusting, that's just the truth, yeah.
>
> So, where are you? Well wherever you all are, I think you should all just leave. Not just leave the hall, leave our country. You fucking (indecipherable). I don't want you here, in the room or in my country. Listen to me, man! I think we should vote for Enoch Powell. Enoch's our man. I think Enoch's right, I think we should send them all back.
>
> Stop Britain from becoming a black colony. Get the foreigners out. Get the wogs out. Get the coons out. Keep Britain white. I used to be into dope, now I'm into racism. It's much heavier, man. Fucking wogs, man. Fucking Saudis taking over London. Bastard wogs. Britain is becoming

overcrowded and Enoch will stop it and send them all back.

The black wogs and coons and Arabs and fucking Jamaicans and fucking (indecipherable) don't belong here, we don't want them here.

This is England, this is a white country, we don't want any black wogs and coons living here.

We need to make clear to them they are not welcome. England is for white people, man. We are a white country. I don't want fucking wogs living next to me with their standards.

This is Great Britain, a white country, what is happening to us, for fuck's sake? We need to vote for Enoch Powell, he's a great man, speaking truth. Vote for Enoch, he's our man, he's on our side, he'll look after us. I want all of you here to vote for Enoch, support him, he's on our side. Enoch for Prime Minister! Throw the wogs out! Keep Britain white![1]

The reaction to this outburst was swift. Upon hearing it, photographer, activist and music fan Red Saunders immediately felt the need to reply. Along with friends, he wrote the following letter and sent it to *Melody Maker* and much of the music and socialist press in England:

When we read about Eric Clapton's Birmingham concert when he urged support for Enoch Powell, we nearly puked. What's going on, Eric? You've got a touch of brain damage. So, you're going to stand for MP and you think we're being colonised by black people.

Come on... you've been taking too much of that Daily Express stuff, you know you can't handle it. Own up. Half your music is black. You're rock music's biggest colonist. You're a good musician but where would you be without the blues and R&B?

You've got to fight the racist poison, otherwise you degenerate into the sewer with the rats and all the money men who ripped off rock culture with their chequebooks and plastic crap.

Rock was and still can be a real progressive culture, not a package mail-order stick-on nightmare of mediocre garbage.

We want to organise a rank-and-file movement against the racist poison in rock music—we urge support—all those interested please write to:

Rock Against Racism

Box M8, Cotton's Gardens, London, E2 8DN

P. S. 'Who shot the sheriff?' Eric. It sure as hell wasn't you![2]

As Max Jones and Denis Preston had done with SCIF 18 years previously after the Notting Hill riots, Red Saunders, Roger Huddle and the other letter co-signees followed an identical path. In response to a racist event, an appeal was sent out to the British music press and an anti-racist organisation was formed. Like SCIF it sought to use music as the vehicle to challenge that racism.[3] Their letter, proposing the formation of an anti-racist organisation was 'letter of the week' in *Melody Maker* and welcomed in the other publications where it appeared.[4] The reaction to the Rock Against Racism (RAR) letter, again like the SCIF letter before it, surprised even the writer: "To our amazement, within a few weeks we had 400-500 replies".[5] Saunders, Huddle and the small group around them set out to create an anti-racist organisation using music as its base, they proceeded in Saunders words to: "Put together a lorry load of anti-Nazi enthusiasts, a couple of elastic bands [with] tuppence ha'penny".[6] But, had things changed from the 1950s? Would it be possible to recreate another SCIF in the 1970s?

Red Saunders and Roger Huddle had been mods, their musical and political outlook had been forged in the streets and clubs of Soho of the 1960s, as Saunders recalled:

I was a mod. I was really into black music—more R&B than the blues... There was that whole 60s progressive anti-racist angle. We thought Clapton was part of that. That's why it was such a shock to hear him coming out with the foulest rubbish. That's why we exploded when we heard about it.[7]

The absorption of black music and culture by Saunders, Huddle and other white working-class teenagers involved in subcultures had a profound political effect as they grew up in the 1960s. The next generation of young people, drawn into the same subterranean subcultural world that mods had inhabited the decade before, were to have similar epiphanies in 1976 and 1977 as punk became the articulation of 1970s disillusioned and disenfranchised white working-class youth. But what had changed in the world of subcultures?

Many mods in the north of England, veterans of the 1960s clubs like the 'Twisted Wheel' in Manchester and the 'Mojo' in Sheffield, were unhappy with the hippy and skinhead movements and unwilling to travel down the road of heavy or glam rock. They developed an underground club scene notable for its obsession with the minutiae of African American soul music played at all-night dances. South London soul and R&B record-shop owner Dave Godin, puzzled by the frequency of visits to his shop by these people from the north of England and their evangelical zeal over the soul records he was selling, christened this scene 'northern soul'. Later in the decade, the intensity of the northern soul all-nighters reached legendary status. In the south of England the same hippy/skinhead subcultural vacuum was filled by a thriving soul and jazz funk underground scene of multi-racial soul-boys and girls frequenting west end clubs like the *Bluesville's House of Funk* in the 100 club on Oxford Street, *Crackers* in Soho and later the *Lacy Lady* in Ilford and the *Goldmine* in Canvey Island. Also from Canvey Island were Dr Feelgood, at the forefront of a 'pub-rock' scene which also rejected the current popular music and played rhythm and blues in local pubs with a messianic ferocity.[8] Unlike the 1960s, there was no longer one musical 'pop' market, but there were many variants of musical expression.

Punks backstage at a gig 1977. © Red Saunders

Punk Rock

The genre that was unintentionally to prove so pivotal in the development of punk was progressive rock. Prog rock became hugely influential in the early 1970s with bands like Yes, Pink Floyd, King Crimson and Emerson, Lake and Palmer. They wrote and performed long, really long, meandering and complicated songs, often in the form of 'concept albums' that required high levels of musical sophistication and technical ability to play and copious amounts of drugs to enjoy. Prog's reign, however, would abruptly end in 1976 when a new generation became bored with its protracted ramblings and swept it aside. Punk sought a relevant, urgent alternative to 'the bollocks' on the radio, something that reflected their generation's experiences and something that could be said in a three-minute song, using only three chords.[9]

Musically, punk's influences were varied, some were admitted, and some were concealed. The mid-1960s garage-band sounds that emanated from America had gone almost unnoticed in Britain at the time. Fast and furious, with melodic hooks and attitude, they became essential listening after being captured on Lenny Kaye's sublime and highly influential

Mick Jones and Paul Simenon of The Clash 1977. © Syd Shelton

compilation album *Nuggets* when it was released in 1972. Two other American bands were also important, the explosive New York Dolls, managed by hustler, small-time entrepreneur and promoter Malcolm McLaren, and The Ramones, whose influence upon punk in the UK cannot be overstated. The aforementioned 'pub-rock' with its recalcitrant rapid-fire riffs and asymmetric attitude was another important piece of the musical puzzle for the birth of punk as it showed that music did not have to be an opus performed in a football stadium, it could be stripped down and simplified, played in a local pub, by amateurs.

Sartorially, what defined punk was not so much of what it *was* but more of what it *wasn't*. It wasn't long hair, it wasn't flares and it wasn't 'fashion'. Hair was short and spiky, the trousers were straight and the clothes were the antithesis of the high street. Punks, both male and female, adopted a second-hand wardrobe and rejected fashion as the commodification and commercialisation of clothing. Malcolm McLaren brought the New York Dolls to Britain to gig and both he and his partner Vivienne Westwood were important in the consolidation of the punk image into the public psyche. But where Malcolm McLaren's influence was most visible was in the 'posture' of punk. McLaren was highly influenced by Dadaism in the 1920s and by the Situationists from France in the 1960s.[10] Punk gigs quickly became spectacles where the intention was to shock rather than entertain and the band McLaren was now managing, the Sex Pistols, used every device possible for maximum impact to outrage a bewildered public; this concept was quickly taken up by the rest of the burgeoning punk movement. This shock tactic would later become a problem with RAR and the Anti Nazi League (ANL) when punks began wearing swastika armbands and Nazi insignia from WWII to adorn their clothes. However, alongside the swastikas were also anarchist symbols, images of Karl Marx and inverted crucifixes; these images sat next to slogans such as 'no future' and 'destroy' and the rationale was to do anything to offend and anything to shock.[11]

Image and attitude worked in tandem for punk and not just for the bands performing at gigs. The main form of communication for punk was the fanzine, which was lifted wholesale from Dadaism, and collages were used for striking visuals. Everyday items such as maps and train tickets were utilised for artistic effect in the same way as razor blades, safety pins and bin liners were used to embellish clothing. The rejection of prevailing attitudes and fashions, the anti-authoritarian stance and the DIY ethos of punk would dovetail perfectly with RAR's militant anti-racism and much of the imagery from punk and RAR overlapped and merged in the heat of the two temperature-breaking summers of 1976 and 1977.

Like punk, RAR had a striking visual identity from the outset and this was deliberate. Imbued in the tradition of Russian constructivist art, RAR member David King was a graphic designer and friend of Red Saunders and Roger Huddle. King had designed amongst other things, the covers of The Who's *Sell Out* album and Jimi Hendrix's *Axis: Bold As Love* in 1967. He created the RAR 'star' logo and later the ANL 'arrow'. The artwork was supposed to capture people's attention and to

Anti-Nazi League and Rock Against Racism logos.

TEmPORARY HOaRDINg

ROCK AGAINST RACISM

20p.

We want rebel music, street music. Music that breaks down people's fear of one another. Crisis music. Now music. Music that knows who the real enemy is.

Rock against racism.

LOVE MUSIC
HATE RACISM

Temporary Hoarding, first issue, 1976. © The TH team from the collection of Syd Shelton

offer a more vibrant, dynamic and attractive representation of politics than people were accustomed to.

As Roger Huddle recalled: "The RAR star soon appeared on everything—posters and badges. I think badges are so important, show what you think on the tube".[12] Badges showing allegiance to the bands one supported were also an important part of punk identity. RAR badges were produced in their hundreds of thousands and these badges, like much of the artwork and other merchandise, could be obtained from the official RAR newspaper *Temporary Hoarding* (*TH*) which ran for 14 issues between 1977 and 1981. Designed by a variety of photographers, artists and graphic designers: Ruth Gregory, Syd Shelton, Andy Dark amongst others, *Temporary Hoarding* used photomontage, Russian revolutionary art and shared punk's love for Dadaism and DIY as the basis for its creative outpourings; at its height it was selling 12,000 copies per issue.[13] On the cover of the first edition was the statement 'We want rebel music, street music. Music that breaks down people's fear of one another. Crisis music. Now music. Music that knows who the real enemy is. Love Music Hate Racism'.[14]

It was RAR's mission statement, but *Temporary Hoarding* was not filled with empty slogans and propaganda. It performed three functions: 1) it was a handbook for music enthusiasts and RAR activists and it carried practical guidance of how to set up a gig for local organisers; 2) it featured concert reviews and gig guides, timetables as well as interviews, letters, reportage, posters and materials for gigs; and 3) it always had articles relating to history, politics, racism and current affairs.[15] RAR was aware of what was happening on the streets and constantly monitored the activities of the neo-fascists. The NF had set up a youth organisation, Young National Front (YNF) with its own newspaper, *Bulldog*. In response, the ANL and RAR created *SKAN* (School Kids Against the Nazis), an organisation and fanzine that distributed tens of thousands of leaflets and badges and ran for six issues over nine months in 1977-1978.[16] Another design influence on the visuals of RAR and *Temporary*

Hoarding came from the album artwork of Jamaican reggae bands and the growing influence of Rastafarianism among black youth in Britain at the time. In order to understand how punk and reggae worked together and why it became an essential part of RAR it is necessary to discuss a brief history of reggae music.

Reggae

A new word entered the Jamaican vocabulary in 1968 with Toots & the Maytals song *Do the Reggay*. Musical developments occurred rapidly in the 1960s West Indies—rocksteady had already slowed down the tempo from ska, and reggae altered the pace again. Reggae moved the focus of the music away from the guitar 'skank' and the bass guitar became the driving force.[17] Initially a localised Jamaican music, by the end of the 1970s reggae would reach every part of the planet with Bob Marley becoming arguably the world's most famous musician. The political and economic situation in Jamaica at the beginning of the 1970s reflected its history. The legacy of slavery and colonialism had left a society profoundly divided by race and class. Even as independence was celebrated in 1962, Jamaica held the distinction of having the world's highest level of economic inequality.[18] Against a backdrop of poverty and near civil war, an increasingly militant and politicised reggae, heavily influenced by Rastafarianism came to the fore.

Imagined as a spiritual and social opposition to the exploitation and oppression that colonialism and slavery had wrought on Africans, Rastafarianism owes its creation to a combination of two things: Ethiopianism, a breakaway religious movement from the Anglican and Methodist churches and the Back-to-Africa movement, articulated by Marcus Garvey and his Universal Negro Improvement Association (UNIA). By the early 1970s, DJs or 'toasters' were politicising Jamaican life and playing at sound systems across the country. Reggae artists such as Big Youth, The Abyssinians, Bob Marley, Peter Tosh,

Record shop, 1977. © Red Saunders

Burning Spear and Jimmy Cliff all come to prominence in this period with tales of oppression and resistance.

Caribbean music was already established within the black communities and white subcultures of London, Liverpool and Birmingham and this new Jamaican music did not take long to find its way to the streets of other British cities. However, with little radio play, a total absence from television, and nightclubs hostile places for black youth, the music needed other ways to find an audience. Blues parties and sound systems had been an integral part of black British life going back to the 1950s. They were a musical and dancing forum, a means of cultural communication back to the Caribbean and a way to share the experience of being black and living in Britain; but for the first generations of black British-born youth, these musical parties were also a school of political education. All of the politicised reggae acts from the UK that would form in the 1970s—Steel Pulse, Aswad, Misty in Roots, Black Slate and Linton Kwesi Johnson—came from this tradition.[19]

Despite progressive legislature, discrimination against black people was still evident across all walks of life. The 'no coloured' signs may have come down but the prejudice that lay behind them remained steadfast. Between 1973 and 1976 unemployment rose twice as sharply for black people as compared to whites.[20] What employment there was tended to be 'below the level of their qualifications and experience'.[21] Housing still had echoes of the 1950s, with overcrowding and accommodation lacking basic facilities disproportionately affecting black and Asian families.[22] By the mid-1970s a whole generation of black youth had been criminalised in the UK. This was done using two interrelated policing policies, firstly, the selective use of statistics relating to street crime, notably 'mugging', that enabled the police to justify an identification of black youth as the main culprits of this offence.[23] Secondly, what became known as the SUS laws. The 1824 Vagrancy Act (passed to stop destitute soldiers returning from the Napoleonic wars begging on the streets) was re-interpreted for the 1970s to enable the police to stop anyone they thought 'likely to commit a crime' or anyone they deemed 'suspicious'

RAR gig 1978. © Red Saunders

(where the SUS laws took their name). In practice this meant the disproportionate targeting and arresting of young black men, and accompanying this racial profiling was a violent enforcement that was witnessed up and down the country and entrenched into British policing.[24]

The racism and brutality perpetrated by the authorities, in both Britain and Jamaica, was called a different name by those experiencing it—Babylon. Reggae would become pivotal in the fight against racism in British society and as a subculture, it adopted an open hostility to 'Babylon' in its lyrics and the use of Rastafarian symbolism in its music. The essence of this musical resistance came in three parts: firstly, the Fundeh drum, which is the root or base of the music; second, the improvised Peta drum which signifies hope; and thirdly, the bassline which symbolises blows against Babylon.[25] But Trenchtown wasn't Brixton and the lingering effects of British rule in the Caribbean were not felt in the same way in 1970s Britain. By 1975 two out of every five black people in the UK were born in the UK.[26] The racism endured by these young black British people needed to find its own oppositional voice, a voice that was also to distinguish them from their parents' generation in one important way—they were not willing to acquiesce. They began to articulate their own experience of racism and, most importantly, build their opposition to it. Reggae had a duality as a political and musical stance against racism, but also as a rebel music in the subcultural tradition of the generation gap. Some of the parents of the reggae generation, the Windrush émigrés who struggled so hard to be accepted and integrate into British society, could not understand their children's rejection of the country they now called home.

Although historically associated with white youth and fashion, subcultures became multi-racial as Britain became multi-racial. As discussed with mods and skinheads, black music and black fashion became increasingly influential in young, white subcultural society. In Jamaica, Rastafarianism was a religious and political movement that occasionally used

Subcultural style, Fred Perry and Gabbicci meets anti-fascism. Black youths in Lewisham about to confront the National Front. © *Mike Abrahams*

reggae as a musical expression of the faith and philosophy. In Britain, reggae becomes a subculture in its own right. Its music is a defined genre, its outlook has a clear political stance, and the clothes associated with reggae had a definite and recognisable style.

Whilst much of the early reggae fashions were influenced by Jamaica and especially the Jimmy Cliff film *The Harder They Come*, the rest of the look developed from the cross-cultural experience of 1970s British life. The hair was the most important aspect, the dreadlock, the symbolic representation of the Lion of Judah, closely followed by the ubiquitous hat. But like all subcultural styles preceding it, reggae begged, borrowed and stole from across the globe. Gabicci cardigans, a style created in England, but heavily borrowed from Italy, Farah trousers and snakeskin shoes, Adidas and Puma sportswear and trainers from Germany and American combat jackets from army surplus stores. For some, African clothing was adopted. Jamaican colours were omnipresent. There was a less discernible style for young black women listening to reggae and high street fashion was prevalent. Fan Beverley Woodburn remembers: "fashion choices were similar to white people, cheesecloths, wide skirts, sometimes with trousers underneath, platform shoes, Clarks shoes were big, they had a factory in Jamaica... but... I'd say it mostly centred on the hair... styles included 'the Gatsby, cornrows, canerows and the 'flick'."[27]

Reggae provided the style and the music for much of black youth in Britain in the 1970s and nowhere was this more evident than in the summer of 1976, the year RAR was founded, as Junior Murvin's *Police and Thieves* provided the soundtrack to the riots at that year's Notting Hill Carnival.[28] The radical stance of reggae chimed with the anti-authoritarian attitude of punk and British youth simmered with unemployed discontent and racial tension throughout the long summer of 1976. The reggae influence would later filter into punk and new wave bands such as The Clash, The Ruts, The Members, The Police, Public Image Limited and The Slits and was described in the Bob Marley and the Wailers' song *Punky Reggae Party*:

> Come-a, come-a and rock your boat
> 'Cause it's a punky reggae party...
> Wailers be there
> The Damned, The Jam, The Clash
> Maytals will be there
> Dr Feelgood too...[29]

But whilst there was a shared discontent among black and white youth that was beginning to articulate itself musically, this symbiosis was yet to manifest itself at gigs. That bridge would only be crossed with the input of an 'outside force'. Reggae and punk bands playing together only occurs after the intervention of Rock Against Racism.

RAR as an Active Organisation

The first events organised by RAR were small-scale affairs and again mirrored what SCIF had done back in the 1950s. The link from RAR to punk though, had not yet been forged. According to Huddle: "RAR started off as a kind of retrospective—soul, funk, pub rock—'cause that's what we thought we could do. That was the prevailing independent music, away from the big pop stars".[30] The early RAR activists worked with the music they were familiar with and the musicians they knew. At the behest of Roger Huddle, RAR began to organise gigs at the centre of where the fascists were most active, in London's east end. These were to be pub gigs played by friends or associates of the activists and the publicity was spread largely by word of mouth. The first official RAR gig occurred in November 1976 at the Princess Alice pub in Forest Gate, east London with white blues singer Carol Grimes. A month later a second gig, this time at the Royal College of Art in central London, saw Carol Grimes perform again, but this time supported by reggae band Matumbi and soul band Limousine. The white band/black band formula had been established.

As was the case with the early SCIF gigs of 1958, violence, or the threat of it was never far from the events RAR staged. 'Security' in the form of local trade unionists was an essential part of the early gigs, certainly in London, but whilst the fledgling months of RAR bore a resemblance to SCIF (small-scale concerts, organised around pubs on the gig circuit), very quickly RAR took off in a way that SCIF could only have dreamt of. By January 1977 RAR was holding gigs at universities around the country and the first large-scale concert was held in the Roundhouse, which had been one of the most important music venues in London during the late 1960s. For the Roundhouse gig RAR had enlisted the support of Mitch Mitchell and Noel Redding from the Jimi Hendrix Experience, Paul Jones, actor and one-time singer from Manfred Mann, Pete Townshend of the Who and Ronnie Lane, bass player from the Small Faces.

Also on the bill were up-and-coming reggae band Aswad, alongside poet and activist Linton Kwesi Johnson. All-female punk band the Slits and punk band the Adverts performed as well. The already politicised Aswad and the Slits with their rapidly politicising punk, 'alerted RAR to the latent synergy between these two forms of music'.[31] The potential of punk as a focus for disaffected youth would be later confirmed when the Sex Pistols outraged the nation with their profane appearance on ITV's *Today* programme during which they swore their way into infamy.[32] Huddle and Saunders realised the importance immediately:

> We both understood that there was a shift and if we didn't orientate on that, then we would miss the audience...It was our experience politically, that we just knew that something was happening, and the next gig had to be a punk band and a reggae band.[33]

Punk band 999 perform at RAR gig 1978. © Red Saunders.

In his work *There Ain't No Black in The Union Jack* Paul Gilroy contends that punk supplied: "an oppositional language through which RAR anti-racism could speak a truly populist politics".[34] Gary Bushell, erstwhile columnist of music weekly *Sounds* and one-time contributor to *Socialist Worker*, had this to say:

> Punk's aggression reflected the anger of a generation who had graduated from school only to serve their time on street corners and the dole. It was working-class rebellion...a violent reaction to a society collapsing around them...a real revolutionary movement.[35]

Temporary Hoarding was able to secure an interview in 1977 with Johnny Rotten, lead singer with the Sex Pistols, shortly after reaching number one with the anti-monarchy single 'God Save the Queen'. He had this to say about the NF:

> I despise them. No one should have the right to tell anyone they can't live here because of the colour of their skin or their religion or whatever the size of their nose. How could anyone vote for something so ridiculously inhumane? [36]

The gigs quickly spread out to the suburbs. Letters asking for support from wannabe independent organisers flooded into RAR headquarters. Red Saunders recalled:

> Somebody would write to me from Aberystwyth and say, "We read your letter in the *Melody Maker* and we think it's fantastic. We're a bunch of fifteen-year-old schoolkids and our teacher's a fascist. How can we get involved?" And I'd write back saying, "Great. You are Rock Against Racism Aberystwyth. Get on with it".[37]

As punk music and fashion left London, it lost its art school and elitist edge and attracted many more that would become the audience *and* the musicians of RAR gigs. Once out of the confines of Soho and Manchester and the scene around the Buzzcocks, punk evolved into new wave. This development had a wider scope both musically and sartorially and attracted many bands that, whilst sympathetic to the general ethos of punk, were not wedded to the totality of the genre.[38]

Because of the extraordinary level of activity up and down the country during RAR's existence, it is impossible to discuss each gig or aspect of the campaign, so confines of space necessitate we identify the key moments of the whole campaign and try to draw some conclusions from there. However, this does not mean that the small-scale, locally organised gigs were insignificant, quite the opposite, as they became part of an effervescent and omnipresent backdrop to the musical and political landscape in late 1970s Britain; indeed by 1978 there were 52 RAR clubs putting on gigs in 52 towns and cities up and down the country.[39]

In spite of their ad hoc nature, or possibly because of it, RAR gigs proliferated as 1976 became 1977. Indicative of the spirit of these early gigs are the comments from John Baine:

> A group of us at Kent University set up a Rock Against Racism society with a £50 grant from the Student Union. We produced leaflets and put on gigs: The Jam in '76, 999's first gig, the Stranglers, the Damned supported by the Adverts, Misty, and the Enchanters...we covered the room[s] in home-made slogans sprayed on bits of paper: Black and white unite and fight, smash the National Front. We didn't have a direct link with central RAR. We just sent off for badges and stickers from *Temporary Hoarding.*[40]

The music was central but so was the political message. Across the country in university common rooms, youth clubs and pubs, small groups of people, some politically affiliated, some there because they disliked racism and some simply going to watch bands, were congregating at events called for the specific purpose of opposing racism and on a scale hitherto unknown.[41] However important these localised gigs were, the political profile of RAR was raised to a higher level by a series of massive carnivals and festivals that were organised in England, Scotland and Wales over the next four years. Elevated from reports in the local and music press, RAR rose to nationwide prominence with regular features from Fleet Street to the BBC. However, as mentioned earlier, crucial in this growth is the intervention of another anti-fascist organisation created on an unabashed and purely political basis with the sole intention of physically opposing the far right, the Anti Nazi League.

Anti Nazi League

Rock Against Racism did not exist as a solitary anti-racist/ anti-fascist organisation during this period, there were other groups and individuals who were politically active at the time. Of these other groups, the largest and most significant was the Anti Nazi League (ANL), a combative, single-issue campaign organisation, set up in 1977 with the sole purpose of undermining the National Front electorally and confronting them on the streets whenever they marched. For its entire existence the ANL worked side by side with RAR and in some instances the two were indivisible; however, they were two *separate* organisations and whilst sharing a common goal and indeed having a membership of often similar people, their tactics and strategies were different.

By the spring of 1977 the NF claimed over 20,000 members.[42] They had put up 413 candidates and received almost 25,000 votes in the May local elections and 119,000 votes in the Greater London Council elections of that year.[43] There had been marches in Battersea, Leicester, Newham, West Bromwich, Bradford and Southall. In Wood Green, a multi-cultural part of north London, on 23 April 1977 the NF organised a march attended by over 1,000 supporters. They were opposed and confronted by some 3,000 anti-fascists, and in the violence that erupted, only the intervention of the police stopped the NF from being routed. After Wood Green, campaigners against the far right sought to form some sort of national network that could co-ordinate an organised resistance to the marches that had been rising exponentially throughout the previous years. In May 1977, 23 anti-fascist committees came together to form an All London Anti-Racist Anti-Fascist Co-ordinating Committee (ALARAFCC) at a meeting in London. Despite its best intentions the new organisation failed to gel and was riven by internal disagreements over tactics and strategies.

At the same time, in Lewisham, south London, growing discontent from the black community to the systematic harassment from the Metropolitan Police and their stop and search tactics was beginning to surface:

> Some 14,000 people were stopped and searched in Lewisham, alone. Over 200 Special Patrol Group police—an elite unit—armed with pickaxe handles and Alsatian dogs, raided 60 black homes in the area. The police called it "Operation PNH—Police Nigger Hunt".[44]

Much of the NF's propaganda at the time was the spurious assertion that street crime and mugging in particular was committed by young black males and, alarmed at the black resistance to the hated SUS laws, the NF, mimicking what Mosley had done in Cable Street in 1936, organised a highly provocative 'anti-mugging' march in Lewisham.[45] A counter demonstration was called which saw over 5,000 in attendance. Comprised of local black residents and the anti-fascist left, they opposed the 800 neo-fascists and the NF march was split into two by a military-like intervention by black youth and anti-fascists. ALARAFCC had also called a counter demonstration to the NF on the day but at a different time and at a different location, thus rendering it ineffective to the NF march, although hundreds did move from the first demonstration to the second

Lewisham demonstration against the National Front 1977. © *Socialist Worker Archive*

that sought to confront the NF. This effectively undermined ALARAFCC's influence thereafter and opened the door to a more focused and militant anti-fascist organisation which was to become the Anti Nazi League.

Formed at the suggestion of the Socialist Workers Party (SWP), a new broader political alliance was created that looked outwards from the narrow confines of the traditional communist left.[46] With the support of 40 members of parliament, trade unionists, religious leaders and high-profile left-wing activists such as Tariq Ali and Arthur Scargill, the new organisation was launched at the House of Commons in the autumn of 1977. From the onset the ANL was to be a non-sectarian, united front, single-issue campaign and the three executive positions of the ANL were taken by Labour Party member and anti-apartheid activist Peter Hain, trade union official and Labour Party member Ernie Roberts and Paul Holborow from the SWP. Other members of the committee included four Labour MPs, one of whom was a young Neil Kinnock, a member of the Young Liberals and Jewish actress Miriam Karlin. However, the ANL's creation was not universally welcomed and there was some scepticism from the sections of the centre left, arguing that the ANL was a 'front' organisation for the SWP and their confrontational tactics undermined the fight against racism.[47]

The 'front' accusation does not stand up to any scrutiny and it is necessary to note the wide level of support the ANL had in order to counter these claims. Amongst the ANL's supporters were 50 local Labour Party constituencies, 30 union branches of engineering workers, 25 trades councils, 13 shop steward's committees and 11 National Union of Mineworkers lodges. Similar numbers came from other trade unions including the TGWU, CPSA, TASS, NUJ, NUT and NUPE. Twenty six union executive committees also voted to support the ANL. There were 600 trade union workplace organisations in direct contact with the ANL including British Leyland Longbridge, Fords Dagenham and the Yorkshire miners. There were branches of civil servants and local government workers involved. In the Fleet Street union SOGAT there was an ANL bloc, as there was in both the national and regional TV unions. Locally FBU branches backed the ANL, as did the postal workers' white collar union ASTMS. Also in support were members of other unions including: knitwear workers in the NUHKW, the cinema and technicians unions ACTT, and the rail unions, the RMT and ASLEF.[48]

For some of those not involved in trade union politics, the ANL's link to RAR alleviated their suspicions that it was not a legitimate organisation and the association with RAR gave it significant cache to be taken seriously. The ANL would grow in the coming months at a rapid pace. The direct involvement of the SWP in setting up both RAR and the ANL was in marked difference to the relationship between CPGB and SCIF in the 1950s. Whilst members of the CPGB played important roles in SCIF, there was no political decision by the CPGB to prioritise anti-racist initiatives and immerse their organisation into the fight against oppression.[49] The CPGB's political emphasis was 'class' and work within trade unions; the fight against racism was subordinated to this. What makes the SWP's position different in 1977 was to identify racism and the opposition to the NF as *the* most important political issue at that time, consequently the focus of its work was directed toward the ANL and RAR.

Steel Pulse perform their song 'Ku Klux Klan' at Carnival, 1978. © *John Sturrock*

Carnival

The first large-scale musical event RAR organised in conjunction with the newly formed ANL was at Victoria Park, Hackney on 30 April 1978, but this was to be no ordinary gig in a park. The first decision RAR made was to re-name the gig and call it a carnival. Deliberately using the language of the Caribbean community, RAR intended the Victoria Park carnival to be an active celebration of shared culture, but it was to be political too. With a PA donated by The Who after the offer of Pink Floyd's rig proved impractical, the gig showcased some of the prominent musical acts of the period. Tom Robinson Band, X-Ray Spex, Patrick Fitzgerald, Steel Pulse and confirmed at the last moment, The Clash.

Rather than simply staging a concert where people passively attended, the intention, as Claudia Jones had done with the first carnival in 1959, was for the carnival to be an act of political defiance. The format was thus: a rally in Trafalgar Square, central London, followed by a political march to Victoria Park, Hackney, some six miles away where the concert would be staged. Co-organiser David Widgery later stated the intention was to:

Make the politics more fun, and the music more political...RAR's unannounced ambition was to turn the event into the biggest piece of revolutionary street theatre London had ever seen, a 10th anniversary tribute to the Paris events of May 1968.[50]

RAR used Notting Hill carnival as its template, floats were employed to carry bands along the route so there was live music and politics all the way to the park. New wave bands The Members, The Mekons, The Piranhas, Gang of Four and The Ruts all played on floats along the route as did reggae band Misty in Roots. They all followed the leading float which displayed giant papier mâché heads of NF leaders John Tyndall, Martin Webster and one of Adolf Hitler; these were made by Roger Law, later of *Spitting Image* fame. At best the organisers thought 10,000 would turn up, but estimates on the day say there were over 80,000, and some reports say even 100,000.[51] Forty nine coaches were booked from Manchester, 10,000 travelled down

Joe Strummer of The Clash at the RAR Carnival Victoria Park, 1978 © Syd Shelton

1978 Carnival. © John Sturrock

from Scotland, dozens of coaches came from Liverpool, Leeds, Sheffield, Middlesbrough, Newcastle, Aberystwyth, Bristol, Norwich and Oxford.[52] Many more made the journey by train, by car, by bus and on foot.

Mass mobilisations for demonstrations were a regular occurrence in British politics and large-scale concerts had developed after the Rolling Stones' free festival in Hyde Park in 1969. However, rarely were there politics at gigs and music on political demonstrations. Most festivals, whilst having political undertones, were not overt in their stated political objectives, if indeed there was a single objective at all. Many festivals like Woodstock in America or the Isle of Wight festival in 1970 were the coming together of like-minded people who shared a broad political outlook and/or just wanted to enjoy the music. The RAR carnival was different; the political demonstration and the music festival were inextricably linked. This combination had never been attempted before on such a scale and were there anyone in any doubt as to the political nature of the event, as he took to the stage at the start of the carnival, compère Red

Saunders cleared up any ambiguities: "This ain't no fucking Woodstock. This is the carnival against the fucking Nazis".[53]

Much has been made about the internal politics of who headlined the carnival and the wrangling over the band running order. Whether The Clash, Tom Robinson Band or Steel Pulse concluded the afternoon is in many ways a moot point. That upwards of 100,000 young people marched the six miles from Trafalgar Square, through the middle of known NF strongholds in east London to attend an openly anti-racist concert is tribute to the commitment of those who attended and the success of the organisers of the event. No doubt the music was of importance, but people marched as well. What happened when people arrived was also important too. Billy Bragg, later to become a singer/songwriter and political activist himself, remembered:

> We were standing under a banner that said 'Gays Against the Nazis' and when Tom [Robinson] sang *Sing if you're glad to be gay* all these blokes started kissing each other on the lips. I'd never seen an out gay man before. My immediate thought was, 'What are they doing here? This is about black people.' And literally in the course of that afternoon I came to realise that actually the fascists were against anybody who was in any way different.[54]

Also in the audience was Gurinder Chadha, who would become the renowned *Bend it Like Beckham* filmmaker:

> I saw hundreds and hundreds of people marching, side by side in a display of exuberance, defiance and most importantly victory. I couldn't believe my eyes, these were white, English people... marching, chanting to help ME and my family in my adopted homeland... so the sight of them along with all the other women, black and Asians in that moment made me feel I belonged. I had found my tribe, my kindred clan... from that moment, I became the political film maker that I am today.[55]

Another young person attending his first political event was Colin Byrne:

It was our political Woodstock. It was the first time that you felt you were part of a mass populist movement... it wasn't full of depressing-looking lefties and donkey jackets. It was fun... Rock Against Racism was reaching out to people who didn't see themselves as political.[56]

What the carnival did was threefold. Firstly, it offered a glimpse into a world free of prejudice; this wasn't just a multi-racial musical celebration. 'Queer-bashing', so prevalent in the last subculture skinheads, was absent from the present one, punk. The environment created by punk, reggae, RAR and the ANL enabled an atmosphere where musician Tom Robinson, an openly gay singer, was headlining, singing the song *Glad to be Gay*, and eliciting the support and participation from an otherwise heterosexual audience. Secondly, the Carnival showed that the racist ideas people hold in their heads are not static, it proved that they can be challenged and changed. The Port of London Shop Stewards Committee, those same dockers who had marched in support of Enoch Powell and immigration controls just ten years prior, donated their union banner to the ANL to be carried from Trafalgar Square to Victoria Park.[57] Thirdly, the carnival drew a line in the sand and clearly demonstrated that a mass movement had been born that would resolutely oppose the fascism and racism of the NF wherever they tried to organise. Carnival was a runaway success, wildly beyond the hopes of the organisers and it made the first item on the national news of the BBC that evening. Geoff Brown from Manchester who had attended the Victoria Park event, said: "After the Carnival...we decided wouldn't it be a good idea if Manchester had a carnival".[58]

The Manchester carnival was to happen fortuitously according to organiser Geoff Brown on 15 July 1978, the Saturday after a local by-election being held in Moss Side, a

March to Manchester Carnival 1978. © *John Sturrock*

predominantly black inner-city area of Manchester. The NF fielded a candidate, Herbert Andrew, and ran another highly provocative anti-immigration campaign. RAR had already established regular anti-racist gig nights across the city renting out 'community or leisure centres...[to]...take it to the council estates to reach out to the kids there'.[59] A tradition had already been established in Manchester where local bands such as The Fall, Joy Division and John Cooper Clarke would play at concerts specifically organised in places 'where the kids who are racist live'.[60] The Thursday night before the carnival, Graham Parker & the Rumour even took time out from their gig supporting Bob Dylan to play a warm up RAR gig.

Like the Victoria Park event in London earlier that year the Northern Rock Against Racism carnival would tread a similar path. There was an initial rally outside Strangeways prison at noon to listen to political speeches and reports of the by-election and from there some 15,000 people marched the three miles to Alexandra Park in Moss Side, 'in a sea of ANL lollipops'.[61]

On its journey, flatbed trucks carried a Manchester steel band and local punk groups The Mekons and the Gang of Four who played to the marchers. The demonstrators were met with applause and waves of support from shoppers and pedestrians along the way. Student Andrew Madaras remembered: "I honestly don't remember any hostility or animosity expressed by anyone we passed".[62] When they arrived at Alexandra Park the 15,000 marchers were met by another estimated 25,000 already there waiting for the gig. Upholding the RAR tradition of multi-racial acts appearing on the bill, Manchester reggae band Exodus played alongside Mick Hucknell's first band the Frantic Elevators, white reggae band China Street, and the headline acts Steel Pulse and the Buzzcocks. Whilst this was obviously a musical event, organiser Geoff Brown recalled:

> The Northern Carnival was a political event. Everybody was carrying these 'No Front' lollipops. It had a really sharp edge to it. It was the strength and ability to combine the politics and the music...the following Monday, every corner of Manchester had got kids who had been there...Manchester didn't have a problem with Nazis after that.[63]

Following on from the success of Manchester, local activists around the country, supported by RAR and the ANL, launched many other events. Wales and Scotland had their own carnivals where 5,000 attended in Cardiff and 8,000 in Edinburgh.[64] A second carnival was held in Brixton, London in 1978 where over 100,000 people saw Aswad, Misty in Roots, Stiff Little Fingers and Elvis Costello and the Attractions. Playing on the floats accompanying the march to Brixton were The Enchanters, The Members, The Ruts and The Straights. Mike Simons, RAR organiser in Newcastle in the late 1970s states that: "By December 1978, the number of RAR events organised since launch [topped] 300 local concerts and five carnivals".[65] In just over two years, with meagre funds, RAR managed three gigs a week, *every* week, the length and breadth of the country and as Simons goes onto say: "There could have been many, many more we simply didn't know about".[66] Indeed, full-time RAR organiser Wayne Minton estimated:

> There are 273 UK bands on my list [of bands that performed at RAR gigs]. There would be an average of three to four people in each band. Giving us over 1,000 RAR people. Each RAR person would have a social diaspora of boyfriends, girlfriends, mates, siblings, ex's etc. Let's say around 20 each, that gives us a potential of around 20,000 RAR people. Let's say each band does an average of six RAR gigs and picks up a dozen or so supporters. That would give us around 240,000 potential RAR members based all over the UK from Acton to Ayr, Belfast to Bristol, and so on…[67]

Whilst this method of gathering statistical data may not be conventional nor adhere to quantitative research methodology, there is a certain logic to it and as no formal records exist of RAR activities or gigs, the memories of participants have to be relied on with the usual provisos for oral histories: unreliability, fallibility and bias. Irrespective of the accuracy of numbers at RAR gigs, there is sufficient evidence that the concerts did occur in the music press archives.[68] The success of these concerts is supported by the fact that they continued week in, week out, in villages, towns and cities in every corner of every country in the British Isles. That such a musical organisation could evolve from a single letter of protest in *Melody Maker* and grow into a nationwide campaign is remarkable in itself. For that campaign to then engage young people in political discourse, often for the first time, and then onto political activity in all its various forms is unprecedented. SCIF had attempted to organise gigs and galvanise anti-racists and anti-fascists in the 1950s, but in a localised form. This was partly in response to the activities of the WDL and the UM whom they were opposing and who were focused on London. In the 1970s the NF were numerically larger and operating all over the country; therefore, the response from the anti-fascist left had to be nationwide too. But there was no inevitability about this response, the initiative had to come from somewhere and whilst the spontaneous support for RAR that occurred throughout the country enabled a network of semi-autonomous RAR groups to exist, without the overview, the organisational and political intervention of the SWP, the level of support and the success of the endeavour would arguably not have happened.

However, this does not mean that there were no issues amongst the performers and supporters of RAR. In Roger Sabin's criticism of punk and RAR, he highlights instances of racism from members of punk bands and provides a list of dubious song lyrics, titles and outright examples of racism.[69] Sabin states that 1970s Britain was a society riddled with racism; prejudice was 'on the map' with racist joke books and TV programmes such as Love Thy Neighbour and Mind Your Language.[70] Yet Sabin seems surprised when this accepted casual racism in society is occasionally expressed by some punks in bands. He exposes what he sees as a glaring racist contradiction in punk yet is unaware of contradicting himself in the same sentence. Quoting an interview The Clash did in *Record Mirror* Sabin says: "The band were busy outlying their anti-racist views, when the subject of anti-Asian violence arises and band manager Bernie Rhodes chips in with: 'There's a lot of Paki's that deserve it', however, Rhodes: 'Was soon corrected by other members of the group'."[71] Nothing more perfectly demonstrates the nature of punk and the reason why RAR existed. When racist ideas arose, they needed to be challenged. No members of RAR or ANL ever espoused the idea that punk was inherently anti-racist; in fact David Widgery clearly points out in *Beating Time* that punk as a subculture, "could have gone either way".[72] The whole point of RAR was to understand that there were racist views in society and then set about challenging them. The motives behind the two-pronged attack against racism and fascism were clear from the different perspectives of the ANL and RAR. The ANL was an organisation

*Anti-Nazi League protest against
the National Front, Southall 1979.
© John Sturrock/reportdigital.co.uk*

Poster © The TH team from the collection of Syd Shelton

Below, Pete Townshend of The Who performing at the Southall Kids are Innocent gig at The Rainbow theatre, London 1979. © Syd Shelton

that campaigned against fascism and was willing to physically confront it and stop fascists marching on the streets. The NF demonstrations of the 1970s had the support and attendance of more committed racists and fascists and the ANL argued their job was to stop them in their tracks. The role of RAR was different, it was to use music to stop the 'soft' prejudices of young people developing into a hardened racism and a further evolution into fascism.

In March 1979, RAR launched the Militant Entertainment Tour in the run up to the 1979 general election. Forty different groups played 23 concerts and covered 2,000 miles on the road. Included in the line-up were the Tom Robinson Band, Sham 69, Steel Pulse, Aswad, The Members, X-Ray Spex, Stiff Little Fingers, The Angelic Upstarts, The Ruts, The Specials and The Clash.[73] In the middle of the tour the NF staged a series of highly provocative meetings designed to provoke counter-demonstrations and attract maximum publicity for their candidates in the forthcoming general election. On 20 April 1979, 2,000 police officers, including over 60 mounted, were deployed to 'maintain order' at an NF meeting in Islington Town Hall, north London. The following day in Leicester, 5,000 officers from 21 forces escorted 1,100 neo-fascists to a rally at a local girls' school. In Newham, east London on 25 April, over 7,000 officers were placed to oversee 400 fascists attending an election meeting. This pattern was followed with 5,000 officers deployed in West Bromwich on 28 April and 5,000 in Bradford on 30 April.[74] The Home Secretary and police commissioners around the country justified such huge logistical and financial undertakings by evoking Voltaire: "I don't agree with what you say but I will defend to the death your right to say it".[75] Voltaire was strangely missing though when the same right to assemble and march was denied to anti-fascists during this period, and the Metropolitan Police refused permission outright for anti-racists to stage a demonstration that planned to march past the NF headquarters. Moreover, the Metropolitan Police dispatched some 8,000 officers to protect the NF headquarters should any spontaneous demonstration arise.[76] All the above National Front events secured column inches in local newspapers, but it was 23 April 1979, St George's Day, that would gain notoriety and become the most significant date in this tumultuous period.

In the town hall of a predominantly Asian town, Southall, west London the NF held an election rally. 2,756 police officers, assorted dogs, horses, vans and a helicopter were drafted in to protect the neo-fascist meeting. Despite massive local opposition to the meeting, the police were determined that the event should go ahead. A counter demonstration against the NF of over 5,000 was organised by the local community and the ANL. Although the protest staged close to the town hall was peaceful, the police baton-charged the demonstrators, some on foot, some on horseback and some in vans:

> The police violently broke up [protesters]...drove their vans into the crowd...bludgeoned people at random as they scattered and ran... [the police] ...vandalised the premises of Peoples Unite, a black meeting centre, arrested 342 people, injured hundreds—and beat Blair Peach to death with unauthorised weapons.[77]

Much violence erupted outside the town hall and the surrounding area and the police had identified the record label and black activist headquarters *Peoples Unite* for special treatment. The house was used as the base for the demonstration and despite being almost half a mile away from the town hall, the entire building was smashed up by the Special Patrol Group, the paramilitary arm of the Metropolitan Police. Much of the band Misty in Roots' equipment was broken and their manager Clarence Baker was savagely beaten by the police and put in a coma for over five months. Following the day's violence and arrests, a campaign to support those facing trial was initiated and in July of that year, RAR staged a 'Southall Kids are Innocent' gig at The Rainbow, one of London's leading concert venues. The Who's Pete Townshend headlined, supported by The Clash, Aswad, The Members and The Ruts.

The demonstration in Southall, and in particular Blair Peach's death, received enormous media coverage at the time. Despite Peach's death and the fact that the NF meeting did occur, the demonstration against the NF was still considered a success by RAR and ANL as it was indicative of how RAR, the ANL and local black and Asian community groups met and organised together with a common purpose. However, a criticism levelled at RAR at the time was its alleged narrow cultural stage and the absence of Asian music in its focus. This was infamously summed up by NME journalist Julie Birchill: "You've got no Asian bands. That proves you're racist".[78]

Black & White Unite?

The Windrush generation had been in the forefront of new musical genres popular in post-war Britain. In fact, in 1948, musician Lord Kitchener was filmed by *Pathé News* as he disembarked from the Empress Windrush singing *London is the Place for Me*, a song he had written especially for the occasion. The organisers of the 1951 Festival of Britain brought the Trinidad All Steel Percussion Orchestra to these shores and the calypso craze peaked in 1956-1957 in both the UK and America with Harry Belafonte's album *Calypso* at number one in the US charts for a staggering 31 weeks.[79] Artists as varied as Robert Mitchum and Bernard Cribbins recorded calypso tunes and for a while it seriously overshadowed rock 'n' roll as the go-to choice for British youth. Before the Beatles, the rite-of-passage for British acts to learn their trade in Hamburg was initiated by Liverpool-based calypso band Lord Woodbine and his Trinidadians.[80] As already noted, youth subcultures such as mods and the early skinheads openly embraced Caribbean culture and black and white musicians had occasionally shared stages even before the Windrush docked.[81]

For the Asian community this musical history did not exist. Ravi Shankar had recorded his first album in Britain in 1956, toured the UK and then Europe and played at the Monterey Festival in 1967. He was name-checked frequently by artists as varied as John Coltrane and The Byrds, but he did not cross the cultural barrier to major success. A similar fate was experienced by his nephew Ananda Shankar who released his self-titled ground-breaking sitar-rock fusion album in 1970. Some British artists had begun to explore music from the Indian subcontinent in the late 1950s, for instance folk/jazz guitarist Davey Graham. But the interest in the Indian Raga was only later developed in rock music by proponents such as Donovan, the Rolling Stones and most famously George Harrison with The Beatles' albums *Rubber Soul* in 1965 and *Revolver* in 1966. Ten years later the adoption of Asian music into British culture was still to occur; in 1976 there was no bhangra explosion, nor fusion with wider musical styles like hip hop. Asian music, at least outside of the Asian community, remained a relatively obscure genre and we would have to wait until the 1990s to see acts like Asian Dub Foundation, Fun-Da-Mental and Apache Indian make the transition into national radio and national consciousness. Consequently, as ANL activist Balwinder Rana remembered: "Much of the Asian music at the time was still about singing the Bollywood film songs, mainly at wedding receptions or other Asian community celebrations like the Indian Independence Day or Diwali".[82]

RAR was not attempting to create an embryonic WOMAD festival, it sought to deliver a political message to the widest musical audience it thought open to its ideas. "RAR did not, and never intended to, offer a platform for *all* culture".[83] The point of the exercise was not to offer an inclusive, liberal smorgasbord of ethnic idioms and musical oeuvres that ticked the boxes of an imagined checklist of cultural oppression, it was to challenge racism and that meant the racism of *white* people. As Syd Shelton recalled: "The problem was not a black problem or an Asian problem, the problem was a white problem. They were the people whose minds we had to change—white youth, not black youth".[84] RAR's mission was to engage with as large a fan base

*Anti-Nazi League protest
against the National Front,
Southall 1979. © John Sturrock'*

as possible, using the medium of popular music, but specifically, a popular music that met RAR's criteria of social relevance and political resistance. Reggae and punk fitted the bill completely, so this was where its orientation lay. RAR spent little or no time organising around the many 'disco' clubs that existed at the time, nor was there any engagement at heavy rock or heavy metal gigs. RAR would not have worked with glam rock or progressive rock, which represented (according to Widgery) "the worst excesses of a bloated corporate music industry".[85] The "oppositional nature of both punk and reggae" were the perfect vehicles for an adversarial movement against racism.[86]

Irrespective of the involvement of Asian music at RAR events, key to the organisation of myriad RAR and ANL events up and down the country were local Asian community groups and Asian youth. The Indian Workers Association (IWA) was one such group. Founded in 1937 its dual purpose was: "to raise consciousness of the struggle for Indian independence among working-class Indians in Britain, and to protect and enhance their welfare".[87] Ten years after independence in 1947, the organisation was reborn with its concentration now on improving conditions for migrant workers and gaining influence inside the British labour movement. By the late 1970s there were in effect three IWAs operating in Britain. Of the three, two were under the influence of two competing factions of the Indian Communist Party, one based in Birmingham and one in Derby. The third, based in Southall, was led by Vishnu Sharma, also a member of the CPGB.[88] The IWA was involved in the organisation of the first RAR Carnival in 1978 and had booked a number of coaches, and a local Asian band were to perform on one of the floats from Trafalgar Square to Hackney.[89] Balwinder Rana had been the founding president of the Indian Youth Federation of Gravesend in 1969 and later became full-time Asian organiser for the ANL in 1977. He was chief steward in Southall for the demonstration where Blair Peach was killed and worked in and alongside the IWA. He was also at the Victoria Park RAR carnival:

A number of older Asian men and women and some children [had] come...I was quite concerned that they may feel left out as there was no Asian music that they would understand and enjoy. But, to my surprise...they all seemed to be quite happy to see so many young people enjoying themselves...and were content to just soak up the atmosphere. It was a great day of solidarity and to see all those young people 'Rocking Against Racism' must have sent a shiver down the spine of even the most hardened racists and must have worried them that the end of their project was now in sight.[90]

Furthermore, Rana and other members of the ANL would travel to towns and cities up and down the country where the NF proposed to march and visit mosques, temples and Asian organisations in the weeks before the event to try and encourage local opposition to the NF when they arrived.

In Greater Manchester a similar story is told: "The Bolton Asian Youth Organisation (AYO) was established in 1976, they came to all the carnivals and Prav Parmer ran the Bolton RAR disco weekly for some years".[91]

Also oblivious to the alleged lack of Asian involvement was Ramila Patel, present at the Manchester carnival. Ramila had staged a defiant solo demonstration against a march by NF leader Martin Webster in Hyde, a small industrial town just outside Manchester the previous year. The racially inflammatory NF march had been banned by the Home Secretary on the grounds of possible violence.

Webster, who was protected by 3,000 police officers, staged a one-man march for 500 yards, carrying a Union flag and a sign reading 'Defend British Free Speech from Red Terrorism'. Ramila was also a keynote speaker at the Manchester carnival, and she had this to say about the event:

It was very moving to see the massive crowd in front of me who were there to oppose the National Front...I will never forget the thunderous welcome from the huge crowd that had

gathered in Alexandra Park. It was an emotional moment and
I felt an acute sense of solidarity with the crowd.[92]

The IWA was to carry on working alongside anti-racist
groups throughout the period and was key to organising events
around the country and at their conference on 17 July 1978,
they issued a call to all their members to set up Asian self-
defence groups and to join (en-masse) the ANL; this, according
to Rana, "was widely reported in the Asian press".[93] Lastly,
mention must be made of Alien Kulture, an Asian punk band
in existence from 1979-1981. Articulating the frustrations of
second-generation Pakistanis in Britain and the fight against
racism, they played many RAR gigs and also released an album
and single 'Asian Youth/ Culture Crossover' on the Rock Against
Racism record label.[94] Simon Frith's assertion that 'RAR had
an off-putting effect on Asian youth' also seems to have gone
unnoticed with this band.[95]

The political experience of Asians *inside* RAR/ANL was
different to that of Afro-Caribbeans because their lived
experience *outside* was different. Their *present* was different
because their *past* was different. The experience of slavery
in the Caribbean and colonialism in India were not identical,
nor was the legacy. British rule in the West Indies took on a
different character to that in the Indian subcontinent. Imposed
upon Caribbean people were the English language, its customs,
culture, dress and religion, all at the expense of *any* African
heritage.[96] To an extent this cultural symmetry enabled an 'easier'
transition into life in Britain when West Indian subjects became
citizens post-Windrush. Imperial rule in India had fermented
the opposite ethos and to enable rule over such a vast country
in size and population, the British sought to maintain and
exacerbate differences in indigenous culture and customs. They
nurtured sectarian divisions in religion as a means to control
the population, as earlier attempts by missionaries to convert
Indians to Christianity did not result in the increased leverage
for political control that was desired. The fostering of 'separate'

food, costume, religion and language, essential for divide and rule policies in India, would consequently make the transition into British life all the more difficult for Asians when they came to the 'motherland' in the post-war period. Nevertheless, by the time of RAR's existence, the impact of immigration had changed many things and although it was far from being an inclusive and non-racist society, Britain looked different in 1979 than it did in 1959. The 20 years between SCIF and RAR had seen black and white youth forged together in some musical and subcultural ventures and a joint engagement in political life, albeit from a defensive, anti-racist position.

The 1979 General Election

In May 1979, the month following the death of Blair Peach in Southall, the Conservative Party won the general election with a majority of 43 seats. Margaret Thatcher was now Prime Minister. The economic crisis, loans from the International Monetary Fund (IMF), industrial unrest and increasing polarisation over immigration were all played out in the election. The NF fielded a record 303 candidates and were confident that they would build upon their previous gains in local elections. In the event, the NF lost all of their deposits and were humiliated in the election, unable to secure a single seat. How had this happened? Why did the far right vote decline so dramatically? Opinions are divided on this issue, but many commentators, certainly those on the right of British politics point to an interview with Margaret Thatcher in an episode of ITV's current affairs programme *World in Action*, screened in January 1978. Thatcher said:

> If we went on as we are then by the end of the century there would be four million people of the new Commonwealth or Pakistan here. Now, that is an awful lot and I think it means that people are really rather afraid that this country might be

rather swamped by people with a different culture and, you know, the British character has done so much for democracy, for law and done so much throughout the world that if there is any fear that it might be swamped people are going to react and be rather hostile to those coming in.[97]

Thatcher reintroduced into mainstream political discourse a vocabulary that had been the property of the neo-fascists and the Monday Club since Enoch Powell's expulsion from the front bench in 1968. Immediately after this interview national opinion polls recorded a dramatic surge in support for the Tories, who jumped to an 11-point lead over Labour, who they had previously been trailing by two points.[98] Journalist and ex-Conservative MP Matthew Paris, who in 1978 was Margaret Thatcher's correspondence secretary, recalled:

We had been averaging 500-700 letters a week when, discussing immigration in a TV interview, Mrs Thatcher used the word 'swamped'. In the following week she received about 5,000 letters, almost all in support, almost all reacting to that interview.[99]

Fraser Nelson, now editor of *The Spectator*, celebrated Thatcher's use of this phrase, arguing:

She killed the National Front that night, as voters who were concerned about immigration believed they had, in her, someone who understood them... and a proper democratic leader will hear their concerns... Maggie's plain-speaking crushed the National Front.[100]

The Daily Telegraph concurred: "The comments were... responsible for a collapse in support for the National Front, which had been gathering momentum in working class communities".[101] Many of Thatcher's comments from this period are familiar racist tropes: "Too many Asian immigrants were being allowed into Britain...it is quite wrong that immigrants should be given council housing whereas white citizens were not...[although she had]...less objection to refugees such as Rhodesians, Poles and Hungarians, since they could more easily be assimilated into British society".[102] Thatcher's words would have consequences, as Alok Biswas, an Asian man from east London attested. Commenting on the racist murder of his friend Altab Ali on the night of the London local elections in May 1978, shortly after Thatcher's interview, he said:

> Who is responsible? I am clear in my mind, that's Mrs Thatcher. She talks of us as aliens. She says we must be kept out and made to leave—says that everywhere we are a problem people. So, it's just no good for her to throw her hands up in horror when some crazy kids wound up by her, do this murder.[103]

If Margaret Thatcher's victory in the 1979 general election and her opportunistic racism were linked, then so was the Labour government's loss of the election to other factors. Labour's handling of the economy, cuts in public spending, industrial unrest, the IMF crisis combined with rising unemployment and the sense of betrayal felt by workers over the 'social contract' all played a part in Labour's unpopularity and ultimately in Thatcher's triumph.

The Conservative Party's shift to populist racism did play a part in undermining the vote for the NF in the general election, but to then make the assertion as *The Telegraph, The Times* and *The Spectator* did, that Thatcher alone 'defeated fascism' is too simplistic, cannot be proven empirically and constitutes a hagiographic misreading of history as it neglects the other factors at play. It also ignores the campaign RAR had begun against the far right in the years prior to Thatcher's speech and the effect it had on the lives of many young people holding racist views, as Peter Hain recalls:

Posters for RAR gigs.

I remember meeting punks and skinheads who were becoming openly political and saying: "I was on the point of joining the National Front and the RAR and the ANL came along. I went to see my band and I suddenly started thinking, 'What am I doing? Do I hate black people? Why do I hate black people? No, I don't actually'."[104]

Lewis Young, a young schoolboy punk from Southall in 1978 echoes Hain:

We were supporters of the Young National Front, everyone I knew was a racist, we were all racists, hard core. We engaged in petty intimidation and bullying of Asians and much graffiti work, putting up stickers and such like. But everywhere we went those fucking yellow lollipops [ANL placards] appeared and their fucking stickers. Every time we put up an NF sticker an RAR or ANL one would appear over it, or ours would be scratched off altogether. Those fucking lollipops man, you couldn't get away from them at school. In the end it sort of ground us down, too many black and Asian people against us, the white people who we thought of as traitors at the time, kept putting forward arguments that started to make sense to us. But ultimately, it was the music that did it. If Strummer and Costello and Malcolm [Owen, from The Ruts] were against us and we loved, really loved them, then maybe it was us who was wrong?[105]

One television interview with Margaret Thatcher did not turn the tide and stop the NF. Nor did it politicise tens of thousands of young people and bring them into activity for the first time. Thatcher's comments did not help white anti-racists arguing against racist ideas in the playground, the workplace or the pub. They did not give confidence to young black and Asian people to face down the violence, intimidation and attacks by gangs of racists and fascists routinely roaming the streets of their communities.

Musician Homer Harriott from Leeds reggae band Bodecian draws this conclusion:

> I believe Rock Against Racism did change a lot, it made a lot of the people more aware, it made me open my eyes politically about what was happening and who was involved rather than just the black and white issue, cos when you're younger you just think that white people hate black people and that's it... when you go out there and see all these people fighting your cause you realise it's not a white/black issue, it's a racist issue.[106]

Legacy

Rock Against Racism brought the political arguments about racism and fascism out from the shadows of left-wing meetings and black and Asian community groups. Racism and the opposition to it became centre stage. It was in the local *and* national media, it was on the TV and in films. It was on albums and singles, it was at gigs and carnivals, it was the music in the air. No longer was it the sole property of socialist and community activists.

Anti-racism, or at least the discussion of anti-racism, was everywhere. It had encouraged a generation of young people into engaging with a political discourse they may not have entered without RAR as the catalyst. Arguably, if you liked popular music, whether you wanted to or not, you *had* to engage with the polemic around racism, the NF and RAR. SCIF had tried this in 1958 and 1959 with some success, but RAR had created a climate whereby there was no part of the UK or musical environment that was not affected by it in some small way.

By 1979 much had changed, not least in the world of subcultures. From their onset, British subcultures had celebrated the 'now', they had taken the music and fashion that was current to each of their generations, they utilised it or updated traditions from the past. Broadly speaking they were forward looking, they were modern. By the middle of the 1970s, the promise of a better society than the one their parents had endured was beginning to look shallow.

In the decades that followed WWII each generation had seen their standard of living gradually improve; by 1976, after the OPEC crisis, with inflation running at 30 percent and unemployment dramatically rising, this seemed an unachievable goal. Punk had spurned everything society offered, it rejected its politics, its fashions and its music and for good reason, 1976 was called 'year zero' by the music press.

Alongside the punk explosion though, other young people had reached different conclusions about the world around them, and with dramatically different results. With both the present and the future seemingly unable to offer anything remotely optimistic, a romantic vision of the past began to enter into the popular vernacular. A proliferation of themed 1950s movies, plays and music start to appear. The film *That'll Be the Day* was released in 1973, *Stardust* in 1974, *Grease* the musical began on Broadway in 1972, *Happy Days* the TV show first aired in 1974. Openly nostalgic 1950s bands like Showaddywaddy, Mud, The Rubettes and Wizzard all had chart success in the UK throughout this period. As the decade unfolded, a 'nostalgia industry' was born. In Liverpool the first Beatles convention was held in 1975 and slowly developed into the behemoth that it is today.

Alongside these cultural reminiscences, a teddy boy revival occurred centred around the Kings Road in central London that was equally popular in suburbia. Backward looking in its fashion and music and embracing the same racist philosophy as their sartorial forebears, the new teddy boys opposed immigration and any of those they deemed 'other' or unacceptable, notably punks, and much violence ensued.

One mutation from the punk explosion was a skinhead revival and many of these second-generation skinheads abandoned all references to the Jamaican culture of the first generation and focused on violence: racist, football or the inter-subcultural variety. This misinterpretation of original skinhead culture would later be challenged in 1979 with the arrival of the Two-Tone movement, a record label and collective of black and white musicians who had grown up listening to both new wave and Jamaican music.

Two-Tone was fronted by The Specials, a multi-racial and highly politicised punk/ska fusion band from Coventry. By the end of 1978, emanating out of the success of new wave band The Jam, a mod revival was also underway and became a national phenomenon the following year after the release of The Who's film *Quadrophenia*, a fictional account of the life of a 1960s London mod. Finally, a rockabilly revival was also taking place with its emphasis on the clothes and music, and (to some extent) the politics of the 1950s. For the time being British subculture was stagnating, faced it seemed with no direction forwards, the conclusion was to look backwards and raid the clothes and music of previous generations.

However much young people wanted to escape the harsh realities of 1970s British society by entering the land of nostalgia, the world around them would rudely interrupt their daydreams. Thatcher's election victory in 1979 unleashed a series of economic policies that resulted in swingeing cuts to public services, as she declared her own political war on the post-war consensus, and unemployment went to heights seen only in the depression of the 1930s. Britain would be very different when she left office 11 years later.

The far right was attempting to come to terms with their crushing humiliation in the 1979 election and their poor result led to further infighting about how they were to go forwards. In January 1980 the inevitable split took place between traditional Nazis and the 'modernisers', whom we shall meet in the following chapter. Veteran neo-fascist leader John Tyndall was in no doubt that the 'unfavourable publicity' generated by the ANL and RAR over the previous four years were the key reasons for the NF's decline.[107]

SCIF had trod a similar path to RAR, they organised gigs,

produced a newspaper, used the music press and media to expose the racism of the neo-fascist groups they opposed. They invited people to become active in both the music and the politics of the time, on a local level. RAR achieved all this and more, but on a national level, their presence was far greater and consequently so was their impact.

RAR was inextricably linked to the wider anti-fascist left, notably the ANL and it operated in union with other 'progressive' anti-racist forces. Aside from its occasional work with the CPGB, SCIF was primarily an independent enterprise. The end of both organisations is also markedly different. SCIF had quietly faded from view by the end of 1959, but RAR's profile and the impact of its work would not allow it to simply slip away.

In September 1980 RAR's greatest hits was released on the Virgin record label and the final edition of *Temporary Hoarding* was published when Rock Against Racism was formally disbanded in the autumn of the following year. However, there was one more carnival, a last hurrah to celebrate activities of the previous five years and to look optimistically into the 1980s.

On 4 July 1981 the final RAR event was held in Yorkshire. Leeds had staged one of the earliest RAR gigs back in 1976 and had started its own RAR club in 1978. It had hosted hundreds of gigs with local punk and reggae bands and the last RAR carnival began with a political march accompanied by the now perfunctory 'bands on floats'. To a defiant multi-racial audience in Potternewton Park, Leeds, Aswad, Misty in Roots, the Au Pairs and headline act The Specials played to 30,000 people. For those who had been there at the beginning, in 1976, The Specials symbolised what RAR had set out to achieve. Ruth Gregory recalled: "Two-Tone was like a dream. Suddenly there was energetic music that was neither black nor white. It was a mix".[108]

This was not different black bands and white bands sharing a stage, this was a band made of black and white people. This was the fulfilment of the RAR project, multi-racial music and the defeat of the fascist threat, at least for now. It was an unqualified success. The last word in this chapter should go to the author of the letter that started off the process, Red Saunders:

> When you saw Two-Tone you went, job done…that's it! This is what we dreamt of in 1976. Two-Tone music and their spirit and their story and everything Jerry Dammers went on to do for Nelson Mandela. It trumped the whole fucking lot of us.[109]

Chapter Five
From Thatcher to Blair: 1980s & 1990s

The euphoria of the multi-racial Specials headlining the last RAR carnival in Leeds was soon nullified by the desolation of the socio-economic landscape as the new decade began. Ironically, The Specials would articulate this mood too, as nothing captured the despair and despondency of the early 1980s quite like the song *Ghost Town*.

> This town's becoming like a ghost town
> Why must the youth fight against themselves?
> Government leaving the youth on the shelf
> This place, is coming like a ghost town
> No job to be found in this country
> Can't go on no more, the people getting angry.[1]

Within two years in office, by May 1981 the Conservative government had overseen a rise in unemployment from 5.3 percent to 10.2 percent, a level not seen for 50 years.[2] As the decade progressed, the welfare state regressed, and massive structural reform was introduced. Later, the privatisation of essential services, the breaking up of the public sector and dismantling the trade unions became a panacea for Thatcher's government. Suppressing wages, lowering inflation, reducing public borrowing and the weakening of any organised working-class opposition would be conducted in the name of 'popular capitalism'. The philosophy of Friedrich Hayek and the dogma of free enterprise ruled supreme in the Conservative Party and they would remain in office for almost 20 years and would only fall with the election of Tony Blair and New Labour in 1997.

Whilst some of the radical rhetoric of the incoming Conservative government signified real change, underneath the hyperbole, it was very much carry on as usual when it came to the issue of race. The use of SUS laws rose to new heights in Brixton for its largely Afro-Caribbean community in the spring of 1981 and discontent grew. Already in March of that year there had been a mass demonstration against racism, a 'Black People's Day of Action'. This was a protest of 25,000 people marching the six miles from Deptford, south London to Hyde Park in anger at the police's indolent response to a fire in New Cross which had claimed the lives of 13 young black people.[3] Much of the anger from the black community was directed at the reluctance of the police to investigate the fire as a suspected arson attack by the NF who were very active in the area at this time.

Resistance to Racism

Already suffering in the grip of a world recession, black people living in Brixton, south London, experienced a disproportionate rise in unemployment, continued bad housing and a symmetrical rise in levels of crime. In an attempt to drive down these crime rates the Metropolitan Police launched *Operation Swamp 81.* This was a policing strategy which involved the deployment into the area of an extra 100 plain clothes officers, the paramilitary Special Patrol Group and a dramatic increase in SUS. This tactic had been attempted before in Lewisham just a few miles down the road in 1977 and the results have already been discussed in the previous chapter. Unsurprisingly, a renewed and more vigorous implementation of the SUS laws was not wholly welcomed by the local community and on 10 April 1981 the simmering discontent of black youth boiled over into rage on the streets of Brixton, but this was not simply a riot, it was an uprising and its effects would reach much further than the streets of south London. Following years of repressed anger, the disturbances in London found an echo across the country. By the summer of that year the revolt had spread and between 3 and 11 July 1981, serious rioting broke out across the country at Handsworth in Birmingham, Toxteth, Southall, and Moss Side in Manchester. Bedford, Bristol, Edinburgh, Gloucester, Halifax, Leeds, Leicester, Southampton and Wolverhampton all witnessed unrest too.[4]

Fryer lists 39 towns and cities where riots took place and estimates there were at least two dozen other towns where significant disturbances occurred.[5] In the middle of the summer's riots on 10 July 1981, The Special's *Ghost Town* reached number one in the charts. Racism and racist policing lay at the heart of these uprisings. The subsequent Scarman Report commissioned to ascertain the causes of the disturbances found unquestionable evidence that the disproportionate and discriminatory use of 'stop and search' powers against black people was behind them. Scarman also added that there were "acute socio-economic problems faced by black youth in inner city areas and unless this racism was addressed the very survival of society was at risk".[6] For Thatcher, this was worrying, not because of the levels of deprivation, for as Thane points out she: "...believed inequality was the natural and desirable state of society" and not because of alleged black criminality as this was "not political, but a consequence of family structure and environment".[7] The main concern for the Tories was to stop the development of a political understanding that linked race *and* class and explained the conditions which led to the riots. An anti-racist, class-based analysis "...was most threatening for Thatcher, when wedded to a critique of capitalism".[8]

The Race Relations Act of 1976 had made it illegal to discriminate against a person because of the colour of their skin, their ethnic background or their nationality, but there were caveats, one of which was exemption from this law for policing. The use of SUS throughout the country saw black people overwhelmingly more likely to be stopped than whites at a ratio of 15:1.[9] Despite these statistics the Scarman Report was unable to find any institutionalised police racism in the wake of the riots, although the introduction of the Police and Criminal Evidence Act (PACE) in 1984 would make this easier for Sir William Macpherson to locate the next time a report was commissioned. Thirty three years after Windrush, the black community in the UK were still living in sub-standard housing, suffering unemployment rates of 29 percent for men and 25 percent for women and being discriminated against by a hostile police force.[10]

The governmental and industrial drive for recruitment of Commonwealth citizens in the years 1948 to 1964 demonstrates the thirst for labour not satiated by British workers in that period. The jobs existed, so the people came. In 1963, only five years prior to his 'Rivers of Blood' speech, health minister Enoch Powell launched a recruitment campaign in India and Pakistan that resulted in some 18,000 trained doctors migrating to the UK to work in the NHS.[11] With a buoyant economy this need for labour continued through the 1960s and only with the world recession after the 1973 oil crisis did the economy begin to slow. However, despite the need for labour, successive government legislation was created in order to restrict immigration with a series of bills that *specifically* targeted black workers and their families.[12]

Furthermore, as the graph below demonstrates, net migration remained negative or negligible for the 30 years when black immigration was at its highest. Despite these statistics, black Commonwealth immigration was continually legislated against. Only when 'white' immigration from the EU began to grow at the beginning of the 21st century did net immigration dramatically alter and the ratio was reversed.

These figures suggest that the introduction of the successive immigration acts were driven not by unemployment or over-population but by political and racial motivations. The 1991 United Kingdom census, the first to include information

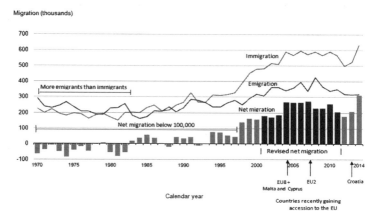

UK Net Migration 1972 to 2014.[13]

regarding ethnicity as a percentage of the population, returned the following statistics: a total of 5.9 percent of the British population were classified as having non-white ethnicity and of those people, 1.6 percent identified as black Caribbean/African and 4.27 percent as Asian.[14]

Discrimination existed everywhere: in employment it was rife and Cabinet Office figures for the 1980s and 1990s show that Caribbean and Asian unemployment rates were consistently twice that of their white counterparts.[15] Housing also remained problematic for black people: the 2001 riots in Oldham, Burnley and Bradford involving white and Asian youth had their seeds sewn in the housing policies of the 1980s.[16] The charge of 'self-segregation' and ghettoisation of Asian communities was found to be fallacious when a formal investigation conducted by the Campaign for Racial Equality into the housing polices of Oldham council established that systematic discrimination and segregation had existed for years within the local authority's housing department. Oldham council was not alone.[17] A 1997 report commissioned by the housing charity *Shelter* concluded: "BAME groups are disproportionately likely to suffer from poor housing; they are seven times more likely to live in overcrowded conditions than white households".[18]

The experience of black and Asian people in Britain since Windrush was a dizzying cycle of invitation, assimilation, marginalisation and discrimination. Recognition for any cultural, economic or political input into society was rare. In the 1980s and 1990s this began to change, albeit in a non-linear fashion. On the one hand as the above evidence suggests, there was still structural inequality in housing, employment and policing, but in terms of a public profile, black representation increased dramatically. There were now newsreaders, fashion designers, actors, artists and musicians. In 1987, four black politicians were elected as members of the British House of Commons, but nowhere was the profile higher than in football. There was a proliferation of black British footballers during these two decades playing at club level and for England. But with this raised profile came a deluge of racism from the terraces of clubs up and down the country. Monkey chants directed at black players and bananas thrown onto the pitch were met with indifference from the Football Association. Whilst individual fans at clubs opposed this racism and attempted to organise against it, official organisations opposing racism in football would not be formed until *Kick It Out in* 1993 and *Show Racism the Red Card* in 1996.

Racism in society had not disappeared with the defeat of the NF in the 1979 election, it had simply changed its clothes. When questioned in the early 1980s about Conservative Party policies regarding race Tory MP for Northampton North Tony Marlow replied, "People criticise [our] measures because they say they are racialist, as if racialist is a word of abuse".[19] Derek Laud, aide and speechwriter to Margaret Thatcher and the first black member of the Conservative Monday Club, was unequivocal when he described the Tories of the 1980s, "...they are the ultimate racists because they deal in stereotypes".[20] Margaret Thatcher's recital of St Francis of Assisi from the steps of Number 10 Downing Street after her 1979 general election victory already sounded hollow to the black community of Great Britain; what hope there was had already turned to despair.[21] Then in the 1983 general election, riding on a wave of patriotic fervour following the Falklands War the previous year, the Conservative Party was elected to a second term of office.[22]

Music as Political Opposition

Thatcher and her cabinet had a clear industrial strategy for the coming years. She had witnessed both miners' strikes in 1972 and 1974 and was determined to destroy the union strength that had brought down the Heath government the year before she became leader.[23] The 'Ridley Plan' was a document based on a report undertaken in 1977 by Conservative MP and free market zealot Nicholas Ridley. It outlined the strategy and tactics that a future Conservative government would need to adopt in order to defeat a major union in a nationalised industry. Thatcher orchestrated an industrial confrontation that resulted in the bitter and protracted dispute of the miners' strike of 1984-1985. An increasingly paramilitary police force provoked confrontation and violence on the picket lines. They were supported by a partisan judiciary and a compliant media and this meant that for the duration of the strike, the National Union of Mineworkers (NUM) were portrayed as pariahs rather than men defending their jobs and livelihoods. Solidarity was to come from a variety of places during the strike, from trade unions, both national and international and on Saturday mornings in high streets up and down the country, bucket collections became a familiar sight.

Support also came from another unlikely source and was to play a major role in popularising the plight of the miners and raising money for those on strike. Miners' Support Groups (MSG) proliferated during the strike and fundraising became a central issue as the NUM's funds were sequestrated and those on strike were prohibited from any financial assistance from the government. Across the country gigs were organised to collect money for the NUM hardship fund. In many respects these gigs were identical to RAR concerts in the late 1970s, combining a political issue and live music.[24] The concerts created a sense of solidarity, collected money and attempted to raise the political consciousness of those attending. Some of those playing at MSG gigs had also performed at RAR gigs and the similarities were further compounded with the same call to action through self-activity and self-education. Whilst it was important to attend concerts in support of the miners, people were also encouraged to become part of the dispute in whatever way they could and build solidarity. Billy Bragg later recalled the gigs, "In political terms it allowed you to feel you were not alone. It was exactly the same experience I had at Rock Against Racism".[25]

The use of music to forward a political objective became commonplace in the 1980s. Responding to the televised scenes of famine in Ethiopia in 1984, Bob Geldof, one-time singer with new wave band The Boomtown Rats, was moved to organise a 'super-group' of over 40 musicians to record and release a single whose proceeds would be donated to Ethiopian famine relief. Geldof's passionate pleas demanding money for the famine led to a massive campaign supported across the music industry and led to a direct confrontation with Margaret Thatcher's government who initially refused to waive VAT on the sales on the record.[26] The single was successful beyond the scope of anything Geldof and collaborator Midge Ure could have hoped for. This was not the first time music had been used to raise money for famine relief. Ravi Shankar and George Harrison had organised the Concert for Bangladesh in 1971 which was followed by a live album of the gig.[27] Bob Marley and several British reggae bands had also played an Ethiopian famine relief gig in the 1970s, without any accompanying press coverage. What was different about the Band Aid project was the sheer scale of the event. The single sold over two million copies, raised over $24m in revenue and the concept was copied in Canada, France, Spain and the United States.[28]

The following year on Saturday 13 July 1985 two interlinking concerts were held in Wembley stadium in London and the JFK stadium in Philadelphia, whilst similar initiatives occurred in the Soviet Union, Canada, Japan, Yugoslavia, Austria, Australia and West Germany. Across 160 nations an estimated audience of 1.5 billion people or nearly 30 percent of the world's population watched the show.[29] According to UNICEF the whole Band Aid project is thought to have raised over $150 million.[30] Band Aid was a truly global event unsurpassed in its scale; little SCIF gigs at youth clubs in 1950s Notting Hill and even the 1970s RAR carnivals of 100,000 were dwarfed by this level of organisation. The focus of these previous groups was different though, as both SCIF and RAR sought to mobilise young people and politicise them into some form of activity, whilst the purpose of Band Aid was to raise money not consciousness. Geldof wanted a financial contribution, not a physical contribution, as he said direct into camera live on BBC on the evening of the Live Aid concert, "Don't go to the pub tonight…stay in and give us your money".[31] Band Aid was about supporters and consumers, SCIF and RAR were about performers and participants. Band Aid's version of political music went from the counterculture to the culture of the counter. Sales became the objective and the subcultural underground was no longer of importance.

At the end of 1985 a strident Conservative government was midway through their second term of office and launching their privatisation of nationalised industries. With the defeat of the miners fresh in people's minds, some on the left began to think about the next general election in 1987 and how they were going to ensure a Conservative defeat. One tactic saw the unveiling of an organisation on 21 November 1985 at the Palace of Westminster. Operating under the name of Red Wedge, it was another attempt to fuse the musical and the political and was formed after a number of early 1980s initiatives involving musicians playing gigs in support of the Greater London Council (GLC), the Campaign for Nuclear Disarmament (CND) and a 'Jobs and Industry' campaign. Musicians Billy Bragg and Paul Weller were the driving force behind Red Wedge with Bragg

THE WORLD OF ARTS
for a world of difference

Red Wedge booklet, 1986

Red Wedge logo and the following layout

DON'T GET MAD
GET ORGANISED

"Peace, bread,

work and

freedom,

Is the best

we can achieve,

And wearing

badges is

not enough,

In days

like these'

Billy Bragg 'Days Like These'

Red Wedge is a broad left alliance set up by young artists, musicians, actors, writers, and others involved in the worlds of entertainment, sport and the media.

We want young people to realise that politics is part of their everyday life, not something remote and irrelevant. For so many, politics is something you turn off the TV to avoid.

We want young people better informed about politics: about the political process itself, about the issues which particularly affect them, and about the practical policies on offer.

Red Wedge believes that a Labour victory at the next General Election is vital to the welfare of young and old alike. But we don't expect any one just to take our word for it. We are setting up a series of 'Listening To Youth' events to bring young people and party officials – MPs, councillors, trade unionists and the like – face to face.

Red Wedge will be pressing Labour to develop positive and up-to-date policies on issues that directly affect young people; Youth Training Schemes, educational grants, benefits, job creation.

We will also be urging the party to form a socialist policy on those aspects of the arts and culture which particularly concern the young. That means a new approach to things like TV and radio, the press, cassette levies, funding for youth arts, venues, independent record labels, performing rights payments, sports facilities and similar issues.

We think the arts belong to everyone, not just a select few. Self-expression and creativity are part of youth's fight back for something better than the no-hope, no-future society the Tory government have delivered.

Red Wedge will be pushing Labour councils to make more premises available for use as studios, venues etc. With the abolition of the metropolitan councils in March 1986, the need for this kind of support will be that much greater.

Red Wedge is establishing a national network of like-minded young artists and those involved in youth culture. We will act as an agency for benefits, putting campaigns in touch with performers, PA companies, DJs, and the publicity machine. Priority will be given to campaigns organised by young people in the labour movement.

We'll also be organising a series of nation-wide do-it-yourself sessions on everything from rapping to playwriting, film-making to fashion. On hand to give advice and the benefit of their experience will be a supreme team of talent.

Artists who have already pledged their support for *Red Wedge* include: Animal Nightlife, Bananarama, Billy Bragg, Jill Bryson, Lloyd Cole, Richard Coles, Jerry Dammers, Ray Davies, Ben Elton, Everything But The Girl, Dawn French, Junior Giscombe, Heaven 17, Lenny Henry, Gary Kemp, D.C. Lee, Madness, Zeke Manyeka, Johnny Marr, Lorna Quarter, Tom Robinson, Sade, Jimi Somerville, Dave Stewart, Helen Terry, Stephen Tin Tin Duffy, Paul Weller, Working Week.

"You don't

have to take

this crap,

You don't have

to sit back

and Relax,

You can

actually try

changing it"

The Style Council
'Walls Come Tumbling Down'

Red Wedge line up, 1986.

acting as the front man. Red Wedge was a similar marriage of music and politics to the CND/GLC gigs above and had echoes of RAR. Billy Bragg later commented that the similarity between RAR and Red Wedge was:

> In feel rather than in organisation. RAR had been an inspirational force in pop culture and we aspired to achieve that. As a vehicle for engaging youth in politics, you could argue that we followed in their footsteps.[32]

NME editor, supporter of RAR and co-founder of Red Wedge Neil Spencer later said: 'Rock Against Racism fed into Red Wedge. If the Trots could do it why couldn't we'?[33] There followed a succession of gigs and a highly successful nationwide tour which saw sell-out concerts with Q&A sessions afterwards involving the musicians and politicians from the Labour Party. The gigs were a homage to the Stax-Volt and Tamla Motown revue tours of the 1960s and a variety of bands performed across a range of genres.[34] The events were overtly political and before the concerts, local unions, youth service providers, anti-apartheid groups, unemployed centres and youth initiatives were organised under the 'Red Wedge Regional Development' programme. Strategies were formulated around how to engage Britain's youth in the political process and ultimately to vote for the Labour Party. This was a remarkable development in popular culture and political terms, there was a direct correlation between pop music and party politics; the campaign was about getting people to vote, albeit by using unconventional methods.[35] The image of young highly successful pop stars advocating and canvassing votes for the Labour Party was as much a departure from normal politics as the then leader of the Labour Party Neil Kinnock appearing on Top of the Pops in a music video by singer and comedian Tracey Ullman.[36] Although revolutionary in its approach and design— Red Wedge took its name from a 1919 painting *Beat the Whites with the Red Wedge* by Russian constructivist artist Lissitzky—that was where its revolutionary politics ended. Whilst the organisation attempted to engage young people with politics in general, its focus was on getting votes for the Labour Party in the 1987 general election and this caused some consternation. Some bands criticised the campaign from the left, not least because the Labour leadership had not supported the miners in their strike and was at the time in the process of purging the socialist *Militant Tendency* from the Labour Party.[37]

Formed in the same year as Red Wedge was Artists Against Apartheid (AAA). The inspiration behind it came from Steven Van Zandt, the guitarist from Bruce Springsteen's E Street Band in America and Jerry Dammers, from Two-Tone band The Specials in Britain. AAA also sought to use music for political purpose and its first activity was to record and release a single called 'Sun City' to draw attention to the situation in South Africa and to promote the economic and cultural boycott of the Apartheid regime.[38] However, the song suffered from sustained political censorship in America and created only ripples of interest in the UK. A different approach was needed to connect with an increasingly salient boycott movement and to grow an awareness of Apartheid around the world. Jerry Dammers had already written the anthemic 'Free Nelson Mandela' which reached number nine in the charts in 1984, so he was the first choice for music producer Tony Hollingsworth to approach after he had conceived the idea of a 70th birthday party concert for Mandela. After securing the support of some of the world's most famous artists a gig was organised for 11 June 1988 at Wembley Stadium.[39] The BBC were the first to agree to air the concert and in total it was broadcast to 67 countries, with an audience of over 600 million. Robin Deneslow declared in 1989 with some justification that the concert was "...the biggest and most spectacular pop-political event of all time, a more political version of Live Aid with the aim of raising consciousness rather than just money".[40]

However, aside from veteran anti-racist campaigner and singer Harry Belafonte, who demanded Mandela's release in the opening speech, all of the artists were censored from making any overt political statements before or during their performances. Moreover, in order to sell the event to broadcasters around the world the concert organisers had to declare it a 'non-political' event and market it as simply a birthday party. The trade-off for this, Hollingsworth was later to say, was a promise from broadcasters to cease referring to Mandela as a terrorist.[41] A second Wembley concert entitled 'Nelson Mandela: An International Tribute for a Free South Africa' was held two years later, two months after Mandela was released and he spoke for 45 minutes to the 72,000 present and a broadcast audience of millions more in over 60 countries.[42] He called for further sanctions and the release of those still languishing as political prisoners on Robben Island.

By the end of the 1990s there was an established formula of musicians recording charitable songs, performing at concerts and raising money for disaster relief or political campaigns that endures to this day; every tragedy has its own theme tune. Since the first Band Aid single was released in 1984 there have been over 150 charity records released in the UK alone.[43]

Subcultures

What was happening in the world of subcultural Britain whilst these records were being made and concerts were watched by millions of people? As the economic situation in Britain worsened during the late 1970s and early 1980s, so the desire to escape its harsh realities heightened. One subculture, the new romantics, echoed the flamboyance of flappers and dandies of the 1920s in an economic climate redolent of the 1930s. The escapism of lavish Hollywood musicals post-Wall Street crash was played out in London clubs of the late 1970s and early 1980s, what journalist Robert Elms described as 'dressing up as an alternative to feeling down'.[44] As the scene evolved it became fixated on outrageous and androgynous clothing worn to shock; design gurus John Galliano, Dylan

Jones and Kim Bowen all were stalwarts of the scene.[45] The music played in clubs such as *Billy's* and the *Blitz* was primarily electronic and many of the bands that grew out of the clubs adopted synthesisers for their signature sound, but the early exponents of new romantic music had also been around the punk or the soul/jazz funk scene.[46] The indigenous bands that grew from this new subculture, Culture Club, Spandau Ballet and Duran Duran went on to enjoy worldwide acclaim. Two faces from the scene, Midge Ure and Boy George went on to have important 'political' roles in Band Aid.

Acid house or rave was the most far-reaching of subcultures in the 1980s and early 1990s. The peak of acid house was 1988, often referred to as the 'second summer of love' and an explosion of rave parties and mass events proliferated around the country. Importantly, much of the rave scene was unfettered by racism and there was a significant representation of all ethnicities as one raver from Birmingham remembered "...here, white people found themselves dancing with black people for the first time. There would be Sikhs, Muslims, you name it everyone would be there".[47] This was now the third generation of black British teenagers who had grown up in the UK and whilst 1960s skinheads and 1970s punks had enjoyed a limited cross-cultural sharing of clothes and music, this rave generation of white and black youth had gone to school together, grown up together and were now going to clubs together, on a mass scale.

The following decade the rave scene took on the most overt of political postures, albeit an enforced and defensive one, as the Conservative government attempted to censure the very lifeblood of the scene with the introduction of the Criminal Justice Bill. The bill introduced the concept of 'collective trespass and nuisance on land' which, amongst other repressive measures, were the loss of the right to silence and increased police powers of stop and search were specifically designed to criminalise raves.[48] The bill, which became an act in 1994, also contained a bizarre clause allowing police to arrest "...twenty or more people listening to music which includes sounds wholly or predominantly characterised by the emission of a succession of repetitive beats".[49] This was a first for any government, to legislate on cadence and tempo in popular music as a way of controlling British youth and would set a precedent for legal control of music that is discussed in the next chapter. A sustained campaign in opposition to the bill culminated in a mass demonstration of 40,000 people in Hyde Park in October 1994 which ended in a riot.[50] This demonstration coincided with the stirrings of a new British music at odds with the electronic beats of house and garage and out of step with the mournful sounds of 'grunge' emanating from the north-west coast of America. 'Britpop' combined the musical influences of 1960s pop music, elements of glam rock, punk rock and the indie scene. More than just a music, it incorporated other cultural forms and Britpop coincided with the maturing of the so-called 'Young British Artists' such as Damien Hirst and Tracey Emin who were as likely to be seen at gigs as musicians Daman Albarn and Jarvis Cocker were at art galleries.

The phrase 'Cool Britannia' became ubiquitous in the mid-1990s and a celebration of British culture in all its forms occurred. The Union flag, so long the property of the far right, became an ideological football.[51] A new generation tried to 'reclaim' the flag, arguing that it no longer belonged to the NF or to the British Empire, but to a new generation, living in a multi-cultural world on the cusp of a new century.[52] In opposing the 'conservatism' of the government of the day, Britpop found itself aligned to the 'left', although for some this was intentional, for example, Blur's Damon Albarn, Pulp's Jarvis Cocker and Creation records owner Alan McGee.[53] They had been brought up on a diet of 1960s 'social realism' songwriters like Ray Davis and 1970s political wordsmiths like Paul Weller, who was enjoying a renaissance in the 1990s as a solo artist. Britpop, however, was not Red Wedge and it certainly had none of the elements of RAR. It reflected the cocaine fuelled celebrity-based orientation of 1990s 'lad' culture propagated by *Loaded* magazine and found itself supporting New Labour by default. What politics there were, were anti-Conservative rather than pro-Labour, old or new. Britpop reached its zenith in 1997 which coincided with Tony Blair's victory in the general election and the celebration party in Downing Street saw Oasis songwriter and guitarist Noel Gallagher sipping champagne with Tony Blair. The fusion of Britpop and New Labour became the defining image of Cool Britannia.

Love Racism, Hate Music:
The BNP and Music

As much as Britpop was 'accidentally' political, the same cannot be said for another music that developed out of new wave. As discussed previously, the skinheads associated with the revival of the late 1970s grew out of punk and were disillusioned by the commercialisation of that subculture. Post-1979, some skinhead revivalists rejected the multi-racial and left-leaning overtones of bands like The Specials and The Selecter and began to show more interest in the NF and a particularly violent neo-Nazi organisation called the British Movement (BM) founded by Colin Jordan in 1968. Some skinheads became increasingly estranged from the ethos of the original skinhead subculture and alongside an assortment of jaded punks a new subculture called Oi! evolved. Skinhead clothes also changed with their political stance. None of the attention to detail of the original skinheads was present, there were no longer sharp suits worn over button-down shirts and an increasingly militaristic style was adopted. Shoes and Sta-prest trousers were replaced by army issue boots and fatigues and jeans were cut high to display the top of the exponentially rising boots. Clothes were now worn solely as an expression of violence and political affiliation, T-shirts with white supremacist and fascist slogans were worn underneath MA1 flight combat jackets.[54] The hair was no longer closely cropped but shorn completely and with this new look skinheads became disparagingly known as boneheads.

Historically burdened with an association with neo-Nazis,

many of the first bands labelled with the epithet Oi! were either apolitical or actually hostile to the far right.[55] But some *were* openly racist; one example was The Dentists from Leeds who performed on stages festooned with swastikas and whose repertoire included the songs 'White Power' and 'Master Race'.[56]

Much of the subject matter dealt with in the lyrics of Oi! bands were comments on issues that faced young, white, working-class men and women such as street violence, unemployment, crime, police harassment, football, sex and alienation. These were exactly the issues that the NF and BM were keen to exploit. Attempting to emulate what Oswald Mosley had tried with the teddy boys in Notting Hill in 1958, the NF sensed an opportunity to exploit teenage dissatisfaction and set up the Young National Front (YNF). The NF had undertaken membership drives at universities earlier in the decade, but in 1978 they refocused their attention trying to recruit schoolchildren and particularly six-formers and this tactic would continue into the 1980s. They created a regular newspaper entitled *Bulldog*, written and designed specifically for young people, and 'educational' meetings and seminars directed at children were organised.

British Movement skinheads, 1982 © Getty Images

Membership of the YNF was open only to those aged 14-25 and the focal points for male recruitment were music and football. NF Leader Martin Webster told BBC's *Panorama* in 1979, "I think there's a lot you can do with soccer hooligans".[57] Few football clubs in any division escaped the fortnightly ritual of neo-fascists selling copies of *Bulldog* and handing out leaflets at home games. The YNF also organised football tournaments between their branches up and down the country. Young women were encouraged to join the YNF by becoming a 'Bulldog Bird', a feat they could achieve by sending in scantily clad photographs of themselves to the *Bulldog* newspaper, 'the sexier the better'.[58] The photos were accompanied by comments directed at young men suggesting this was 'one good reason for joining the YNF'.[59]

Alongside football matches, gigs were seen as a potential recruiting ground. The far right had seen the success that RAR had enjoyed and sought to emulate it. The NF/BM began to infiltrate concerts and distribute their literature, as an edition of *Bulldog* reported in March 1979:

> For years, white British youths have had to put up with left-wing filth in rock music. They have had to put up with the anti-NF lies in the music press. They have had commie organisations like Rock Against Racism trying to brainwash them. But now there is an anti-commie backlash.[60]

There was a concerted attempt by the far right to forge substantial links to youth culture. Some punk bands such as Sham 69 had already been adopted by racist skinheads irrespective of whether the band welcomed the following or not.[61] This dilemma later recurred with the Two-Tone movement and Selecter, Madness and Specials concerts often became battlegrounds not only between mods and skinheads, but left-wing and right-wing too.[62] The YNF distributed their literature inside and outside gigs and these interventions were regularly reported in *Bulldog,* according to Paul Sillett, an anti-fascist skinhead at the time "...most skins in London thought it was cool to be racist and call yourself NF/BM...they were vicious and organised and attacked all manner of gigs...but there were skins on the right side...Skins Against the Nazis".[63] NF/BM members were encouraged to write to the music press to raise their profile in that media. In Leeds, a magazine called *Punk Front* had been launched in 1978 and its creator Eddy Morrison went on to help develop a new organisation Rock Against Communism (RAC), a campaign specifically formulated by the YNF to counter RAR. Oi! bands fitted seamlessly into Rock Against Communism.[64] Although only holding sporadic gigs after its formation in 1978, RAC took on a new life in the 1980s helped by the summer concerts held in the grounds of Conservative Party activist Edgar Griffin, father to future BNP leader Nick Griffin.[65] Further developing the fusion of music and politics of RAC, the NF/BM helped to develop the White Noise Club and Blood & Honour, two openly neo-Nazi music organisations that staged private gigs and played at political rallies all over Europe.[66] These gigs paradoxically display the strengths and weaknesses of the far right during this period. On the one hand they indicate a sizeable number of activists willing to travel and assemble at secret political and cultural events at short notice, often at considerable personal risk. Conversely, they demonstrate the inability of the far right to *openly* organise fascist or white power events to showcase the bands and highlight their broader political programme.

Despite the subterfuge involved in the organising of these secret neo-Nazi gigs, they did act as a focus for solidifying the far right in the 1980s and the music played a central part:

> [Oi!] played an important symbolic role in the politicization of the skinhead subculture. By providing, for the first time, a musical focus for skinhead identity that was 'white'—that is, that had nothing to do with the West Indian immigrant presence and little obvious connection with black musical roots—Oi! provided a musical focus for new visions of

skinhead identity [and] a point of entry for a new brand of right-wing rock music.[67]

Joe Pearce, leader of the YNF during this period, reflected in 2013 that the music was a conduit to the politics and as a result "...many of the second-generation skinheads had adopted white nationalism and either joined the Front or otherwise supported it because of the gigs".[68] The BNP would later go on to form its own in-house radio station and record label *Great White Records* (GWR) which sold CDs of 'inspirational lectures' and some of Nick Griffin's self-penned and no-doubt poignant songs. The records released by GWR were never likely to trouble the charts, nor become part of any accepted scene in subcultural terms and this is not just a reflection of the unpalatable politics. The more alienated the people involved with Oi! became, the more alienated the music became. Consequently, the onomatopoeic White Noise club proved to be more of a description rather than a designation.

There has never been a happy marriage of modern music and the right-wing. Fascist leaders before WWII rejected the 'modern' and harked back to a mythical world where quaint rural people, creatively unsullied by Jewish or black influence, made earthenware pots and sang simple folk songs. In 1930s Germany, under the control of the *Reichskulturkammer* (Reich Cultural Chamber), all music had to conform to the Nazi ideal and as jazz was associated with black Americans it was labelled 'degenerate' and verboten.[69] Mussolini decided that Italy was 'allergic' to foreign musical influences, especially jazz.[70] Guitarist Django Reinhart was banned by the Vichy government for being 'decadent'.[71] In McCarthyite America, black 'race' music, irrespective of its genre, fared little better.[72] One Chicago radio station received over 15,000 letters complaining that the rock 'n' roll they were playing was 'dirty' ie it was black music. In the UK the *Daily Mail* declared in a 1956 front page editorial that rock 'n' roll was 'the negro's revenge'.[73] Colin Jordan from the White Defence League agreed and in open opposition to

SCIF's musical celebration of black music, declared: "Rock and pop were a manifestation of the jungle, a musical counterpart to the broader Afro-Asian influx that had facilitated Britain's national decline".[74]

Stanley Cohen in his work *Folk Devils and Moral Panics* observed that: "All subcultures are about the relationship between the white working class and black music".[75] In the period Cohen was writing in, this statement has validity; the further away a subculture strayed from black music, the more the likelihood of racism increased. This was true with Teds in the 1950s and Oi! in the 1980s. Today this can clearly be seen with the 21st century version of skinheads, the casuals. Concentrated around football and football violence and with little outward interest in music, the link between casuals, violence and racism is stark. The street-fighting forces of the far right in the last ten years, the English Defence League (EDL) and the Democratic Football Lads Alliance (DFLA), recruit almost entirely from the casuals' ranks and they will be discussed in the following chapter.

The British National Party

The general election of 3 May 1979 had been an unmitigated disaster for the far right in Britain. Overall, the NF secured 1.3 percent of the total vote, significantly down from their high of 3.1 percent in 1974.[76] Their membership, according to Copsey, fell to under 5,000 from a high of 15,000 and a post mortem began in earnest.[77] It took only eight months after the election for the recriminations to begin and fissures to surface that resulted in an acrimonious three-way split. Part of the problem was image. Photographs of Tyndall, Webster and Jordan in full Nazi regalia obtained by the anti-fascist magazine *Searchlight* had been widely circulated by the ANL/ RAR from 1976 onwards and as Thurlow points out, in reaction to this, there was a concerted attempt by the NF leadership to present themselves in a more 'rational and reasoned' way.[78] Roger Eatwell concurs, stating that Tyndall tried "..hard to hide

[the] neo-Nazism from public view, fearing it might damage popular support".[79] Interestingly, Paul Gilroy accuses the ANL of pandering to English chauvinism by circulating the Tyndall 'Nazi' photos and equating the NF with Hitler and the Holocaust. He suggested that the ANL:

Manipulate[d] a form of nationalism and patriotism as part of [their] broad anti-fascist drive... British Nazis were merely sham patriots who soiled the British flag...it is hard to gauge what made [the NF] more abhorrent to the ANL, their Nazi-ism [sic] or the way they were dragging British patriotism through the mud.[80]

Gilroy's comments are refuted by numerous sources: Goodyer, Renton and Street and contemporary issues of *Temporary Hoarding* or ANL materials offer no suggestion that this was the case.[81] Arguably, what the constant comparisons to Hitler, the 'Nazi' photos, the badges and NF = Nazi Front stickers did show, was a direct link between the NF's politics and the politics of the gas chambers. By 1979 this connection had registered in the consciousness of a wide range of British people. Much damage had been done to the image of the NF and a significant section of the party was in the process of realigning itself toward a more 'moderate' Strasserite position.[82]

After an unsuccessful leadership battle, prominent member Andrew Fountaine resigned in November 1979 to form the National Front Constitutional Movement, claiming some 2,000 members.[83] Tyndall followed suit in June 1980 and founded the New National Front and claimed that a third of the NF's membership defected with him.[84] Webster, at the time embroiled in a series of allegations that he had been making sexual advances to the party's young male cadre, wanted to focus on the recruitment of skinheads and football hooligans and build a street army to continue with the confrontations that had culminated in the Southall riots in April 1979.[85] Webster was hegemonic inside the NF until 1983 when he was dethroned by a new faction led by the openly Strasserite Nick Griffin. The arguments over strategy and tactics did not disappear with the new leadership and there continued an internal debate which effectively saw these two groups unhappily co-existing alongside two others, the 'Flag NF', an aggressively anti-immigrant and racial purist faction and the 'Official National Front' which sought to re-brand the NF as an anti-capitalist, radical and youthful party.[86]

Further complicating matters were the BM who had an altogether different perspective and rejected electoral politics completely. Occasionally working alongside the NF from 1968 onwards, the BM grew out of Colin Jordan's National Socialist Movement (NSM). The BM were openly fascist and from their inception had been associated with attacks on black people and left-wing activists. Their emphasis was on direct action, which almost inevitably ended with violence. The BM encouraged paramilitary training and their members, both male and female, were urged to join the Territorial Army. By 1980 the BM claimed over 4,000 members in 25 locations.[87] These members were often disgruntled ex-NF members and skinheads who preferred violence to political campaigning, and a revolving door between members of the BM, the NF and other fringe groups operated throughout the 1980s.[88]

The differences between these disparate groups and the inter-party fighting ensured they stayed small and relatively weak through the two decades relevant to this chapter. However, the most important faction that developed from the remnants of the 1970s far right is the British National Party (BNP). Created by Tyndall after leaving the NF in 1982, the BNP would attempt to rebuild and rebrand British neo-fascism in the coming decades. Very influential in this makeover was the growth of the Front National (FN) in France.[89] Tyndall and the new generation of fascists around Patrick Harrington and Nick Griffin developed an interest in the *Nouvelle Droite* and ideas of Alain de Benoist.[90] Playing the long game, the FN had sought to slowly broaden their appeal and had developed a 'sophisticated critique' of liberal democracy which sought to create a society based on 'national roots'. There would be less emphasis on race and they would develop a nuanced and codified language on 'culture' and 'cultural differences' that explained the integrational difficulties that France faced.[91] Harrington and Griffin had been cadre-ised in the NF as 'political soldiers' and had both been to university. They began to cloak themselves in the language of the *Nouvelle Droite* and argue not for racial purity and superiority but for 'racial differentiation'. Caution again should be exercised here as one of the difficulties in establishing a narrative for the BNP is the lack of a coherent political line. Griffin was seemingly able to move to the *Nouvelle Droite* position in the late 1980s, to then advocate the opposite in 1993, stating that the BNP "should *not* be a postmodernist rightest party".[91] He became increasingly influential inside the party and after another disastrous election for the BNP in 1997 wrested control of the party from Tyndall. Following this Roger Eatwell observed that Griffin did another volte-face and "set about turning [the BNP] into a modern right-wing populist party on continental lines".[93]

Britishness and the 'loss of national character' would replace racial superiority as the motif of the new party. The BNP engaged in a range of issues not commonly associated with the far right in this period, environmental politics, the Countryside Alliance, issues of local concern such as lower speed limits on housing estates and organising against closures of local swimming baths. They presented to the British public, a different BNP committed to a 'new modernist nationalism' and by the end of the 90s they had '...jettisoned much of the protectionist and corporatist economic policies and became more influenced by market economics'.[94] In a further unexpected shift the BNP began eulogising Nation of Islam leader Louis Farakhan and Libyan leader Muammar Gaddafi. Louis Farakhan was a black separatist, a position the BNP could readily support and Libya was seen as 'a model of direct democracy in a dual and practical form'.[95] Arabs were seen as part of the heroic struggle against capitalism and communism, codified language for world Jewry. Ironically this position has now been reversed and the antisemitism has been replaced with Islamophobia. In 2021 Tommy Robinson and the British far right support the state of Israel against Palestine, Arabs and Islam in general.[96] The BNP declared that the British electorate now had the 'chance to vote for a party like the Front National'.[97] They also produced two new newspapers for the new millennium, *Identity* and *Freedom*. But under their new 'cultural' veneer, the old racism was just below the surface. In January 2001 *Identity* declared:

> As illegal asylum seekers pour into Europe, how many more can we take? They will keep coming until Britain simply ceases to be Britain—or until the British people say 'stop' and turn to the only party that will take any notice of what ordinary voters want: the BNP.[98]

The September 2001 issue of *Freedom* continued: "The British are going to become a minority in our own country within the next 100 years and already in some parts of inner-city Britain anti-white violence was so bad it was a form of ethnic cleansing".[99] The true nature of their politics was not just hidden inside their newspapers. Over the period when this 'modernisation' was supposedly happening, the BNP's campaigns belied their non-racist epiphany.

Engagement in elections were sporadic throughout the 1980s and 1990s. In the 1983 British general election, the BNP canvassed only five seats, it abstained in the 1987 general election and stood 13 candidates in the 1992 general election. However, the party was successful in the Millwall by-election in the Isle of Dogs, east London the following year. The campaign was based on a 'rights for whites' platform erroneously stating that preferential treatment was being given to Bangladeshi residents in social housing.[100] Derek Beackon, the BNP candidate, won the seat, beating Labour by seven votes. In response, a campaign by local residents, a re-formed ANL and Anti-Fascist Action (AFA) ensured that he only held this seat for eight months and it was lost in the 1994 local election. The confrontations that occurred in both of Derek Beackon's campaigns were due to the formation of a BNP 'self-defence' unit styled on Mosley's 'I Squad', but redesigned for the 1990s. Griffin had stated that the BNP must be "...a strong disciplined organisation with the ability to back up its slogan 'Defend Rights for Whites' with well-directed boots and fists".[101] A paramilitary group called Combat 18 (C18) supplied the boots and fists. C18 was formed as a 'stewarding group'; although its name refutes this claim. The C was for combat and the 18 is derived from the initials of Adolf Hitler, A and H being the first and eighth letters of the alphabet. C18 was supposedly a defensive organisation but was in fact a terrorist cell that was notoriously violent and known to attack anyone they deemed 'degenerate'. They were also linked to attacks on left-wing activists, the murder of immigrants and even that of their own members. From its inception C18 had direct links to casuals in football hooligan firms, indeed they could boast members of the Chelsea Head Hunters and the Millwall Bushwackers amongst their ranks.[102] C18 attempted infiltration of football firms and superintendent Adrian Appleby, head of the Football Unit of the National Criminal Intelligence Service, claimed that the BNP had also targeted several football clubs with some success. These clubs included Heart of Midlothian, Glasgow Rangers, Leeds, Blackburn, Burnley and Oxford United. Many of those active in football firms went on to become BNP members.[103]

In 1989 the BNP moved their headquarters to Welling, in the London borough of Bexley. Following the move, racist attacks in the area increased by over 200 percent and four young black men: Rolan Adams, Orville Blair, Rohit Duggal and Stephen Lawrence were murdered between February 1991 and April 1993.[104] All of these deaths were proven to have a racial motivation, but it was the death of Stephen Lawrence, a teenager murdered whilst waiting for a bus on his way home, that was to have far-reaching consequences in British politics in the years that followed. Initially his death was overlooked in the mainstream media, but a tireless campaign run by the Lawrence family was determined to seek justice.

It gradually gained ground and with help from local community groups, socialist organisations, trades unions, the re-formed ANL and the newly-formed Anti-Racist Alliance (ARA), Stephen Lawrence's death and the police culpability over a lack of convictions were thrust into a media spotlight.[105]

The response from the Metropolitan Police to Stephen Lawrence's death captured as many headlines as the murder itself and would result in wide-reaching reform. The police had been given information on possible suspects by members of the public which they failed to pursue. They overlooked and destroyed evidence, obfuscated and impeded inquiries and appointed undercover agents to spy on the Lawrence family rather than the suspected killers.[106] As the case unravelled and under mounting political pressure, Jack Straw, the then Labour home secretary launched a judicial inquiry into the police's handling of the case. The resulting Macpherson Report released in 1999 concluded that there was: 'institutional racism' at the heart of the police force and that there had been a "...collective failure of an organisation to provide a professional service...through unwitting prejudice, ignorance, thoughtlessness and racist stereotyping which disadvantage minority ethnic people".[107] Political scientist Inderjeet Palmar described the report as "...the most wide-ranging inquiry into police-ethnic minority relations since the Scarman Report of 1981".[108] The results held a mirror up to the police force and sent shockwaves throughout the British establishment and of the 70 recommendations from Macpherson's report, 67 were implemented.

Prior to the Lawrence murder there had been disquiet about the rise of racism in London and concerns about the growth of the BNP and their headquarters in Welling. One organisation seeking to counter this growth was Anti-Fascist Action (AFA). Formed in 1985 they were a militant combative organisation, that saw physical confrontation as the key to stopping the growth of neo-fascism. AFA was forged through a variety of anti-fascist individuals and notably, a group called Red Action, one-time members of the SWP, who were expelled from the organisation for 'squadism'. The direct and violent action of small 'squads' of activists prepared to physically fight fascists had been used by the ANL and SWP to protect its meetings in the late 1970s and had its origins in Italian anti-fascists fighting Mussolini in the 1920s, but after the defeat of the NF in the 1979 general election, arguing the threat of the far-right had receded, this tactic was seen as unnecessary.

AFA disagreed with the analysis of the now disbanded ANL and the perspectives of the SWP, and they were not alone. At its founding meeting in 1985 in attendance were many active anti-racist individuals and several groups: Searchlight, the Newham Monitoring Project, the Jewish Socialist Group as well as future Labour Party leader Jeremy Corbyn, who became its first honorary president. Combining leafleting campaigns in working class communities against neo-Nazi propaganda and 'direct action', AFA became, albeit on a smaller scale, a similar organisation to the ANL in its heyday. But, whereas the ANL saw the building of popular campaigns and mass mobilisations to confront the far-right, AFA argued that symmetry with the far-right was required and small groups of activists would physically attack the BNP wherever they appeared.

In adopting these tactics, AFA stood in the tradition of the 43 Group and the 62 Group mentioned in previous chapters. As racist attacks grew in the late 1980s, so did attacks on the left. The perpetrators of these attacks came from the aforementioned, Blood and Honour, an extremely violent neo-fascist 'musical' organisation.

A series of gigs in London were targeted by Blood and Honour, three in particular, The Pogues, the Angelic Upstarts and Jamaican ska artist Desmond Dekker were violently attacked, and several people were injured. In response, in 1988, AFA set up a musical organisation of its own, Cable Street Beat

(CSB). Like Rock Against Racism before it, CSB began organising gigs in pubs across London and set up its own magazine Cable Street Beat Review. This was AFA's forum for discussion on anti-fascist tactics and an organiser and advertiser for the gigs they were putting on. Notable successes occurred. Gigs in Brixton by The Blaggers and The Neurotics, and another at the Sir George Robey, a pub in north London with a notorious far-right clientele, where The Upstarts and The Blaggers played. Blythe Power and Atilla the Stockbroker performed at Lyndhurst Hall in Kentish Town and a sell-out concert at Camden Town's Electric Ballroom, headlined by The Men They Couldn't Hang with The Neurotics and Atilla the Stockbroker was a highlight.

There followed a nationwide 'Dance and Defend Tour' which was organised to fund the defence of activists arrested at a counter-NF march the previous year on Remembrance Sunday. Alongside the confrontational tactics, AFA and CSB were also engaged in petitioning campaigns such as one against a shop in Carnaby Street which was selling 'under the table' Nazi memorabilia, and was allegedly a front for Blood and Honour. The campaign culminated in a mobilisation of hundreds of supporters who marched down Carnaby Street and picketed outside the shop. Westminster Council would later revoke the shops licence after this pressure.

Blood and Honour gigs became an important focal point for the far-right throughout Europe at this time and these gigs would be consistently opposed by AFA, CSB and individuals associated with the anti-fascist left from all over the country. The most notorious incident occurred in opposition to a proposed Blood and Honour gig in September 1992. Attempting to assemble the worst and most violent neo-fascists in Europe for a night of celebration and morale boosting, Blood and Honour organised a gig to be held in a secret location in London. The destination was due to be announced at an assembly point at Waterloo train station. Hundreds of anti-fascists descended on Waterloo station and its surrounding environs. Neo-Nazi skinheads came under a barrage of attacks from the AFA organised counter-demonstration and running street battles occurred over a period of hours. Many fascists, particularly those from abroad, who were unfamiliar with the location, were severely attacked and some hospitalised. Although the gig was finally held, with a reduced audience, in a pub in south-east London, the 'Battle of Waterloo' was a considerable defeat for the far-right and undermined its ability to stage similar events in the future.

Aside from organising counter demos, CSB also promoted musical festivals of their own and staged three carnivals in the early 1990s. The first 'Unity Carnival' was staged in October 1991 in east London to counteract the 'Rights for Whites' campaign being run by the BNP. Over 10,000 people attended the carnival, and it was followed later that year by another 4,000 anti-racists marching in Bethnal Green against racist attacks.

A second carnival, featuring bands Five-Thirty, Soho, 25th May and Honey Chile was held the following year in Hackney Downs, just round the corner from where the RAR carnival had been held only 14 years earlier and much of the organising for the Battle of Waterloo—two weeks later—took place here. A third carnival was held in Newcastle headlined by The Shamen

British National Party demonstration 2001. © Jess Hurd

and Fun-Da-Mental with an estimated attendance of up to 10,000 people.

Many were arguing that there was a direct link between the BNP moving their headquarters to Welling and the rise in racist attacks and murders and several small demonstrations had been organised in opposition to the party relocating there. A resuscitated ANL launched a campaign to close down the BNP headquarters with immediate effect. A demonstration was called in October 1993 which saw 45,000 people attend to demand the BNP 'bookshop' was closed down. Despite a route being agreed between the demonstration organisers and the police, on the day, the police blocked the marchers and kettled them. There then followed successive waves of mounted police charges and over 70 people were injured.[109]

Bexley Council finally closed the HQ down in 1995. Despite the Lawrence family's fight for justice, the successful campaign to close down the headquarters of the BNP, the Macpherson report and blanket coverage of institutional police racism, the BNP still managed to be runner-up in the Bexley South by-election of 2000. They received 26 percent of the vote, their biggest success since Derek Beackon. The BNP saw this as a dress rehearsal for the election the following year.[110]

2001 General Election

The 2001 British general election was fought with immigration at the top of the agenda. A number of international crises and civil wars saw increasing numbers seeking refuge in the UK from a succession of countries such as Kosovo, Sierra Leone, Iraq and Sri Lanka.[111] Legislation passed by the Conservatives restricting entry to the UK was continued by Tony Blair's government and the 1999 Immigration and Asylum Act. The number of countries where a visa was required for entry into the UK leapt from 19 in 1991 to 108 in 2005.[112] Amid a sea of scaremongering stories about refugees and asylum seekers, the political environment was once again highly charged with racist and xenophobic invective. The tabloid press was awash with headlines such as *The Sun's*: 'Britain full up' or 'Blair supports bogus asylum seekers' and from the *Daily Mail* 'Romanian gipsies begging on the streets of Britain to pay for dream home'.[113] Not for the first time did a leader of the Conservative Party adopt the language of the far right and William Hague declared in the election campaign: "Elect a Conservative government and we will give you your country back".[114] Similarly, shadow home secretary Anne Widdecombe stated: "Britain should close its doors to a flood of bogus asylum seekers".[115]

Labour Home Secretary Jack Straw had argued in 1999 that the Macpherson Report should be "a watershed in attitudes towards racism…a catalyst for permanent and irrevocable change".[116] Just two years later, this was forgotten as he campaigned to change the 1951 United Nations Convention of Refugees and curtail the right to asylum in Britain.[117] The Labour Party think tank *Policy Network* declared: "Angry young men were about to desert Labour for a [Jean Marie] Le Pen like figure unless the party embraced their hostility on asylum and immigration".[118] Peter Mandelson, architect of 'Third Way' thinking inside the Labour Party insisted there should be no ambiguity, Labour must "…crack down on immigration".[119]

BNP leader Nick Griffin exploited the refugee and asylum 'crisis' in the 2001 British General Election and provocatively stood in the Oldham West and Royton constituency where racial tensions were high after riots between white and Asian youth had broken out earlier in the year. Griffin won some 16 percent of the vote and the next year, just 20 miles to the north of Oldham, the BNP won three seats on Burnley council.[120] This was the beginning of what would prove to be the most successful political intervention made by a fascist or neo-fascist party in British history and, arguably, the success was due to the shift in presentation and the influence of the French *Nouvelle Droite*. The nature of the fascist threat had changed and the people SCIF and RAR opposed at gigs and on demonstrations, the teddy boys of the WDL and the skinheads of the NF, had been replaced by besuited and 'respectable' politicians who presented their arguments in a more 'refined and nuanced' way. The nativism was still there but had been replaced by 'cultural incompatibility' tropes. The BNP exploited the general hostility toward asylum, immigration and race and their results in local and general elections were evidence to some on the political left that the far right were gaining ground and there was a need to counteract them. Once again music would be used as a platform upon which another organisation would be built to form opposition to the growth of the new fascist threat.

Chapter Six
Love Music Hate Racism

Love Music Hate Racism (LMHR) was formed in 2002 in response to a surge in popularity for the BNP in the UK local and general elections the previous year. LMHR sought to combat racist and neo-fascist ideas using music as its focus. It followed the template set down by RAR in the 1970s and was a national *and* local campaign of individuals and groups who organised events and gigs to counteract the popularity of the BNP and their ideas. The BNP had grown significantly toward the end of the 1990s and appeared to be on the verge of 'respectability' and of becoming a mainstream political force in British politics. Substantial gains were made by the BNP in the UK local elections of 2002. They won 16 percent of votes and would sustain this level for the years to come.[1]

Three BNP candidates were elected in Burnley with an average share of 28.1 percent. In Oldham, the party polled its highest share of the vote (35 percent) in St James ward, and (30 percent) in Chadderton South. In total the BNP fielded 67 candidates and polled 30,998 votes in 26 local councils.[2] They won hundreds of thousands of votes and, later in the European elections of 2009, even secured the election of two MEPs.[3]

Alarmed at these historic gains, a discussion took place between active anti-fascist organisers and leading members of the SWP. A decision was made to launch a new musical opposition to the BNP and the general anti-asylum seeker/ refugee feeling prevalent at the time. A subsequent meeting with ex-Specials keyboard player Jerry Dammers and Billy Bragg's manager Peter Jenner resulted in a larger meeting of sympathetic music industry people at the University of Westminster.[4] Also, like SCIF and RAR before it, "LMHR was meant to be a cultural front against the BNP and focused on people in the arts and music industry".[5] A steering committee was formed with artists from Roll Deep, Get Cape, Wear Cape and Atlantic records boss Paul Samuels, who attended the first RAR carnival.

Like SCIF and RAR before it, LMHR was to be a single issue campaign and the steering committee were against "widening out its remit, believing it would split the organisation".[6] LMHR national organiser Lee Billingham recalled: "We wanted LMHR to focus on combatting the BNP".[7] Any disagreements over the war in Iraq or the state of Israel for instance were placed aside in order to concentrate on the fight against neo-fascism: "Paul Samuels did not take the same position on Israel as others…[on the steering committee]…any support for the Palestinian cause would have split LMHR…no position on Israel was taken".[8] The LMHR steering committee was weighted to ensure that there was a representation of different political opinions present and no one political organisation dominated proceedings. Alongside the SWP presence there were Labour Party members and others who were not aligned to any particular political party.

LMHR was formed in the tradition and spirit of RAR, indeed, its name Love Music Hate Racism was taken from the statement on the cover from the first edition of RAR's publication *Temporary Hoarding*: "We want rebel music, street music. Music that breaks down people's fear of one another. Crisis music. Now music. Music that knows who the real enemy is. Love Music Hate Racism".[9] But circumstances had changed since the 1970s and the campaign against the National Front. The racial nationalism and provocative demonstrations of skinheads into largely BAME neighbourhoods had been replaced by the French FN-inspired cultural asymmetry and incompatibility tropes against Muslims. Nevertheless, LMHR

Poly Styrene, left, lead singer of X-Ray Spex, at the LMHR 30th Anniversary Carnival in 2008 © Jess Hurd/reportdigital. co.uk and opening the RAR Carnival in 1978, below © Syd Shelton

spokesperson Weyman Bennett commented: "Racism is just as much of a problem today…[but]…things are more covert… racists wear suits and look respectable".[10] In support of the new LMHR initiative, DJ, film-maker and RAR veteran Don Letts agreed: "It used to be a black and white issue, but now it's more complicated. Today there's more racism against Muslims or eastern Europeans for instance".[11]

So did this change in how the far right operated necessitate a change in tactics for the left? Would it be possible to simply recreate another RAR in the new millennium? It was not just that the fascists had changed their clothes, Britain's youth were no longer gripped in a world of self-imposed subcultural separation. The tribalism that once dominated British youth had slowly merged into an amorphous high-street identikit. Musically, the digital age had opened up a vast array of musical styles that were accessible to everyone at the touch of a computer key. Gone were the days of endlessly rooting through dank and dimly lit specialist record shops searching for elusive B-sides or albums by bands that high street record shops had never heard of.

As a name and as a concept, Rock Against Racism simply did not fit the new musical climate of the 21st century. Therefore, the new title that was found had to reflect this and LMHR replaced the narrower musical confines of RAR. A statement issued at its launch said:

> LMHR is a non-partisan campaign which aims to promote unity through the power of music. Our message is simple, there is more that unites us than divides us. Nothing demonstrates this more than the music we listen to. LMHR uses the energy of the music scene to celebrate diversity and promote anti-racism.[12]

The focus would again be on young people, but there were no identifiable mass youth trends that LMHR could target as a focus of resistance to racism like punk and reggae were for RAR. Where did young people go to listen to music collectively?

Furthermore, a large percentage of the attacks from the far right were against Muslims. If Muslims were involved in LMHR it would be impossible to organise RAR-type gigs in the back room of pubs when alcohol was not a part of Islamic life. The pub had long been the stalwart of the British left and untold interventions and demonstrations began and ended in the pub. There needed to be a reassessment of where LMHR gigs would be staged.

Initially LMHR used the experience of RAR to establish itself. Whereas the link between SCIF and RAR had not been made in the 1970s, this time many of those RAR veterans concerned about the rise of the BNP and racism were still politically active and their experience and the lessons learnt in the 1970s could be utilised in LMHR. Local gigs and club nights were once again set up around the UK. The first event was a carnival in Manchester on 1 September 2002 headlined by Ms Dynamite, Doves and Billy Bragg with The Shining, Miss Black America, Heartless Crew and Phi-Life Cypher in support. LMHR had initially approached Burnley council to stage the carnival where significant 'race riots' had taken place the year before. Just as SCIF member Claudia Jones had done in 1959, with the first Notting Hill carnival, LMHR wanted the 2002 carnival to be a political statement, but also a celebration of diversity and have a calming effect on the antagonisms inside the town. Permission was refused by Burnley Labour council on the grounds that it could provoke conflict, despite giving ex-NF leader John Tyndall permission to hold a meeting of neo-fascists in the town centre only months before. Local LMHR activist Jess Edwards told the NME this:

> We want to give confidence to the anti-Nazi majority, to say look, we're here, we're on the streets, come and join us. You don't just have to sit at home thinking 'Oh god, this is really terrible, what's happening to my town?'. We've got to cut through that and say—no, you should be proud of where you live, because you live in a place where the majority of people aren't racists.[13]

Following the Manchester carnival, a series of concerts from youth clubs to football stadia were organised around the country, but towns and cities were targeted where BNP councillors had won seats or where popular support for them was growing. During the 2004 London Assembly elections, The Libertines headlined the London Love Music Hate Racism Festival, at Finsbury Park.[14] Carnivals and festivals grabbed the headlines and tens of thousands of people attended, but the work that went on in local areas was of equal importance. LMHR did not just host mass events and then disappear back to London. Gigs were organised by local people, often in less glamorous locations than football stadia. One such gig, on 19 April 2007, was held at Balne Lane Working Men's Club in Wakefield, West Yorkshire. The club was in a mainly white working-class estate where the BNP were campaigning for the local council elections on 3 May that year. The gig was organised specifically to counter the BNP activity.[15]

The purpose of the gig was threefold. First, to make a political statement that whenever the BNP stood, they would be opposed and second, that the music people enjoy is as

LMHR 30th anniversary RAR carnival 2008. © Guy Smallman

multi-cultural as the town in which they live. A third, unseen intention was more subtle but lay behind the tactics of all of the organisational work discussed in this chapter: to undermine the confidence of neo-fascist activists and their supporters. The objective was to wear down neo-fascists by a constant sticker, poster and gig campaign alongside standard political activities such as canvassing and demonstrations, the idea being that this constant opposition relentlessly chips away at their morale. LMHR gigs also stood in the RAR/ANL tradition of linking the anti-racist movement with organised labour and the LMHR gig in Wakefield was sponsored by Unison's West Yorkshire police service branch, Wakefield TUC, as well as local council and health Unison branches. Nurses, local hospital workers and council workers were present at the gig as well as Wakefield Unite Against Fascism.

Carnival II

To commemorate the 30th anniversary of Rock Against Racism, LMHR staged the LMHR Carnival at Victoria Park on 27 April 2008, where the first carnival had taken place. The funding of the event was also a clear indication of how much had changed in the intervening years. Trade unions had been vocal in their condemnation of racism with SCIF in the 1950s and RAR in the 1970s, but the issue of race and racism was not treated as a priority in the union movement. Money was certainly not forthcoming to sponsor events such as the 1959 or 1978 carnival. The 1980s and 1990s had seen significant advances in representation of black members in unions and 'black sections' in the Labour Party. Racism was now treated as one of the key issues on the left and the 2008 LMHR carnival demonstrated that. The bulk of the funding for the carnival came from trade unions, including PCS, CWU and the South East region of the TUC.[16] Unite the union sponsored the second stage, which featured acts including Patrick Wolf, Akala, The Paddingtons and Adelaide Mackenzie. PCS hosted the dance

LMHR gig posters.

marquee—which was packed right from the start of the carnival with ravers shouting, 'Fuck the BNP!' to bassline house and jungle. Several union leaders spoke at the event, including the general secretaries of Unite, Derek Simpson, the CWU's Billy Hayes, Mark Serwotka of the PCS and Frances O'Grady, the deputy general secretary of the TUC.

The funding was different, but so was the event. Whilst there remained a 'main stage' as in the 1978 carnival, it was now augmented by a second stage and a 'dance tent', similar to large-scale music festivals like Glastonbury—it was a reflection of how the musical world had changed. Poly Styrene of X-Ray Spex, who opened the 1978 Carnival, performed, as did Jerry Dammers, but the old formula of punk and reggae could not be recreated in the new millennium.

At this carnival, musical worlds collided and hip-hop, indie, grime, bhangra, rock, reggae, dubstep, R&B, funky house and jungle all fought for the attention of the audience. LMHR's slogan reflected this change, you no longer 'rocked against racism', now the battle cry was 'Hip-hop, indie, drum 'n' bass, reggae, punk and grime—Love Music Hate Racism'.[17] The digital age had democratised music for its creators and broken the subcultural genre barriers for the audience. Record collections, such as they are, now contain a multitude of genres from around the world and across the musical spectrum. Although the genres of the music were now different, the difficulties of translating politics into digestible portions for the audience remained. London grime artist DJ Target of Roll Deep was as aware of this as RAR's Dave Widgery 30 years before him: "Kids of today would prefer to listen to a song than to a politician they can't relate to. A concert is a good way to communicate the anti-racism message".[18]

Over 100,000 people attended the carnival, and it was a resounding success, although not all were impressed. *New Statesman* journalist Daniel Trilling criticised the event for being 'too corporate', stating:

I wasn't around 30 years ago, but this seemed a far cry from the original Rock Against Racism concert. The punk bands that played back in 1978—The Clash, X-Ray Spex, Buzzcocks—promoted a culture in which people were encouraged to be active participants, rather than passive spectators. 'This is a chord, this is another, this is a third. Now form a band,' went the famous punk slogan. In today's music industry, it would be more like: 'These are the results of our marketing demographics survey. Now generate some income'.[19]

Trilling's next comment, however, describes the exact thing he said was missing: "A teenage rap group called Little Rascals protégés of the grime star Dizzee Rascal [who] showed off their lyrical skills and boasted about their (lack of) age".[20]

The following year, on 30 May 2009, LMHR organised another carnival in Stoke. The BNP had won three more seats in the local elections in May 2008 and now had a total of nine seats in Stoke-on-Trent council.[21] More than 24,000 people crowded into the Britannia Stadium to see host Eddie Izzard introduce Pete Doherty, Beverley Knight, Reverend & the Makers, Kelly Rowland, Jerry Dammers, DJ Ironik and Chipmunk.

In 2010 LMHR and Barnsley Metropolitan Borough Council teamed up, with the aim of sending a clear message that racism is rejected by the majority of Yorkshire people. Ten thousand people saw UB40, Reverend & The Makers, Chipmunk, Mumzy Stranger, and Devlin perform.

There was also a programme of LMHR fringe events occurring in a dozen music venues across the town. Self-activity was still the most important element for LMHR. The LMHR website informed people that:

There are many ways you can help. Help raise awareness of the campaign eg on social media or by displaying a poster. Host an event in your local community or workplace. Attend existing LMHR activities in your area.[22]

The music and musicians were important to attract
people initially, but the intention was to use their celebrity as
a springboard to thrust young people into anti-racist activity
themselves. LMHR followed the template set out by RAR in the
1970s when it came to the self-organisation of gigs and events,
but now this advice was online and immediately accessible:

> Love Music Hate Racism has a range of resources to help and
> inspire people who want to support the campaign. Whether
> you are a music fan who wants to put on their own event or a
> teacher looking for educational resources, you can download
> materials to support you in tackling racism. *Click here to visit
> our Education page.*[23]

The gigs and campaigns that LMHR ran were not done
in isolation and music alone was not going to defeat the BNP
in forthcoming elections. In 2003 after discussions with the
National Assembly Against Racism (NAAR), which was formed
in 1995 after the collapse of the Anti-Racist Alliance, the ANL
merged with NAAR and its component parts.[24] A broader anti-
fascist movement was formed to counteract the BNP threat.
This new organisation was called Unite Against Fascism
(UAF).[25] "We want to start an anti-racist movement that'll
drive the Nazis back into the sewers where they belong", said
organiser Julie Waterson.[26]

Like LMHR, it was clear from the onset that UAF was to be
a single-issue campaign; no conditions were placed upon any
person or organisation wanting to be part of the anti-fascist
movement other than anti-racism. Secretary of UAF Weyman
Bennett stated: "The aim was to build an anti-racist atmosphere
and arm the movement with a set of arguments they could use
against the fascists".[27] He added: "Our second strategic strength
comes through Love Music Hate Racism, the cultural wing of
our movement. We can get the stars to speak out against the
BNP in the media and the press".[28]

The Electoral Threat of the BNP

A pivotal event for the far right globally was the 9/11 terrorist attack in New York and the ensuing 'war on terror' led by the US administration, under George W Bush. Islam would become the political focus for neo-fascists and afforded them many opportunities to organise around. The tactics adopted by the far right in the 1990s to concentrate on 'cultural issues' came to the fore. The terrorist attack in New York on 9/11 changed foreign policy around the world and in particular, perceptions of Islam. One response to this attack was to energise a media already hostile toward Islam into overdrive and there followed a political realignment that would inform political debate around Muslims and immigration that continues to this day.[29] In response to the 9/11 attack, on 7 October 2001, the invasion of Afghanistan began, soon to be followed by a second war in Iraq in March 2003. British Prime Minister Tony Blair was complicit with the US. President George W Bush's desire for revenge, and Tony Blair provoked the largest political demonstration in British history as over one million people marched in the streets of London to protest against the so-called War on Terror. The 7/7 bombing, in London in 2007, further fuelled hostility to Islam which became normalised by the media, and the fight against a real or imagined Islamic nemesis continues unabated.[30] The massive wave of support that carried Tony Blair to power in the 1997 British general election would ebb with every successive election he subsequently fought.[31] There were many reasons for this; domestic policy would play a part as New Labour floundered as an alternative political and economic strategy, but his support of the war in Afghanistan and Iraq would have a profound effect on the perceptions of Blair's leadership qualities.

Support for the BNP grew throughout the 2000s. Immigration would again play a large part in far right successes and they fed off media and popular discontent. The enlargement of the European Union (EU) in 2004 saw the admission of new Central and Eastern European states into the union.[32] The Schengen Agreement was an EU arrangement that enabled the free movement of people in its member states throughout the continent. Although Britain neither signed the treaty nor accepted the principle of free movement, the remote possibility of large numbers of people migrating from these newly admitted states, especially those containing Slavs, was of great concern to the media. Between May 2004 and March 2007, 630,000 people registered to enter Britain. Those coming to Britain to seek work were overwhelmingly young and in good health. The government created a Worker Registration Scheme to monitor these 'economic migrants' as they became known and although the majority were working and paying taxes, accusations of 'scrounging', 'benefit fraud' and 'health tourism' became commonplace. Despite the reality that migrants and refugees suffered restricted access to healthcare and benefits, immigration disinformation once again dominated the British political discourse. The terms *economic migrant* and *refugee* became adjectives to vilify people in the press.

As was witnessed in the 1950s and 1970s even small increases in immigration can cause infrastructural problems with housing, healthcare and education if not properly planned for. The lessons of previous waves of immigration had not been learned or at least acted upon and people seeking work or fleeing poverty and injustice were often placed in parts of Britain that were witnessing crises of poverty and injustice of their own. The issues were not addressed but the political fallout was. Further to its 1999 Asylum Act, the Labour government introduced more legislation designed to placate a febrile media and an increasingly anti-immigrant atmosphere. The extent to which Tony Blair liaised with the media over immigration can be demonstrated by the relationship New Labour had with the *Sun* and its campaign against asylum. It was exposed in the summer of 2003 when Downing Street's 'media planning grid' was leaked. It showed that the week beginning 18 August was to be *Sun* 'Asylum Week' where the newspaper would publish a series of anti-refugee stories and ministers were briefed to concur with each day's headline, culminating at the end of the week with home secretary David Blunkett echoing the *Sun* editorial promising 'draconian measures to clamp down on bogus [asylum] claimants'.[33]

The following year the Asylum Act of 2004 criminalised foreign nationals entering the country without papers, permitted the use of electronic tagging for asylum seekers and limited appeals against negative application decisions as well as asylum seekers' ability to obtain hospital care. Further anti-terrorism legislation enacted in 2006 saw tighter checks on foreign nationals entering the UK. Polls conducted in 1997 showed only three percent of voters had immigration among their top three concerns but by 2006, 40 percent placed it at the top.[34] After 2005 those seeking to live in the UK had to take a 'citizenship test', a series of bizarre questions on the 'British way of life' which if they failed meant an unsuccessful application.[35]

Although the BNP would ruthlessly exploit this hostile atmosphere, it was an atmosphere they had deliberately helped to create. A long-term tactic employed by the far right is the conscious attempt to drag the political debate and establishment parties to the right. Racism is the decisive element to this. Neo-fascist parties create agitation about immigration or an issue relating to culture/race, which in turn is heavily reported in the media. The traditional parties, the Conservatives, Liberals and Social Democrats, worried that they will lose sections of their electoral base, begin to make concessions to the issue and these concessions legitimise the original neo-fascist position. By adopting even part of the argument, the 'centre' parties normalise the discussion and in effect allow the far right to dictate the agenda. The neo-fascists then push the argument even further rightwards and this validates those holding nascent racist views in the public sphere.[36]

In the 2004 European Parliament elections the BNP received 800,000 votes in a campaign run almost exclusively on immigration.[37] In the British general election the following year, the Conservative Party campaign ran on the slogan 'Are You Thinking What We're Thinking?' and posters declared 'It's Not Racist to Impose Limits on Immigration'.[38] The BNP manifesto for the 2005 general election stated: 'immigration threatened Britain's very existence' and multi-culturalism was 'a profound cultural war against British people'.[39] The BNP fielded 119 candidates and averaged 4.3 percent of the vote.[40] In the 2006 local elections over 220,000 votes went to the BNP and they secured an additional 33 councillors nationwide, again on an anti-immigration platform. The BNP also played on fears of economic and job insecurity and campaigned against European labour in the UK. At the 2007 Labour Party conference Gordon Brown, by then leader of the Labour Party, announced there should be 'British jobs for British workers'— a slogan of the far right going back to the 1950s.[41]

One area of particular concern for anti-fascist campaigners was Barking in east London, which held the dubious title of 'race hate capital of Britain' after the BNP won 12 council seats and became the official opposition in the borough. A carefully orchestrated campaign had been waged by the BNP to win control of the council. In keeping with their strategy of involvement in 'community issues' one tactic adopted was to send activists dressed in high-vis jackets emblazoned with the BNP logo to pick up litter in public spaces. They introduced themselves to parents who had brought their children to parks and offered to clear rubbish from their streets if needed.[42] The idea was that the BNP would develop a 'reputational shield' that showed they were more than just an anti-immigrant party and they were the only party attending to the needs of the 'forgotten white working-class'; this resonated with the residents of a very poor London borough.

In May 2008 the BNP also gained a seat on the London Assembly, polling 130,174 votes or 5.33 percent of the vote.[43] In the 2009 European Parliament elections, the BNP succeeded in gaining two MEPs, party leader Nick Griffin and Andrew Brons.[44] This represented a major electoral breakthrough for the BNP, giving them access to resources, influence, greater respectability, and the ability to work with other far right and fascist parties in Europe. By May 2009 the BNP had 55 councillors across the country and in October of that year, leader Nick Griffin was invited onto *Question Time*, the BBC's preeminent political discussion show.[45] A consistent campaign against the BNP was run throughout the country but in the 2010 general and local elections LMHR/UAF specifically targeted Barking, the BNP flagship council. LMHR/UAF organised 13 days of action leading up to the election, gave out over 200,000 leaflets and mobilised hundreds of people, they also took voter registration forms to accompany the 15 different leaflets they produced. Alongside this, another anti-racist organisation Hope Not Hate (HNH) themselves organised hundreds of people and distributed over 100,000 anti-BNP newspapers. UAF also visited Barking bus garage, Barking and Dagenham College and other workplaces in the area. LMHR had been organising concerts before the 2010 election with artists such as Ms Dynamite playing a series of gigs to school children, and rock band Dirty Pretty Things had played LMHR concerts in the evenings, but in the election campaign there became an obvious need for some cultural opposition to the BNP. LMHR attempted to run events and gigs against the BNP, but the Labour controlled council in Barking refused to grant licences to venues for LMHR to stage gigs. When they finally relented, LMHR staged a concert on 17 April at Barking Broadway theatre. Over 300 local people attended to watch ska band The King Blues perform, although the venue instructed the band not to make any political comments from the stage.

The election results showed that the hard work had paid off; the local and general elections in 2010 were catastrophic for the BNP. They got wiped out in Barking losing all 12 seats, they were routed in a key constituency in Stoke and nationally they managed to keep only two council seats.[46]

Party leader Nick Griffin was also beaten into third place when he stood as MP for the parliamentary seat of Barking against Margaret Hodge. But how was he beaten? The tactics employed by UAF/LMHR and HNH to defeat the BNP are interesting to examine when compared to the local Labour Party leadership's response to the BNP. There was a housing crisis in the borough caused by years of neglect, insufficient funding and the Conservative 'right to buy' scheme that had sold off social housing stock without any affordable replacement. Between 1980 and 2010, 17,523 council houses had been sold off in the borough, a 50 percent reduction in social housing.[47] Of the two main building sites where new housing was being built a mere 31 homes were to be council-run. In the prestigious Barking Riverside project 11,000 private homes were being built at a cost of £3.1 billion.[48] These homes were financially out of reach for local working-class people, so what remained of social housing became the focus of a political battle that the far right dictated. The BNP held immigrants responsible for the housing crisis and were distributing leaflets entitled 'Africans for Essex', falsely claiming immigrants were being given grants of £50,000 to buy houses in the borough.[49] Adam Sampson, spokesperson for the homeless charity Shelter, commented: "Neglect of the [housing] issue over the past 20 years had led to a shortage of council housing, allowing a 'blame culture' to thrive".[50]

Margaret Hodge, Labour MP for Barking responded to the BNP claims by stating: "We should look at policies where the legitimate sense of entitlement felt by the indigenous family overrides the legitimate need demonstrated by the new migrants".[51] Labour Education Secretary Alan Johnson accused Hodge of "using the language of the BNP".[52] In an uncanny re-run of fascist Jeffery Hamm's response to Labour MP George Rogers' comments after the Notting Hill riots in 1958, BNP council group leader, Richard Barnbrook, delivered a bouquet of white lilies to Hodge's constituency office to thank her for backing his party's policy.[53] The note read: "I am indebted to you for having the gumption to tell the truth about housing allocation. We must stop agreeing like this or people will think we are having a political agreement".[54] Labour

Party chiefs considered disciplinary action against Hodge over her comments.[55] Despite Hodge's comments, the work of activists patiently explaining to local people that the housing crisis was not caused by immigration and that the BNP offered no real solutions meant the BNP were defeated. After her election victory Hodge acknowledged that UAF "...was part of the winning strategy in Barking which focused on those areas where the BNP were strongest".[56] She went on to state that LMHR members and UAF had:

> Put in months of work that began before the elections. They knocked on thousands of doors and distributed many more leaflets. This helped to mobilise to beat the BNP and increase voter turnout which made such a difference in reducing the BNP's vote.[57]

Nick Griffin described the election results in 2010 as 'disastrous' and tweeted the BNP had been 'hammered by Labour'.[58] Their wipe-out in Barking was only made worse by the total loss of seats in Burnley, where the BNP had made their initial breakthrough. The election results were the first time in ten years Burnley had been free from neo-fascist councillors.

Things went from bad to worse for the BNP and lurking in the background were recriminations and the internal bickering that appears after every setback. Allegations of financial impropriety had been brewing since 2007 and a succession of splits occurred in 2010 after the election defeat with members leaving to join splinter groups: the British Freedom Party, Britain First and the National People's Party.[59]

There were also concerns about security after the names and addresses on the BNP membership list were accidently published on their weblog and posted online by WikiLeaks. By 2012 leader Nick Griffin was left as the sole MEP after Andrew Brons resigned from the party and in the local elections of that year the BNP vote went down from its high of 240,000 in 2008 to 26,000.[60] In the space of two years, the BNP had lost all of its

Date	Event	Artists	Attendance
06.12.02	LMHR Launch Event, Ocean Hackney	Tim Westwood, Heartless Crew, Taz, Ragga Twins	500
01.09.02	Manchester Carnival	Ms Dynamite, Doves, Billy Bragg, Heartless	30,000
08.02.03	ANL Conference/Festival	Elbow, Hardkaur, Marcus Intalex	800
27.04.03	Burnley Unity Festival	Bassment Jaxx, Tim Westwood, Punjabi Hit Squad	600
26.04.03	Unity Against the BNP, Manchester Apollo	RDB, Chumhawamba, Un-Cut, Alabama 3	3,000
07.09.03	Stoke Carnival	Spooks, The Stands, Metz & Trix	2,500
01.10.03	LMHR CD launch, London Jazz Café	Estelle, Daniel Bedingfield	500
25.02.04	LMHR @ UAF Launch	Billy Bragg, Metz & Trix, Mike Rosen	400
16.03.04	London Astoria	Libertines, Buzzcocks	2,000
03.05.04	Sunderland LMHR Respect Carnival	Futureheads, Genius GZA, D Double E, Mad Professor	4,000
01.05.04	Leeds - United By Music festival	Various	6,000
10.07.04	LMHR @ Marxism Festival	Ashley Walters, D Double E,	500
30.06.04	Unity Festival, Liverpool Academy	Badly Drawn Boy, The Music, Bloc Party, Skeme	2,000
25.06.04	Glastonbury LeftField	Rodney P +more	3,000
12.09.04	Stoke Carnival	Kasabian, Roll Deep	2,000
15.10.04	Europe Against Fascism (ESF) Coronet London	Babyshambles, Cooper Temple Clause	800
16.10.04	Europe Against Fascism (ESF) Astoria London	Karma Sutra, Carbon/Silicon, Hanin Elias, Billy Bragg	1,200
07.12.04	LMHR Brighton Concorde	Chas n Dave	800
15.09.05	Scala London (Who Shot the Sheriff docu launch)	Hard Fi, Roll Deep, The Beat	1,000
19.06.05	Dagenham Seabrook Hall	Gemma Fox, Donaeo, Metro Riots	200
01.05.05	UAF Festival, Trafalgar Sq	Pete Doherty, Estelle	40,000
29.06.05	LMHR @ Glastonbury Left Field	Babyshambles, Kano	5,000
09.07.05	LMHR @ Marxism Festival	Plan B, Sway, Bashy	500
27.10.05	Remember Anthony Walker (Liverpool Academy)	Ms Dynamite, Lupe Fiasco, The Stands, Roll Deep	1,200
29.04.06	LMHR/UAF Carnival, Trafalgar Square	Belle & Sebastian, Babyshambles, Akala	30,000
14.07.06	Barking Abbey School	Ms Dynamite, Billy Bragg, Akala	400
10.11.06	LMHR Fundraiser @ Fabric London	Babyshambles, Mystery Jets, Akala, The View, Grime MCs	1,600
30.09.06	Barking/Dagenham LMHR Festival, Ilford Cauliflower	Dirty Pretty Things, Roll Deep, OT Crew	500
20.12.07	Hull United Against Racism	The View, Lethal Bizzle, Paddingtons	1,200
23.06.07	LMHR Show @ Glastonbury Left Field	Hard Fi, Lethal Bizzle	5,000
19.07.07	RAR 30th Anniversary, Hackney Empire	Misty In Roots, Tom Robinson, Wiley, Lethal Bizzle	1,200
17.10.07	LMHR NME Cover CD	Akala, Noisettes, Lethal Bizzle, Dirty Pretty Things, Manu Chao	-
27.04.08	LMHR - Victoria Park London 30th Anniv Carnival	The Good The Bad The Queen, Jay Sean, The View, Akala	100,000
30.08.08	Hull Freedom Fest	Wiley, Magic Numbers, King Blues	15,000
06.09.08	Rotherham Carnival	Kaiser Chiefs, Reverend & The Makers, Roll Deep, Courteeners	6,000
12.08.09	LMHR @ Sziget Festival, Budapest	Lee Mavers (The La's), LowKey, Drew Mcconnell, Jimmy Pursey	60,000
15.12.09	LMHR Xmas fundraiser, Proud Camden	Tiny Tempah, Get Cape, King Blues	600
01.05.10	Barnsley LMHR Carnival	Reverend & The Makers, Chipmunk, Devlin, Get Cape	10,000

Love Music Hate Racism concerts, 2002 to 2010.[61]

council seats and its membership went down from 11,811 to under 500.[62] *Guardian* journalist Matthew Goodwin was moved to state: "The BNP is finished as an electoral force".[63]

Historically, the two key elements of a fascist organisation have been an electoral and 'respectable' face, campaigning in elections, and a street-fighting force that attempts to intimidate political opponents and target religious or racial minorities. The electoral face of the BNP had been roundly defeated by 2010 and the tactical changes adopted from the FN in France seemingly had failed.

Broadly speaking they had not sought the help of a street army, partly from choice and partly because there wasn't one, as this was an area of weakness for the far right. Successive years of campaigning by the ANL/UAF/AFA and a wide variety of community groups had depleted this reserve. But all this was to change after 2009 with the advent of a new street-fighting organisation, the English Defence League (EDL).

As this first phase of LMHR came to an end, in total there had been over 400 LMHR events organised across the country. There were two massive 50,000-plus LMHR festivals in Trafalgar Square, carnivals in Manchester, Barnsley, Stoke, Finsbury Park and the 30th anniversary of RAR in Hackney where over 100,000 people attended. Some of the concerts organised are listed in the LMHR spreadsheet above, compiled by Lee Billingham, LMHR national organiser.

Alongside these gigs, there were countless seminars, musical events in schools, colleges and youth clubs as well as a 14-day university tour in opposition to the BNP and a double CD released in conjunction with NME.[64] LMHR/UAF had attempted and succeeded in creating a counter argument to the anti-immigration narrative prevalent during that time and were an essential component in the ultimate defeat of the BNP.

The second phase of LMHR will now be discussed, but before this is undertaken, it is important to explain how developments on the far right of British politics changed during this period and how this change informed the operations of LMHR.

English Defence League demonstration, 2009. © Getty Images

The English Defence League

On 10 March 2009 in Luton, a homecoming parade of soldiers from the Royal Anglican Regiment returning from the Afghanistan War were heckled by a small group of Muslim men linked to an extremist religious sect Islam4UK. Shouting their opposition to both the war, and the soldiers, there followed an animated argument and a small skirmish after which the incident would probably have passed unnoticed. Local TV reporters who were there to cover the story passed the footage on to the mass media and within hours the incident was televised throughout the nation. The story became headline news over the following days, and an outraged press who had almost universally supported the war carried the story on their front pages. In Luton, March for England (MFE), a tiny neo-fascist organisation, got permission from the council to hold a demonstration to voice their opposition to the Muslim demonstrators. MFE swiftly pulled out of organising the demonstration and it was taken over by the 'United People of Luton', a group overseen by Stephen Yaxley-Lennon. On the demonstration in May of that year over 500 people marched with virtually no police presence. At the end of the march, what has been described as a 'mini-pogrom' erupted and Asian people were attacked, Asian shop windows were smashed and there were several arrests.[65]

The narrative of the EDL is that it sprang up spontaneously as a result of popular outrage at the demonstration by Islam4UK, patriotic support for the war, and increased anger over the perceived 'Islamification' of Britain. These factors undoubtably played a part, but behind the scenes there was a cynical political operation taking place. Christian fundamentalist Alan Ayling was a millionaire director of a City investment fund who had made extensive contacts with anti-Muslim ideologues around the world through his 'counter-jihad' website called *4Freedoms*. Ayling, operating under the alias Alan Lake, had been searching for a UK-based street group to use as a pressure group to force Islam up the political agenda.[66]

A few weeks after the Luton demonstration, Lake called Yaxley-Lennon and a small group of anti-Muslim sympathisers to his flat where they discussed the formation of a new street organisation, the English Defence League (EDL). It was decided at the meeting that outwardly, the EDL would appear as a spontaneous outpouring of anger at Islamic extremism and 'political correctness' and would develop into the voice of the 'forgotten white working class'. It was also decided that the EDL would be careful not to fall into the traps that had befallen the BNP and would at least on the outside appear to be a multi-ethnic organisation.[67] Furthermore, there would be no manifesto, as this was not an electoral political party but a single-issue street movement opposed to radical Islam. It was decided at the meeting that Yaxley-Lennon would be the figurehead of this new movement but should adopt the pseudonym of Tommy Robinson.[68] All was not what it seemed with Yaxley-Lennon either and he was not simply a patriotic man incensed over the disrespect for British soldiers. Yaxley-Lennon had been around the far right for some time and was a card-carrying member of the BNP for over a year after joining in 2004.[69] The birth of the EDL coincided with the electoral demise of the BNP and consequently the EDL profile rose exponentially; indeed many members of the EDL had been either active or passive supporters of the BNP. Bankrolled by Alan Ayling, the EDL began to grow rapidly by staging a series of highly provocative and violent demonstrations around the country. They organised around football firms, and the inter-club networks previously used to arrange fights were utilised for national demonstrations.[70]

Many of the football firms that were involved with the EDL were casuals. Sometime around 1976 the casual subculture first began to be seen. The original adherents wore a combination of designer clothes and European sportswear, Aquascutum, Burberry, Lois jeans and Adidas trainers. Overshadowed by punk, the first wave of the casual subculture went unnoticed. Cultural commentator Paolo Hewitt says the fashion first appeared with Millwall fans, others place the new look in the north west but wherever it began, it is in Liverpool in the 1980s that the casual look became discernible.[71] This was a subculture based around football. Some music was listened to, primarily soul and jazz funk, but football and clothes were the primary focus.[72] With the advent of acid house, those with a more musical bent would eventually drift off under the influence of MDMA and go to clubs and warehouses. But those others who were more interested in football and clothes would mimic the skinheads in the 1970s and become increasingly involved in fighting and the support of far right politics. The networks of these casuals that were previously used to organise inter-club fighting were utilised by the EDL to great success. But it was the prolific use of videos and political posts on Facebook and Instagram that separated the EDL from what had come before. They were the first far right group to effectively exploit social media.[73]

Over the next six years the EDL organised over sixty national demonstrations, some attended by more than 3,000 people. There were also hundreds of local marches. It had nationwide political structures based around regular meetings and local branches or 'divisions'. For a while they looked unstoppable, but there were tensions in the ranks and a debate ensued about the kind of movement they were trying to build. Some wanted an organisation based on street fighters and others wanted political marches.[74] Paul Corner's study *Fascism in Ferrara* written about the 'Squadristi' gangs of fascists who organised flying columns to attack the left in Italy in the early 1920s is particularly pertinent when discussing the EDL. Corner states that the Squadristi was a dynamic movement that grew very quickly, but it was prone to crisis and internal fighting when it suffered setbacks.[75] A *Socialist Review* article noted:

> There are tensions in its [EDL] ranks. Right-wing street movements have a dynamic—they have to continually move forward to keep their supporters active and maintain a level of excitement and a belief they are on the winning side. Any stalling or reversal of fortunes can lead to splits or implosion.[76]

In which direction would they go? The north-west divisions were increasingly unhappy with Yaxley-Lennon's leadership and things came to a head, literally, at a Blackburn EDL rally in 2011 when Yaxley-Lennon headbutted an EDL member who had accused him of being corrupt. This altercation resulted in a split and an extremely violent faction, the 'North West Infidels', was created. A rupture also occurred in London and some inside the EDL began to target left-wing groups. Yaxley-Lennon personally threatened anti-fee protesting students demonstrating in Whitehall and a London EDL firm attacked the Occupy demonstrators at St Paul's.

In the 2011 London riots local EDL divisions formed vigilante squads to protect the suburbs from 'rioters' (rioters meaning black people). Attacks on Asians and black people became commonplace the bigger the EDL grew. They also attacked trade union offices, left-wing bookshops and striking workers on picket lines. In Trotsky's analysis of fascism, he states: "Fascist movements do not start out as fascist movements, but at the moment this movement begins attacks on the workers, their organisations, their actions and minorities, a fascist movement is born".[77] Indeed, the EDL had moved from a single-issue campaign group against Islam to a broader neo-fascist organisation.

The media, who had struggled to find a label to pin on this latest example of the far right, were reluctant to call them fascists, neo- or otherwise, and this in no part was caused by the confusing nature of some of the statements the EDL made and some of the individuals inside their organisation. They claimed a Jewish division, an LGBT division and boasted some Sikh members who went on demonstrations. Some commentators confuse the racism inherent in fascism as the essence of fascism. As an ideology fascism is more than simply racism, antisemitism or Islamophobia. It is the combination of several political positions as outlined in the introduction.[78]

Conversely, some fascist organisations are misidentified as *not* being fascist simply because they claim black, Jewish or Asian members, as was the case with the EDL. Historically, there are precedents to this. In Germany, in the 1930s, *Der Deutsche Vortrupp* (The German Vanguard) was a Hitler supporting political organisation that had Jewish members. Leading Jewish industrialists were in Mussolini's inner circle and hundreds of Italian Jews participated in the March on Rome.[79] Fascism is an ideology that *can* have a racist element, but it is not an essential ingredient and those who fall victim to fascism can also fall prey to its initial propaganda too.

Ultimately the violence, the direction of the violence and the barely concealed racism on their demonstrations and social media sites left little doubt as to the true nature of the EDL. Publicity-wise they faced a massive setback in 2011 when two members were convicted of plotting to bomb mosques in the UK and in the investigation after the Norwegian terrorist Anders Breivik killed 77 people, he was found to have multiple links with the EDL. Yaxley-Lennon also drew fierce criticism when he addressed a demonstration in London in the same year:

Every single Muslim watching this...You had better understand that we have built a network from one end of this country to the other end, and we will not tolerate it, and the Islamic community will feel the full force of the English Defence League if we see any of our citizens killed, maimed or hurt on British soil ever again.[80]

After a series of dwindling and demoralising demonstrations, the in-fighting in the EDL grew and in October 2013, supported by the Quilliam Foundation, Yaxley-Lennon and deputy leader Kevin Carroll resigned.[81] The unrelenting work of anti-fascists was central in their decision.

Unite Against Fascism & Stand Up To Racism

By 2013, UAF had organised over 250 counter-mobilisations against EDL protests. Many of these demonstrations were in support of small isolated Muslim communities, such as those in Dudley, Blackpool and Preston. Some were large scale

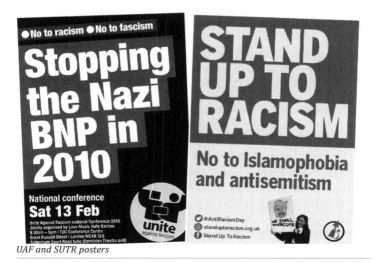

UAF and SUTR posters

mobilisations, such as when 5,000 turned up to physically resist the EDL in Tower Hamlets and 4,000 in Walthamstow. Although the government's 'Prevent Strategy' and the threat of arrest was consistently used by police forces around the country to stop mosques, Islamic community groups and individual Muslims attending counterdemonstrations, many braved the consequences and violence of the EDL to show their opposition. In every location, local trade unions, faith groups and individuals repeatedly resisted the EDL. The anti-fascist demonstrations were later described by UKIP leader Gerald Batten as: "Thugs of the left who promote intimidation and violence... the real fascists".[82] These demonstrations were the public face of opposition to the far right, the physical representation of anti-racism, but behind the scenes other work was also being carried out.

An important part of the UAF strategy was to undermine the morale of EDL activists and supporters. UAF conducted much preparatory work to achieve this demoralising effect. For example, in Tower Hamlets in 2011, when the police announced the EDL were to assemble in Sainsburys car park for their demo, UAF immediately launched a 'Boycott Sainsburys' campaign and within hours the corporation announced the EDL could not use the car park. Likewise, when the police wanted to use Liverpool Street station as a rallying point for the EDL, UAF contacted the railworkers' union the RMT, who threatened to close the station down on health and safety grounds should the EDL appear. When the EDL announced it was meeting in six pubs near Kings Cross station before a demonstration, UAF visited each of the pubs explaining who and what the EDL were and then made it clear a boycott of the pubs would be organised if they allowed the EDL to meet. The following morning all six pubs barred the EDL from their premises.[83] The campaign against the EDL and BNP has to be seen in its totality. The physical confrontations stopped the EDL from marching, the building of anti-fascist activist networks in local areas allowed communication between groups and enabled the response to far right activity. The campaigns around boycotting pubs and enlisting union support undermined the far rights morale and split the hardcore fascists from their softer periphery. In isolation, each of these tactics would be important but it is the combination of all the elements together that was crucial.

For the years that the EDL were active, LMHR had taken a supporting role; different manifestations of neo-fascism required different responses and for UAF the concentration was on physically stopping the EDL from marching. This also caused logistical problems. For instance, at the anti-EDL demonstration in Tower Hamlets on 3 September 2011, when the protesters marched to confront the EDL, the performers on the LMHR stage were left playing to only 20 people. Furthermore, as the EDL was a violent street movement this scared some artists from performing at rallies and demonstrations. The cultural aspect was not abandoned but was a tactic for a different occasion:

> If the [fascists] take to the streets, we will have to confront them...but a cultural struggle never was and never will be enough to beat the fascists. We need to strengthen the political wing of the anti-fascist movement. This means redoubling our efforts to deepen the roots of Unite Against Fascism inside the trade unions, colleges and communities. Things are not better or worse today than in the 1970s. They are just different. So, we need to learn from the past, adapt our tactics today and where necessary develop new strategies for dealing with the Nazis.[84]

By 2013 the EDL was a spent force, and a brief hiatus occurred where the threat of the far right receded.[85] There was also a human element and, according to LMHR activist Mike Simons, the constant organising, activity and intervention led to stress and exhaustion and the continued threat of violence had all taken its toll on many of those involved in anti-fascist campaigning.[86] But the Islamophobia and racism that the EDL fed off did not ebb with them. The 2014 European elections marked a watershed in British politics. UKIP, a right-wing, populist party won over 27 percent of the popular vote, 4,352,051 in total.[87] "The victory marked the first time in modern history that neither Labour nor the Conservatives have won a British national election".[88] As an anti-European party, much of UKIP's focus lay on immigration. Some of the anti-immigration feeling in the 2014 election which may ordinarily have gravitated toward the BNP was deflected toward UKIP, but UKIP was not a neo-fascist organisation. Founded in 1993, they steadily gained traction in British politics in the years that followed. Fêted by the media after taking over the leadership in 2006, Nigel Farage, a self-professed 'anti-establishment, man of the people' became a permanent fixture in the political establishment.[89] Over the next ten years membership of the European Union would become a central issue in British political debate, one which continued into 2020.

Whilst no neo-fascist organisation was operating with any great success during the period 2013-17, immigration, Islam and race still dominated current affairs. In 2012, the coalition government's home secretary Theresa May unveiled a new policy: "The aim is to create, here in Britain, a really hostile environment for illegal immigrants", May informed a press conference.[90] This was to be done by forcing landlords, NHS staff, public servants and bank staff to check the immigration status of those applying for housing, care, a driving licence or a bank account. The following year, in and around London boroughs with high densities of ethnic minorities, advertising hoardings on the back of lorries were driven around displaying large signs asking: 'In the UK illegally? Go Home or Face Arrest'.[91] In total, seven immigration bills were passed under Theresa May's six-year tenure as home secretary. She made 45,000 changes to immigration rules, among which were the removal of appeal rights, the denial of legal aid, asylum support was slashed and families were torn apart. The legacy of these policies is witnessed in the deaths and repatriations of British citizens forced back to the Caribbean in the ongoing 'Windrush scandal'.

Increased levels of structural racism and the growth of UKIP during this period saw the creation of another organisation to oppose them both. Stand Up To Racism (SUTR) was created in 2015 as an adjunct to UAF. Theresa May's hostile environment, however unpleasant, was not fascistic and UKIP was not a neo-Nazi party which relied on mass mobilisations in the streets, so the tactics to resist them were different to the ones used against the BNP or the EDL. The opposition was to be done under an umbrella organisation that would act, like UAF, as an organising focus especially around events like the United Nations day of action against racism which is held in March of every year. Systemic racism and Islamophobia were in the workplace and in schools and colleges and the opposition to them was not necessarily in the form of mass demonstrations. Many of the people involved in SUTR were the same people as in UAF, but it concentrated on institutional racism and Islamophobia and campaigned against them using different tactics to those employed against neo-fascists.

LMHR: Side Two

A revamped LMHR was conceived in 2017, one which had to reflect the changing world around it. With its relaunch came a new website. Part of the recent success of the far right had been its online presence. Successful utilisation of social media conveying a political message works. This was also seen in the Brexit referendum and the engagement of Cambridge Analytica in propaganda for the 'Leave' campaign. If the right had been successful with their online presence, then LMHR needed symmetry to counteract them. Consequently, two possibilities presented themselves that could alter how music would be used to combat racism in ways that were vastly different from SCIF and RAR. First, there began a shift in emphasis away from the traditional focus of gigs toward a campaign that engaged with young people online: "We are increasing our focus on online content because we feel this can have a big impact and spread a positive message far and wide...[although]...regular events across the country is absolutely a key part of the activities of our local groups".[92] Secondly, the music industry could take on a leading role in the direction and control of the organisation, and in particular Paul Samuels. One-time RAR activist in the 1970s and now vice-president of Atlantic Records, head of a multinational musical empire, Samuels had influence in the upper echelons of the music business and access to resources that could enable LMHR to have a far larger reach. According to Samuels: "We have to become a legitimate face of anti-racism, we want to create everyday activists, the whole business should be anti-racism, it should be standard".[93] Rather than being an organisation that was run on a shoestring, relying on donations from individuals, trade unions and the general goodwill of the public, it should, Samuels argued, be properly funded by an industry that not only had the resources but the moral responsibility to act against racism. Paul Samuels reiterates the point:

Stormzy and Ed Sherran, LMHR, Beautiful Resistance, 2019. © Paul Samuels

The industry I work in has all these amazing people, like all these kids who are great online, and I look at us trying to protest against Tommy Robinson on the street...this has to come from the industry, the industry has to fight back, the industry won't survive if the right win. If we don't fight back and if we don't get properly organised, cos they've got millions of pounds, and we're running around blagging trucks and trying to blag people to do things and we have to get pro and we've got to become as good as them, cos unfortunately their online presence is really good.[94]

In March 2017 the new direction began and *#lovemusichateracism* trended on social media and was picked up by music fans the world over. One of the first initiatives was a T-shirt campaign. Top music acts were photographed wearing the distinctive Love Music Hate Racism T-shirts and the website received 56 million hits. A subsequent interview with Ed Sheeran about LMHR received over 300,000 views. A monthly podcast was enacted, and the channel grew in subscriptions. Support also came from YouTube who offered free studio time. Further podcasts 'Beyond Skin' were created with a Spotify/LMHR link up each month. These were short, to-the-point items, as the average 'engagement time' for young people online is allegedly eight seconds.[95]

Between 8 and 22 March 2019, LMHR launched the *Beautiful Resistance* campaign which coincided with the United Nations Anti-Racism Day demonstrations on 16 March. Over 300 venues participated in *Beautiful Resistance*, running the LMHR logo. Hundreds of LMHR branded gigs and the whole of singer Ed Sheeran's tour carried the logo. There were music events, assemblies, workshops and panels taking place in schools and colleges during the fortnight. The activity involved video interviews of artists including Sheeran, Dave, Rudimental, Mahalia and Anne-Marie discussing the role music can play in combating racism. The online video content was complemented by venues across the UK putting up LMHR posters, projecting the logo and running campaign stalls during shows. The artist content was made available to educators later in the year, to form the basis of anti-racist teaching materials.[96]

Branding became central to the modus operandi of LMHR getting artists, venues and companies to support the organisation. Negotiations were held with Stormzy to wear a LMHR T-shirt at future gigs and other bands playing at upcoming festivals may do the same. DHP Family and Melvyn Benn of Festival Republic (formerly Mean Fiddler), two of the leading venue owners in the UK, offered their venues and said: "Do what you want, we'll brand them LMHR if you want".[97] Google, Ben Sherman and other brands including Stone Island expressed an interest in supporting LMHR. Further suggestions were the linking of LMHR with the Professional Footballers› Association (PFA) and 'Kick It Out' football-based anti-racist campaigns.[98]

Although the mass public perceptions of LMHR may have changed to online material and branding, live music and regional events remain an important aspect of the organisation. Gigs are still organised in the spirit of SCIF and RAR as they are perceived to be crucial for both the music and the shared experience that they provide. The online presence and branded events provide mass publicity, but the local concerts are where cohesion can occur for those involved in political activity or seeking to begin it. Before the Covid-19 pandemic a grime show was planned in Luton to celebrate the town's diversity and as a politically defiant gesture to the EDL birthplace.

Part of the move online was a reflection of how young people enjoyed music in the late 2010s, but there are still gigs or 'clashes' for grime artists that pull sizeable crowds. But does the subcultural base that SCIF and RAR thrived on exist in the same way today? Is the scene around grime and drill comparable to skifflers, teddy boys, punks and reggae fans? Some certainly think not, according to Paul Samuels: "The problem now is that it's so fractured that there really isn't a scene that it could stem from, it's very fragmented, everyone has their own little worlds…it was simple back then as the punk and reggae scene meant you could galvanise them because they were rebels".[99] Of the subcultural groups that exist in the 21st century there has been mixed reaction to involvement in musical anti-racist events. Despite being involved in the 'Grime for Corbyn' campaign there has been difficulty getting grime artists fully behind LMHR.[100] But the reasons for this are complex. Samuels suggested that this was primarily because of the reluctance of the artists' management, something that was also a factor with the 1970s punk bands and RAR as discussed earlier. In contrast to Samuels' position, LMHR organiser Mike Simons argues:

> The local control of grime managers and non-major promoters via streaming emphasises the importance on local gigs and local hooks ups because local grime artists will be central to any new cultural fusion that might emerge out of an LMHR movement.[101]

Part of the difficulty in securing grime support was the environment in which these artists had to perform. Whilst music may not be in the vanguard for young white teenagers to articulate their anger with the world as it did with punk, the same cannot be said for young urban black teenagers. The poverty and institutional racism that was identified by the Macpherson Report still exists.[102] This inner-city alienation is expressed musically, notably in grime and drill. Inherent in the music is a palpable anger as artists 'spit bars' to convey their lyrics. Grime and drill are the two subcultural musical genres that are the vehicles for this anger and they both have their origins in hip-hop.

Originating in the 1970s hip-hop casts a long shadow over music, fashion, and 'black politics'. Its influence is so multifaceted that it is impossible to classify it as a subculture, but this is not to say that it did not begin as one. Hip-hop's origins are in the poor neighbourhoods of the Bronx in 1970s uptown New York and its synthesis of electronic music, lyrical poetry, scratching and later sampled beats were revolutionary in 20th century music. Stylistically, hip-hop has constantly evolved and is emulated in every continent on the planet. It remains arguably the most important cultural phenomenon in the world and whilst it cannot be considered a subculture, grime and drill most definitely can.

Sartorially, grime clothing is essentially sportswear, with modified MA1 jackets, hooded sweatshirts featuring prominently, with trainers elevated to theistic status. Women's clothing is similar but with Jamaican dancehall styles also prevalent. Grime is a hybrid music mixing UK garage, jungle and elements of dancehall. Its musical base is electronic and lyrics reflecting urban life are rapped. Throughout the early development of grime, the music was plagued by the notorious government 'Form 696' which was first launched in 2005 in response to a series of shootings at London gigs. Form 696 was a risk assessment that had to be completed before a licence was permitted for a live music event and non-compliance would result in the police refusing permission for the event.[103] Harmless enough, until the details of the form were disclosed, with questions relating to the genre of music being played and specifically to the ethnicity of those going to the event. This form was designed to target garage, grime and R&B performances and young black people. The use of Form 696 stopped in 2017, but the policing of urban music continued, and drill has been the victim of arguably the most repressive policing of music in British history.

Developing out of trap music from the south side of Chicago in the early 2000s, drill is electronic music with bleak observations on the realities of inner-city life. Violence features heavily in the lyrics, justified, drill artists say, as it is a reflection of their everyday lived experience. Evolving as a genre at the same time as an alarming rise in knife deaths in London, drill music has been inextricably linked with the crime ever since. Scotland Yard launched Operation Domain in September 2015 with the aim of taking action against gang-related videos encouraging violence. This campaign has concentrated on drill as a catalyst for crime and in May 2018 Operation Domain intensified when Metropolitan Police chief Cressida Dick called on YouTube to remove drill videos. Despite the many complex reasons why inner-city youth become involved in violence, it is drill music that has been blamed for the rising wave of gun and knife crime in London.[104]

The level of state intrusion into musical performance reached new heights in January 2019 when a worrying development in British musical history took place. The Metropolitan Police announced they had secured a sentence of nine months in prison (suspended for two years) for two 21-year-old drill rappers Skengdo & AM for breaching a gang injunction issued in August 2018. The nature of the breach was performing their song *Attempted 1.0* at a London concert in early December 2018.[105] This is a watershed in British legal history, where a prison sentence has been issued for artists performing a song. Furthermore, another injunction has been placed on any musicians in the 410 Gang, of which Skengdo & Am are part, proscribing the creation of *any* drill music videos.[106] The injunction also prohibits anyone performing or broadcasting songs with lyrics mentioning rival crews, other gangs or their perceived territory, even their postcodes.

The folk devil of the teddy boy and the moral panic over delinquency and increased knife crime, allegedly caused by rock 'n' roll in the 1950s, echoes in 2020 with drill music and black urban youth. Commander Jim Stokley, who oversaw the Metropolitan Police gang crime unit, announced in 2018 that police officers were to be given increased powers to pursue drill rappers who they believed were 'provoking violence' by posting their music online via social media. Moreover, Stokley argued, existing terrorism legislation for which, crucially, there does not need to be a proven link between the incitement of violence and its realisation can be employed to police drill music. In other words, with minimal justification, the police will be able to arrest anyone performing drill music. These powers are singularly targeted at black urban youth and are in effect SUS laws for music.

Back in Notting Hill, where this book began, and in a further unprecedented development, the Metropolitan Police sought and successfully obtained such a Criminal Behaviour Order (CBO) that was placed upon west London drill rapper Digger D and fellow members of Ladbroke Grove gang 1011. This CBO prevents any of their music or videos being released until the lyrics have been deemed appropriate by a representative of the Metropolitan Police. Which member of the police force decides what is appropriate for release remains a mystery. Despite Digger D videos being viewed over 15 million times, war has not broken out in Notting Hill, indeed the relationship between the videos and local crime are unknown as applications to the Metropolitan Police for Freedom of Information relating to crime statistics and drill music are regularly refused. Major record labels such as Polydor have expressed interest in releasing future drill recordings, however, this interest has been thwarted by the censorship of the police. Whilst there has always been state suppression of music, for instance, when the country has been at war, the demand to censor the lyrical content of songs prior to release is a new development in state interference in an art form.[107]

The Future

LMHR stood at a crossroads in the autumn of 2019, whether to maintain its roots as a 'bottom-up' organisation that seeks to mobilise ordinary people into activity or to become a 'top-down' brand that will be led by the music industry into a high-profile media campaign against racism. This crossroads would be traversed by the end of the year. However, in order to understand the direction that LMHR finally took, the journey that led to this crossroads needs to be explained.

By the autumn of 2017, LMHR was juggling a two-tier strategy. One, the major record labels (Warners, Sony and

Universal) were pressing for increased involvement of high-profile major stars endorsing musical and online campaigns. Two, grassroots supporters were orientating around local gigs and local organisations. These two strategies, whilst not mutually exclusive, would lead to much internal discussion in the next two years over where the emphasis of LMHR should be. A further complication was the aftermath of the 2016 European Union (EU) referendum. Ubiquitous on all sides of the EU debate was a discussion over race, racism and immigration. In the aftermath of the 'leave vote' LMHR was approached by anti-Brexit campaigners who wanted to use the LMHR brand and its music industry contacts to promote pro-European Union gigs.

A caricature had been established by sections of the media that a vote to leave the EU was a vote for bigotry and xenophobia. That immigration and racism played a part in the leave campaign there is no doubt, however it is not the case that this alone was the reason every person voted to leave the EU. Decades of alienation from established political structures in the UK and Europe, political impotency at a local level and frustration at the austerity people faced in their daily lives all contributed to the outcome. Furthermore, 30 percent of BAME people in the UK also voted to leave the EU, so the referendum result cannot be explained by racism or xenophobia alone.[108] Many people in the music industry were anti-Brexit, including some of those involved with LMHR.

Conversely, others in LMHR, whilst pro-European, were against the structures of the European Union. However, one thing that did unite the disparate groups, prior to the vote, was the understanding that whatever its outcome, the referendum campaign would stoke racism across the country. For the grassroots LMHR activists, this meant it could not take sides in the referendum. Following the vote to leave, LMHR refused to become involved in pro-EU or pro-Brexit events. LMHR had to be ready to spread a message of unity in the referendum's aftermath. Former RAR and current LMHR campaigner, Mike Simons, explains:

By joining those who claimed 'to be anti-EU was to be, by definition, racist', LMHR would have made it impossible to intervene in those towns and cities that saw the EU referendum as an opportunity to put two fingers up to establishment politics. Far from using music as a bulwark against racism, we would have been driving these people into the arms of the racists.[109]

Another pressure on LMHR came from some of the staff managing the then Labour leader Jeremy Corbyn's election campaign. They wanted to work with LMHR and use its historical connection to RAR to build on the Labour leader's rapturous reception at the 2017 Glastonbury Festival. This pressure was also resisted by LMHR. Labour Party organisers wanted LMHR to be *their* bridge to artists and fans. Their argument was that Jeremy Corbyn is anti-racist, so anti-racist organisations should support his election. LMHR replied that the fight against racism wasn't a matter of which party had a majority in the Palace of Westminster and that the anti-racist movement needed to be independent and should not endorse political parties. For the music industry executives who were supporting LMHR, this call to support Corbyn was also unwelcome, but for different reasons. The companies they worked for did not support the politics of the Labour leader. Some even accepted the spurious argument that Corbyn's Labour Party was antisemitic. It was imperative for LMHR to maintain the separation of an anti-racist cultural organisation from official mainstream politics and any particular political organisation. This meant saying 'no' to demands from some of those around Corbyn that LMHR endorse and throw its weight behind the Labour leader's pre-election campaign.[110]

Corbyn's team saw that his popularity amongst young people could be utilised by the Labour Party, especially those young people attending musical events. Corbyn's reception in 2017 at large concerts like Glastonbury and Prenton Park on the Wirral in Liverpool and his cover-page features in music magazines such as *NME* and *Kerrang!* all demonstrate the popularity he had amongst many young people. The logical step, thought Corbyn's team, was to emulate the success of RAR and LMHR carnivals and set up a Labour Party concert of their own, the Labour Live Festival in 2018.[111] Whilst LMHR agreed with the anti-racist message Corbyn was projecting, its independent stance meant that it did not officially support the initiative. Held in a 20,000-capacity venue in overwhelmingly Labour Tottenham, with its large black and minority ethnic population, Labour Live delivered an underwhelming audience. Despite dropping ticket prices from £35 to £10 and eventually making them free, journalists present at the event put the final crowd at 4,000.[112]

Corbyn supporter Richard Burgon MP erroneously claimed on Twitter: "Labour leader Jeremy Corbyn…[spoke]… at the first ever festival organised by a major political party in the UK to bring people together through music, politics, discussion, culture and fun!"[113] Far from being unprecedented, as Burgon claimed, Labour's involvement in such events was not new as we have examined with the Labour Party's involvement in Red Wedge in Chapter Five. Whatever the history, the contrast between the Labour Live Festival and the RAR and LMHR carnivals was stark. The staging of mass musical events with political overtones had proven to be more difficult than simply booking an arena and selling tickets.

The LMHR music executives were already uneasy about Corbyn's potential involvement in LMHR. LMHR's close links to the trade union movement became a bigger issue when the union UNITE, one of LMHR's sponsors, joined the campaign to boycott the American IT company Hewlett Packard (HP) in July 2019. HP provides IT systems for the Israeli Population and Immigration Authority which is the backbone of the Israeli segregated political system. Industry bosses were uneasy with any criticism of Israel and this unease was exacerbated in September 2019 when TUC conference voted overwhelmingly to join the Boycott, Divest and Sanctions (BDS) movement against Israel and adopted a conference motion to: "…prioritise Palestinian rights to justice and equality…[by]…applying these principles based on international law to all UK trade with Israel".[114] At a time when the defence of Palestinian rights and opposition to apartheid in Israel was being conflated with antisemitism, notably with Jeremy Corbyn and the allegations of antisemitism inside the Labour Party, this fissure inside LMHR would inevitably end in fracture.

LMHR resolutely opposes antisemitism, but like other united front anti-racist/anti-fascist organisations, it does not voice an opinion over Israel. However, the question of Palestinian oppression remained. What was LMHR to say about this? The questions over BDS would prove intractable within the two sides of leadership inside LMHR. Is it antisemitic to support the Palestinian struggle or to oppose Israeli policies? What should be the position of LMHR should artists be asked to appear in concert in Israel? There remains high-profile opposition to any artist travelling to Israel to play concerts, led by musicians such as Pink Floyd's Roger Waters, Elvis Costello and Brian Eno, so this was not an issue that LMHR had to face alone.

The laudable insistence from those like Atlantic's Paul Samuels that anti-racism should be the industry standard would inevitably run into problems where the question of Palestine and Israel and the Labour Party were concerned. Conversely, there were worries that the involvement of major record label management would shift the emphasis of LMHR from local groups involved in community activities into 'corporate interests and corporate control' which ran the risk of weakening the message and the organisation. The money and publicity that the major record labels could supply could propel LMHR into unimaginable places, but at what cost? What would the organisation become and what would be its legacy? Furthermore, activists inside LMHR were not overly enthusiastic about taking instructions from an industry that had yet to face some embarrassing truths regarding its own in-house affairs and the proportion of BAME people working in it, especially at management level. When

LMHR/industry meetings were convened the only black people present were activists from LMHR. Replacing these activists, members of the SWP, Labour Party and trade unionists with Sony, Warner Music and Universal executives on the steering committee would mean a wholly different LMHR. By the end of 2019, the fracture became a split.

With the industry money still to appear, the promises from the social media giants Facebook and YouTube et al yet to materialise and the music industry moguls unhappy with the presence of BDS, LMHR returned to its grassroots base whilst the industry looked to launch a new organisation, Music Against Racism.

In the wider political world, there had also been changes. The Brexit referendum result continued to have a polarising effect on British society and the inability to enact the referendum result led to increased hostility toward parliament and growing exasperation that was reflected in open racism. Racially motivated crime doubled in the years 2014-2018.[115] UKIP turned sharply to the right and enlisted the support of ex-EDL leader Tommy Robinson as an 'advisor'. The Football Lads Alliance (FLA), another street fighting organisation, sprang up out of the ashes of the EDL in the aftermath of a London Bridge terrorist attack in June 2017, with more than 10,000 people attended a gathering that culminated in a wreath laying on the site where the attack took place. The FLA declared that it was 'not left or right, but centre, anti-extremist'.[116] However, no mention was made at the demonstration about the attack on the Finsbury Park Mosque where Makram Ali was murdered by an EDL obsessive five days earlier, nor the murder of Labour MP Jo Cox a year before by a Britain First extremist.

Very soon it became clear the FLA was inhabited by ex-BNP and EDL members and football firms linked to the far right for many years. Its Facebook page with over 65,000 members carried many racist and misogynistic posts about London Mayor Sadiq Khan and Labour MP Diane Abbott.[117] The *Observer* and the *Times* both ran exposures on the FLA and the Premier

League issued a warning about the FLA and their extremist links.[118] The FLA quickly split and a rival group, the Democratic Football Lads Alliance (DFLA), was formed. Both groups have welcomed far right activists like Tommy Robinson and Anne Marie Waters onto their demonstrations.[119] Like the EDL before them they have been highly successful in using social media and drew crowds of over 15,000 on events such as the Free Tommy Robinson demonstration in June 2018.

The 2019 European elections were a success for the newly formed Brexit Party led by Nigel Farage after he left UKIP, although votes for the remain parties, the Liberal Democrats and the Green Party were also strong. Economic uncertainty and lack of political clarity from Westminster created a country in limbo, where many people seeking to identify the roots of their problems lashed out at those who do not bear the responsibility. The historian Robert Paxton has stressed the importance of favourable 'settings and allies' for fascism to grow and advance.[120] Many factors have contributed to a situation in the UK in 2021 where both the environment is suitable, and the accomplices of neo-fascists are sympathetic, for Paxton's scenario to be realised. The shift to the right is palpable.

The importance of social media cannot be overestimated as a weapon for the far right to use as a propaganda and organising tool. The days of the NF standing outside schools selling their newspapers have gone as far right organisations can now potentially reach millions of people with the click of a button and they are bankrolled by a group of very rich 'Alt-Right' supporters like Steve Bannon. The new world of 24-hour media has also changed the formal presentation of politics. One politician understood this shift immediately and for Tony Blair, advisors became more useful than cabinet meetings and a new word 'spin' entered the lexicon of politics. Boris Johnson's appointment of Dominic Cummings continued this trend. Spin symbolised the worst excesses of government and whilst a public distrust of politicians had grown steadily at the end of the last century, it was to accelerate dramatically at the start of the new one. A poll conducted in 2005 after a particularly low turn-out at that year's general election found a: "...well ingrained popular view across the country that our political institutions and their politicians are failing, untrustworthy and disconnected from the great mass of the British people".[121] This disconnect was exacerbated with the expenses scandal of 2009 which further undermined the public's trust in parliament. The 2008 economic crash and the austerity programme imposed on the nation by the Coalition/Conservative government from 2010 onwards, has plunged millions of people into precarious work, squalid housing and desperate poverty. The recent United Nations report on the UK saw the rapporteur commenting on

LMHR carnival 2008 ©Guy Smallman

the 'tragic social consequences' and 'record levels of hunger and homelessness' that Conservative polices had created.[122] 9/11 and the Afghanistan/Iraqi wars were accompanied by an aggressively anti-Muslim media which has created a climate of Islamophobia and anti-Muslim rhetoric that has entered common parlance. Finally, Brexit, the EU referendum, and the lies about immigration from both the leave *and* remain sides and the toxicity of the debate over democratic control and accountability has resulted in an impasse that shows no sign of being resolved.

The combination of all these elements created a poisonous environment that has enabled the far right to become legitimised in the public discourse. Furthermore, Trump's victory in the 2016 American election unleashed a storm of Orwellian double-speak that saw the alt-right/far right in both the USA and Britain presenting themselves as victims of anti-free speech from the media, the so-called 'PC brigade' and an imagined 'fascist left'. This confected 'culture war' continues unabated with the so-called 'war on woke'. However, the shift to the right is opposed. On the night of his defeat in the May 2019 European elections Tommy Robinson commented that he lost because of 'social media interference' that meant he had 'one hand tied behind his back', this despite the fact that a media circus followed him around wherever he went in the north west.[123] Another statement from Robinson was far more telling where he inadvertently disclosed exactly how successful the UAF/SUTR campaign had been against him: "I had run a positive campaign but was repeatedly asked by voters 'aren't you a Nazi'?"[124]

Aside from the Covid-19 pandemic, the most significant event that occurred in 2020 was the re-energising of Black Lives Matter (BLM) after the death of George Floyd in America. The significance of this movement is profound and its orientation toward an activist, street-based movement has already seen results that decades of pressure groups, lobbyists and parliamentary reformers were unable to achieve. Taking to the streets changes things. BLM has implications for music too.

LMHR's concentration on grassroots activism at the end of 2019 now seems prescient and a multitude of musical online events have occurred in the wake of BLM movement. An anti-racist street movement that is willing to work with an anti-racist musical organisation and can link up artistically *and* politically is what SCIF dreamt of and what RAR partially achieved with punk and reggae. The linking of the two could establish a foundation that would resist a growth in neo-fascist ideas.

The threat of the far right has not gone away in 2021. Indeed, there are ominous clouds gathering over Europe as populist and far right parties still present a serious threat in every nation across the continent. For the 60 years covered in this book, there has not been a single moment where neo-fascists were not attempting to organise and grow. At certain points they were strident and achieved electoral success, at other times they were almost winning the battle on the streets, but whatever they won or lost, at every turn there has always been an organised opposition to them. This opposition has taken many forms, but music has always been there. It was sometimes in the forefront of the campaign as with SCIF, RAR and LMHR and sometimes just as a crutch to lean on in the aftermath of activity. Whatever the outcome of the Brexit debacle, Black Lives Matter, the economic crisis and political instability we face from the Covid-19 pandemic, history informs us of one certainty, the far right will always use these issues as an opportunity to build, but equally, there is another certainty, the opposition to fascism will always be there and it will always have music as a weapon in its arsenal to counteract them.

Conclusion

The purpose of this book is to understand the significance of three musical anti-fascist organisations: SCIF, RAR and LMHR. It has examined how and when they arose, the fascist organisations they opposed and the influence of subcultures during their existence. The first premise was to examine a hitherto 'lost' musical anti-fascist organisation, SCIF. What were the social, political, economic and musical circumstances in which this organisation was formed, how did it operate and what success did it have? Hopefully, these questions have been answered. Once this history was established, a second purpose was to examine whether there was a link between SCIF and the two musical organisations that followed, RAR and LMHR.

Having interviewed founding members of RAR, Red Saunders and Roger Huddle, there is nothing to suggest any synchronic or diachronic link, nor any theoretical or organisational connection that relates to any aspect of SCIF and RAR. It is therefore safe to say that aside from one short sentence in David Widgery's history of RAR: "Colin MacInnes, along with John Dankworth, Cleo Laine, Max Jones and other British jazz musicians, had set up the Stars Campaign for Interracial Friendship after the Notting Hill riots in London in 1958", no one else in RAR discussed or was even aware of SCIF's existence.[1] Thus, the second premise has also been achieved: there was no link between SCIF and RAR. It should therefore be logical to then state that there is no link between SCIF and LMHR. However, sometimes, historical artefacts unexpectedly turn up and the advent of the internet in the years between RAR and LMHR enabled materials to surface that had been otherwise lost. LMHR's website had a YouTube hyperlink to the short clip from BBC's 1959 *Panorama* programme which featured SCIF, discussed in Chapter Two, and the whole basis of this book derives from that clip.[2]

Whilst there was no organic connection between LMHR and SCIF, the former was at least aware of the latter and what little history was then known about SCIF was encompassed in the LMHR website and the political tradition of British musical anti-fascism. This 'once removed' connection between SCIF and LMHR has now been replaced by the work contained within this thesis. This book, therefore, provides new evidence that not only presents a history of SCIF for the first time, but also fills the 'gap' in knowledge in the relationship between all three organisations. SCIF can now finally be united with its estranged descendants RAR and LMHR.

The same historical fracture that separated SCIF and RAR did not exist with RAR and LMHR. Many of the people involved in RAR were integral in the setting up of LMHR and the experiences of the activists and musicians involved in RAR were literally handed on to the next generation. Though the 'baton' was not passed from SCIF to RAR or LMHR the remarkable similarities between the three organisations suggests that there is a commonality present, something that unites them all, and this book demonstrates that there are two aspects to this commonality. First, a radical socialist tradition, effervescent in the 1950s and still alive in British politics today, that sought to marry art with politics in its fight against neo-fascism. Secondly, a rich current of subcultural music and style that was abundant in the second half of the 20th century and, although less visible in the 21st century, remains an influence on British youth today.

This book also presents for the first time an interpretation of the symbiotic relationship between neo-fascists, anti-fascists and the subcultures and music of each of the periods SCIF, RAR and LMHR operated in. Whilst there is much that is similar to all three, the 20 years that separates each of the organisations means there is also much that differed. Each group adopted distinctive tactics, and each had varying degrees of success. The first part of this conclusion therefore is to look at how effective these organisations were in undermining neo-fascism, what conclusions can be drawn, and where there is agreement and disagreement over the successes of each group.

Academic Criticism

Whilst 20th century scholars of fascism have concentrated on fascist thought and fascist activity, less time has been spent on the opposition from the anti-fascist left and even less on the musical responses. What commentary there is on musical responses to fascism concentrates on RAR as this is the organisation that is considered the most successful. What is evident throughout almost all the academic discussion on anti-fascism, musical or otherwise, is a broad consensus which at best, questions the achievements of anti-fascist work and, at worst, dismisses it. The academic devaluing of anti-fascist groups is also shared by popular media and can be summarised by *Spectator* journalist Toby Young's comment: "It's naive to think a few well intended musicians can do something about a problem so widespread and endemic".[3]

In each of the periods discussed in this book, academics have raised questions over the effectiveness of anti-fascist opposition. The demise of Mosley's British Union of Fascists in the 1930s, according to Roger Griffin, was due to the withdrawal of support from Lord Rothermere's stable of newspapers.[4] He relegates the opposition of Jewish groups, the CPGB and other anti-fascists, the physical opposition at Olympia in 1934 and the Battle of Cable Street in 1936 to only minor and supporting roles.[5] For Griffin, it was the lack of favourable media coverage that ultimately undermined Mosley. Historian Richard Thurlow concurs: "The ending of Rothermere's support...ensured that public opinion would become increasingly hostile".[6] Nigel

Copsey is another historian keen to question the effectiveness of anti-fascist organisations. Firstly, the 43 Group and their relationship with Mosley immediately after WWII: "What bought fascist meetings to an end at Ridley Road was not the venom of the anti-fascist opposition, but the severe winter of 1947-48".[7] Mosley's supporters seemed to have warmed up by the May Day bank holiday of 1948 when an estimated 5,000 went to see Mosley speak in Ridley Road, and his Blackshirts did not seem cold or demoralised when they attacked a Trades Council meeting in December 1948 with petrol bombs.[8] Copsey's insistence that 'other forces' stopped the far right is at odds with the overall content of his work on anti-fascist groups and unfortunately, he does not seem to have overcome his own subjectivity as his conclusions are in contradiction to the evidence he otherwise presents. In *Anti-Fascism in Britain* he dismisses the activity of the 62 Group but is unable to notice the glaring contradictions in his analysis:

> Shrewdly, the Union Movement responded to the recurrence of violent opposition by holding snap meetings without advance publicity. Adopting this method, Mosley was able to hold orderly meetings in September 1962 at Earls Court, Bethnal Green, Highbury and Dalston [and] Kensington.[9]

However, Copsey continues:

> The Union Movement had not counted on a switch in tactics by anti-fascists. The 62 Group responded to snap meetings by...[launching] physical attacks on individual members of the Union Movement [and to] organise a 'fast call out' scheme whereby stall holders and shop owners would immediately inform 62 Group members when fascists arrived to hold a meeting.[10]

Thereafter, Mosley was physically opposed wherever he tried to assemble indoors and unable to hold meetings outdoors. He finally admitted defeat in 1963 but Copsey states that the: "...important factor in the Union Movement's final demise was the decision by Municipal authorities to deny it premises for indoor meetings".[11] A strange conclusion considering he describes legal and council sanctioned UM meetings in his previous paragraph. Copsey continues with his dismissal of anti-fascist activity through to the 1970s and the NF and echoes Griffin's and Thurlow's comments that the media had the most important role in undermining the far right:

> In point of fact, support for the National Front may have already peaked by the time the ANL was launched...[and]... hostility from the mainstream media impeded the NF more than the activities of opposition groups.[12]

This book disputes the conclusions drawn by Copsey, Griffin and Thurlow. There is no doubt that individual journalists have opposed racism and fascism from the 1930s to the present day using whatever methods they had and sometimes at great personal risk. In all the anti-fascist campaigns discussed, journalists have played important roles. However, the same cannot be said for the editorial boards of mainstream media and their record in opposing racism and fascism speaks for itself. Headlines such as *The Daily Mail's* 'Hurrah for the Blackshirts' in 1934, *The Mirror's* front page, 'New flood of Asians into Britain' in 1976, 'Up Yours Delores' from *The Sun* in 1990 and 'Labour threw open doors to mass migration in secret plot to make a multicultural UK' from *The Daily Mail* in 2010 hardly suggest a consistent and principled stance of anti-racism/fascism.

As recently as 2016, the European Commission against Racism and Intolerance (ECRI) singled out *The Sun* and *The Daily Mail* for hate speech and discrimination, with some articles comparing migrants to cockroaches.[13] It is therefore difficult to conclude as Copsey, Griffin and Thurlow do, that a media responsible for disseminating so much of the racism produced in British society can also be credited with undermining it. Others see the media role as irrelevant and credit the defeat of the NF in the 1970s to Margaret Thatcher, summed up by *Spectator* editor Fraser Nelson: "...she killed the National Front".[14] Her 'swamping' interview on ITV in 1978 was apparently more effective than the efforts of hundreds of thousands of people at gigs or on demonstrations physically opposing the NF whenever they marched across the country.

Thatcher's swamping speech *did* have a role to play in the eventual defeat of the NF, but it was not the main role. If the way that neo-fascism is defeated is simply to undermine and mimic it as Thatcher did in 1979, then where was the 'Margaret Thatcher' character whose 'swamping' speech stole the ground from underneath the BNP in 2010? The general and local elections of that year were nothing short of calamitous for the BNP, a defeat on a scale far greater than the NF suffered in 1979. Yet no demagogue, no Thatcher, no stealer of fascism's clothes was anywhere to be seen. The explanation for the NF's defeat in Chapter Four of *this* book offers a more realistic and objective explanation than the *Spectator's* attempt at historical analysis.

Other historians are so eager to downplay the role of anti-fascists that even when there is a grudging acceptance that the ANL/RAR did have a part to play in the ultimate defeat of the NF, those like Richard Thurlow are still unable to get past the fact that the leadership was socialist:

> The decline of the NF was partially due to the successful undermining of it by the ANL. When the latter itself was blatantly taken over by the Socialist Workers Party the organisation folded as the bulk of the membership refused to tolerate being controlled by a notorious hard-line Trotskyist group.[15]

Had Thurlow attempted the most elementary research into the ANL he would have discovered that this was not the case. His language is also particularly telling: 'blatantly', 'notorious' and 'hard-line' are hardly the comments of an objective historian. Furthermore, his statement is refuted over and over again, by Lord Hain, on the steering committee of ANL, as well as historians Goodyer and Renton.[16] Evidence presented here from members and supporters of the ANL demonstrate that the ANL was formed at the suggestion of members of the SWP, built alongside others on the broad left and not 'blatantly taken over' by any party. Thurlow presents the familiar tropes of 'outside agitation' and 'hard-left infiltration' in political campaigning, unwilling to accept that people can be politically independent and draw their own conclusions rather than infiltrators indoctrinating them. Rather than the ANL 'folding' it was brought to an end in the same way as RAR because the threat of the fascists had receded, but whilst Thurlow criticises the ANL for being 'Trotskyist', academic Paul Gilroy accuses the ANL of the opposite and declares that the ANL pandered to British nationalism.

Paul Gilroy sees no major problem with RAR and what he labels 'radical populism' and the union of punk and reggae, but he states that the ANL in its labelling of the NF as 'Nazis' led them down a path of nationalism. Gilroy alleges that the portrayal of the NF as 'foreigners' used: "...the very elements of nationalism and xenophobia which had seen Britannia through the darkest hours of the Second World War".[17] Neither Renton nor Goodyer or the research conducted for this book has been able to locate any such reference to a 'reclaimed' nationalism in any of the ANL materials examined. Interviews with Lord Hain and former Shadow Home Secretary Diane Abbott also refute this alleged 'nationalism'.[18] Gilroy implies that RAR/ANL in printing photographs of the NF leadership in Nazi uniforms and images of Bergen-Belsen and Auschwitz were trying to evoke a nationalist 'Dunkirk' spirit to defeat the NF. One could equally argue that these photos were simply demonstrating an algebraic formula, the NF = fascist = war = gas chambers.

References to WWII are never far from the surface in almost any part of British life since its end. Overzealous traffic wardens receive the appellation of Nazi for merely carrying out their duties. Officious council workers in the public sector who pursue policy with any degree of enthusiasm and any political leaders, left or right, who are resolute in their opinions, are labelled 'Hitler's'.[19] As the recent spate of accusations of antisemitism inside the Labour Party under Corbyn's tenure demonstrates, the constant comparison to fascism of any individual or organisation deemed unpalatable by those opposing them occurred on a regular basis.[20] The use of Hitler and Nazism as a descriptive metaphor is ubiquitous in British society. In the case of NF leaders Martin Webster and John Tyndall however, it was not a metaphor. The anti-fascist magazine *Searchlight* had published photos of both Webster and Tyndall in full Nazi uniform in the 1960s and many of the splits inside British neo-fascist parties emanate from their dilemma over celebrating their Nazi heritage or hiding it. There is a long history of Hitler fetishism and a predilection for Nazi uniforms on the British right that stretches back to the 1930s with Arnold Leese, through the 1950s with Colin Jordan, the NLP in the 1960s, the NF in the 1970s and continue to 2020 with the EDL/DFLA. Nazi-themed stag nights and sex parties fill the photo albums of Conservative Party activists and members of the royal family to this day.

Gilroy's criticisms continue; he states: "That neither the ANL nor RAR adequately fought the systemic and structural racism that existed inside British society in the 1970s".[21] It is self-evident that RAR did not eradicate racism in British society, although that really is outside the remit of a 'few well intended musicians'. The elimination of racism from society was never a claim RAR made, nor did the ANL declare it would cleanse the world of fascism. The task each organisation set itself was to hinder the growth of fascists operating in the UK and stop racism becoming fashionable. Furthermore, Gilroy's allegations are proven to be unfounded as numerous examples challenging structural racism exist in RAR/ANL publications that do take on the issues of slavery, empire and structural racism.[22]

In any event, fascism has never become popular in Britain because, according to historian Roger Griffin, the British are 'imbued with humanism and tolerance' and are 'complacent, indifferent and non-political' and 'do not like to make a fuss'.[23] This innate 'humanism and tolerance' that Griffin bestows upon the English seems to have been absent in numerous episodes of British history, such as the Amritsar massacre in 1919, Ireland during the potato blight, the Mau Mau rising in Kenya and for the families of Gurdip Singh Chaggar, Stephen Lawrence and the untold others murdered by extremists in Britain. The sort of comments expressed here by Griffin should not pass for serious academic debate as 'national characteristics' and an imagined cultural or biological determinism does not explain the complex political development of any individual or any society. The attempt to denigrate human consciousness to a set of cultural quirks and foibles is beneath contempt.

It may be apposite here to raise the questions of experience and objectivity in the historiography of fascist and anti-fascist literature. How many of the academics, some of whom have written invaluable works into the history and politics of fascism, have actually spent any time involved in a sustained grassroots campaign to oppose it? It is relatively easy to unpick the politics of campaign groups and identify organisational flaws and tactical mistakes with distance and the benefit of hindsight. In the cut and thrust of community politics such luxury is not readily available.

Many people who became involved in campaigns such as SCIF, RAR or LMHR did so out of anger and passionate opposition to fascism, so strategic and tactical perspective was not always available. Through no fault of their own, some activists were not accustomed to the decorum of lectures, seminars and tutorials nor the structured discipline of political, trade union or academic meetings. Simultaneous interruption and shouting are commonplace in community politics and a recognised and universally accepted protocol is less than frequent. Political argument was not conducted in the pleasant surroundings of an academic conference, it happened outside a scout hall, on the back of a bus or in the nearest smoke-filled pub.

Community campaigns are composed of a multitude of political persuasions. There are myriad political organisations involved in such activity-based groups, often in rivalry with each other and sometimes openly hostile to each other. Some have an overarching strategic view and clear tactical outcomes, others without any strategy or tactics, there only to ensure that the former doesn't exercise theirs. Sectarian splinter groups abound with axes to grind on the slightly larger sectarian groups they were expelled from in the first place. There are random non-affiliated individuals, at times perplexed, at other times exasperated, by the seemingly endless and irrelevant arguments between rival groups and factions.

In the case of RAR and LMHR you also have black and Asian organisations, highly suspicious, with good reason, of the British political system and hostile to any white people claiming to support them, even those on the left. In some cases during the 1970s joint action was taken with black nationalists, who for political expediency had overlooked their contentions that all white people were inherently racist, as the need to break the NF was paramount. To navigate one's way through this bewildering array of contradicting and conflicting opinions, whilst trying to keep all onside and focused on the task at hand required skilful political negotiation, patient explanation, reasoned conversation and at times hard political argument.

This had to be done whilst trying all the time to ensure that people wanting to be involved in the campaigns did not get physically hurt, or at worst, as in the case of Kevin Gately and Blair Peach, killed. The spurious contention voiced by Thurlow that this political clarity and search for unity in action can be achieved by a few well-chosen quotes from Trotsky or the relentless repetition of a particular party dogma is not only inaccurate and disingenuous, but insulting both to the memory of those who died and to the experienced activists who spent untold hours of their own time at meetings or demonstrations patiently explaining complicated ideas to young, politically naïve, but enthusiastic listeners.

Furthermore, the accusation that party building was the raison d'être for the left in anti-fascist groups overlooks the fact that it was precisely these activists that put themselves in personal danger, donated what little money they had and spent endless hours in preparation for meetings and gigs and demonstrations irrespective of how many joined their organisations.[24]

For the Marxist left 'social being determines consciousness'. In practice this means workers' political ideas change through their participation in campaigns, strikes and struggles.[25] To be engaged in activity is the most important aspect of this process, recruitment to the party is important, but secondary to the winning of the particular campaign.[26]

Affront or a Front? Anti-Fascist Organisations

The initial letter to the music press in 1958 that led to the formation of SCIF came from journalists and musicians, none of whom were affiliated to any party outside of the Labour Party. The letter sent to the *Melody Maker* over Eric Clapton's outburst that created RAR came from Red Saunders who, although on the political left and expressing sympathies with Marxism, was not involved with any political party. The ANL's nucleus centred around three people: Peter Hain, Ernie Roberts and Paul Holborow, members respectively of the Liberal, Labour and Socialist Workers parties.[27]

The initial decision to set up LMHR in 2002 was arrived at by two SWP members, but enthusiastically supported by Jerry Dammers from The Specials and Peter Jenner, manager of Billy Bragg. The leadership of all three musical anti-fascist organisations discussed in this book were made from a variety of people from different political persuasions. The steering committees of each were made up of political activists and music industry artists, managers, journalists and record label directors. To build a mass musical united front against neo-fascists *was* the idea of the SWP in 2002, although was *not* a political decision arrived at by CPGB leadership in 1958 with SCIF, nor by the SWP or any other left-wing party with RAR in 1976.

The idea of organising politically within popular culture evolved organically out of those willing to be involved in anti-fascist activity at the time. There was even opposition to the setting up of SCIF and RAR from elements of the leadership of the CPGB and SWP as discussed in Chapters Two and Four. In fact, the SWP leadership were critical of one of its member's leading role in RAR. Activist Dave Widgery "saw everything from the standpoint of the mass movement, nothing from the standpoint of the party...Widgery placed a naïve faith in good-will rather than 'hard politics.'"[28]

No analysis exists on SCIF and the relationship between organised political activists and unaligned anti-fascists in the 1950s, but this book has demonstrated that a relationship between CPGB, various black organisations, anti-racist individuals and SCIF did exist.[29]

Does this mean the CPGB used SCIF as a front organisation? There is no corresponding growth for the CPGB in the short while that it worked with SCIF and again, CPGB work around SCIF played little part in their overall activity, an assertion supported by party members Eric Hobsbawm, Claudia Jones and Billy Strachan.[30]

What about RAR/ANL? Were these front organisations set up for the SWP to recruit? The growth of the NF in the early 70s had already seen individuals and organisations from all around the country take their first tentative steps to oppose them:

> It is apparent that RAR was not expanding into a vacuum...a widespread anti-racist and anti- fascist milieu had developed around the time of RAR's inception...a number of anti-fascist committees—sometimes set up at the instigation of trades councils and the radical left, at others by bodies such as local

Race Equality Councils and the Labour Party—had been established across the country.[31]

Copsey concurs:

In sharp contrast to the 1930s, the involvement of grassroots Labour Party members [in] local anti-fascist groups was actively encouraged by Labour leaders who had become increasingly concerned about the [electoral] success of the extreme right in working class areas.[32]

Research from the *Striking A Chord* project at the University of East Anglia details 'cultural and political networks that had grown up prior to, and independently of, RAR itself'.[33] Indeed, Goodyer states: "Far from the SWP or RAR's London centre, calling all the shots in the provinces...it is evident that the networks which forged the music scene, the venues, the retailers, the local media were instrumental in organising RAR".[34] Examples of how RAR operated as an autonomous organisation abound:

RAR in Manchester...[became]...associated with the first Deeply Dale festival, a four to five day, free, outdoor event...in Coventry...a local coalition of lumpen intelligentsia; teachers, social workers, semi-employed, self-employed, artists, writers and musicians formed the basis of RAR...in Bristol, the Ashton Court festival was renamed in 1978 the Rock Against Racism/Free Community Festival.[35]

In Simon Frith and John Street's comparative essay *Rock Against Racism and Red Wedge* they observe that:

Both organisations' musicians operated as spokespeople for youth, but whereas in Red Wedge, the interests of young people were communicated to the Labour Party in order to influence its policy making, in RAR these interests were reflected back on to the audience as a stimulus to direct action.[36]

Frith and Street studied the similarities between the two groups, their emphasis on effecting a change of political consciousness in the participants, and examine the influence of the political parties involved in both, namely the SWP in the former and the Labour Party in the latter. They concluded:

> Labour kept a tight rein on Red Wedge's activities, but the SWP was less concerned with exercising direct control over RAR, preferring to 'educate and direct those involved, to provide theory and practice'.[37]

Some of the artists performing at RAR gigs were less diplomatic. Joe Strummer of The Clash commented on a recruitment attempt: [They were] "...coming up and saying, 'come and join us'. But they can fuck off, the wankers, that's just dogma. I don't want no dogma".[38] Malcolm Owen of The Ruts had this to say: "None of us are Socialist Workers...we just don't like racists".[39] Nicky Tesco, singer of New Wave band The Members told this to Ian Goodyer in an interview in 2000:

> We never had any...'commissar' turning up and basically trying to convert us, or anything like that. And also...you know, punk was renowned for its' nihilism, which was... anathema to a lot of the hard-core Socialist Workers people.[40]

RAR's first full-time paid worker Kate Webb was interviewed by *Sounds,* a weekly music paper that was sympathetic to RAR. Indeed, their 25 March 1978 edition dedicated the front cover and an eight-page article inside to the fight against racism and a centre spread promoting carnival. She had this to say at the time: "I don't know how many times we've got to say it but RAR is completely independent. I'm not an SWP member, other people aren't. In fact, most aren't".[41] Goodyer suggests that, as with SCIF in the 1950s, some journalists played a pivotal role in raising and sustaining the profile of a radical, anti-racist movement, particularly in the music press:

> RAR events, particularly the carnivals, were given prominent coverage in the music papers, with *Sounds* offering RAR space to promote itself in the journal's special report on racism in the music industry...RAR was not simply catching the mood of the moment but was involved in a symbiotic relationship with the music reporters and companies they worked for.[42]

The support and co-operation of *some* journalists in the media, the music industry and people in the wider society necessitated a malleability in activists that a 'dogmatic' party recruitment policy simply could not countenance. Members of the SWP were an absolutely crucial part of RAR in its formation, its execution, its literature and artwork, as Peter Hain commented: "The SWP brought Rock Against Racism, without the SWP there wouldn't have been enough energy",[43] but, the idea that RAR was controlled by and served purely as a recruitment pool for the SWP simply does not hold any water.[44] Similar accusations regarding LMHR and the SWP exist today, and whilst the founding meeting of LMHR was set up by Jerry Dammers and Peter Jenner alongside two members of the SWP (who have given leadership throughout), it has remained independent. Furthermore, the second incarnation of LMHR was, in part, led by the music industry.

Irrespective of this evidence, why are left-wing organisations held to a different standard than those on the rest of the political spectrum? In the 1970s the National Front presented a political programme from which it hoped to secure votes in local and general elections and it also sought to recruit members to its organisation. The Labour Party, then as now, relies in part on the subscriptions of its members. It too seeks votes in elections and attempts to persuade people that its policies are the best and endeavours to recruit them to their party. The trade unions' lifeblood are its members and are constantly on recruitment drives. The Conservative Party in the 1950s and 1970s was also a membership-driven party and even religious organisations involved in anti-racist struggles during this period would not have been unhappy should their congregation swell as a result of their engagement. A reasonable question therefore would be to ask, why is it that socialist and communist organisations should be judged by wholly different criteria? Why is their involvement in anti-fascist struggles questioned, cloaked under the guise of 'front organisations' and dismissed as an elaborate recruitment drive?

The experiences of Germany, Italy, France and Spain showed quite clearly that the first casualties of a fascist government were communists and socialists; they were the first ones marched into concentration camps. One could suggest that these groups had a vested interest in opposing the growth of fascism. Marxists believe in the unity of the working class whatever race or religion and therefore will oppose any attempts at division. Ultimately, they argue, there can be no transformation of society without a unified working class. White socialists opposing racism and engaging in anti-racist struggle should be understood morally, as an opposition to racism and oppression, but also politically, as an attempt to stop division in the working class. Socialist organisations will always seek to oppose divide and rule tactics and one does not have to be black, Asian or Jewish to oppose racism and antisemitism. That members of the CPGB, the Labour Party, SWP, IMG or any other left-wing group involved in this struggle should hope to add to their membership is not unreasonable and certainly in keeping with the practice of other groups concerned.

Cultural Marxism

A further aspect of this book has been to approach the question of art and its relationship with politics, in particular music and anti-fascism. Historically for the Marxist left, culture has presented itself as somewhat problematic, at least in terms of the practical application of the theory. The relationship between creativity and commodity has posed a dilemma for over 100 years. The approach to art has essentially revolved around two things: firstly, Trotsky's contention that: "...art is not a mirror to hold up to society, but a hammer with which to shape it",[45] and, secondly, whether a commodified object can truly be revolutionary. The *Frankfurt School* was very influential in left thinking, but rather than being helpful, the theoretical musings of academics such as Theodore Adorno hindered the movement. His dismissal of popular music and jazz displays his manifest commodity fetishism and in the case of jazz borders on racism:

> The specification of the individual in jazz never was and never will be that of a thriving productive power, but always that of a neurotic weakness, just as the basic models of the 'excessive' hot subject remain musically completely banal and conventional. For this reason, perhaps, oppressed peoples could be said to be especially well-prepared for jazz.[46]

To reduce art simply to alienated labour and distorted social relations under capitalism shows a profound misreading of Marx and is wholly undialectical in its approach. For Adorno: [Art] "...is subordinate to the laws and also to the arbitrary nature of the market, as well as the distribution of its competition or even its followers".[47] Adorno never saw The Clash.

Culturally and politically, a constant thread ran through the CPGB for the entire period discussed in this work, and that was inconsistency. Party members had difficulties maintaining an active and interventionist role, engaging with workers, whilst the leadership (and Moscow) were directing them in a different direction.

Music is a case in point. The CPGB and the Workers Music Association (WMA) had set up the London Youth Choir (LYC) in 1954 which went on to play an important role in the CND. But, like the WMA, a constant source of disagreement ensued over what genre of music should be played at LYC events, folk or jazz.[48] With the financial backing of the WMA, the LYC set up a bi-monthly publication called *Sing* and its role was unambiguous, it advocated political music. It published songs and articles and promoted peace and socialism, but also provided guidance on building and playing instruments for beginners during the skiffle boom. The comparisons to *Temporary Hoarding* and the DIY gig-guides that RAR provided are remarkable.[49]

But the political and cultural contradictions remained: on the one hand, the CPGB was relating to young people listening to skiffle, trad and folk music and providing practical assistance on how to do this; but on the other, their quest for 'proletarian authenticity' and 'cultural orthodoxy' was inhibiting their ability to do so.

RAR/ANL badges. © *Roger Huddle*

The 1960s changed much of this and gave a new confidence to British artists of all genres. Alongside the new generation of artists, a 'new left' had grown up in, and been part of, the counterculture; their relationship with art was different to the CPGB vision and 1960s popular art forms had evolved in a different way than Adorno envisaged. Some of the baby-boomer generation embraced these new expressions fully and understood that the 'process of culture' was as significant as the form of its production and they rejected the mechanical Marxism of 'prolekult'. Art did not have to be didactic in order to be political and it could embrace the 'new'. Byron was as important as Brecht and the Beatles could be as influential as Beethoven. This epiphany carried on into the 1970s as punk and reggae left traditional folk music in its wake. Red Saunders captured the new mood perfectly when commenting on RAR: "'...at last someone said, be proud of using electric modern music and culture to fight the Nazis and racism, not Hungarian linocuts".[50]

Was this new-found cultural freedom universally accepted on the left and how did they relate to the punk explosion? Some political organisations like the Liverpool-based Big Flame supported RAR and put on anti-racist concerts of their own.

The CPGB had organised a music event in the summer of 1977 called Music for Socialism (MFS) but was: "...dominated by an acrimonious debate as to punk's progressive or reactionary tendencies".[51] MFS followed a similar path to the WMA decades before; its insistence was that music—be it free jazz, traditional folk or punk—must first and foremost be political, music that did not fit their criteria was dismissed.

Whereas RAR sought to tap *into* the musical mood of punk and reggae that already existed, MFS sought to impose a rigorous and formulaic musical structure *onto* its audience. Elsewhere, the Workers Revolutionary Party (WRP) said punk:

> ...was tailor-made for the interests of capital; a 'breeding ground for fascism' that served less as a soporific and more

as a deliberate plot designed to provide an 'excuse for the growing police state whose ready target is the revolutionary working class'.[52]

Another left-wing music organisation, the People's Liberation Music, felt able to:

> ...dismiss punk as 'fascist' simply by looking at the cover of The Clash's eponymous debut LP, released in April 1977. Not only was it stamped with the logo of a global capitalist monopoly (CBS), but its sleeve featured a symbol of imperialism (the Union Jack on Paul Simonon's shirt pocket) and propaganda for state forces in its back-cover image of policemen charging at rioters in Notting Hill.[53]

On the day of the Victoria Park carnival in April 1978 with upwards of 100,000 people in attendance and mass coverage in the music press, socialists in the Militant Tendency were handing out leaflets to people in Victoria Park explaining why you should not support the ANL or RAR.[54] For those in the SWP active around RAR, who had organised the carnival, there was no dialectical setlist that bands had to produce in order to be worthy of playing anti-racist gigs. Bands did not necessarily

The Clash's first album [55]

have to be 'political' or sing 'political songs' to be invited to perform at RAR gigs, but the very fact that they did play at these gigs sometimes imbued them with political attributes that were not necessarily present in their lyrics.[56]

Rock Against Racism, the Anti Nazi League and the influence of the SWP was a watershed in British left politics in the 1970s. There was a shift in hegemony away from the Stalinism of the CPGB to the Trotskyist left from the 1960s onwards. The CPGB had formally renounced the revolutionary insurrectionism of its 1930s programme *For Soviet Britain* and replaced it with a gradualist and reformist strategy, adhering to parliamentary democracy and broad left alliances. This was outlined in their 1951 programme, *The British Road to Socialism*.[57] The new generation of counterculture activists had not witnessed the depression of the 1930s and the rise of Hitler. They had experienced May 1968 in Paris, been involved in the anti-Vietnam war movement and new cultural forms such as Pop Art. One of the implications of this hegemonic shift was the re-orientation around the arts as a way to combat fascist activity. Also, the mushrooming of two pugnacious subcultures, punk and reggae, at exactly the same time as the birth of RAR was fortuitous as there was a ready-made audience for RAR to capitalise on. There had also been sufficient shifts within youth subculture to enable at least some multi-racial gatherings at gigs. RAR took every opportunity to kick this slightly ajar door open and flood venues with black *and* white audiences.

Political Music

The left does not hold a monopoly in its use of music for political purposes. Wagner and Stravinsky left no doubt of their political allegiances. The Oi! movement was a musical focus for the far right and forces of teenage reaction in the 1980s. National anthems are used as political tools and rallying calls for nation states the world over. Woody Guthrie's alternative national anthem *This Land is Your Land* was written in direct response to Irving Berlin's patriotic *God Bless America*.[58] Music has always been used as a weapon on all sides of the political spectrum. The Nazis used the 'Horst-Wessel' song to keep the spirits of fascist fighting men high, a tactic directly taken from the KPD's repertoire of revolutionary tunes. Songs were sung by the civil rights movement and by the Ku Klux Klan; music has always been written to promote peace and to wage war.

In Britain, music has been used as a rallying cry for progressive political change throughout the whole period discussed in this book and not just with SCIF, RAR and LMHR but with other organisations as well, on a grand scale Band Aid and on a small scale Red Wedge. However, the desired outcome of using this music has not always been the same. The difference between Band Aid and Red Wedge and SCIF, RAR and LMHR is implicit in both the theory *and* the practice of the organisations.

RAR sought the self-activity of those sympathetic to its cause and urged (partly out of design and partly out of necessity) local groups to organise themselves and promote gigs and events specific to their locale. Wherever possible at RAR gigs white and black bands would play gigs together. With Live Aid, Bob Geldof consciously marginalised black artists. Sade was the only black artist to appear at the Live Aid concert in 1985 and Geldof later opposed African artists playing at the Live 8 concert in 2005 arguing: "There were no African acts big enough to perform".[59] In an attempt to placate outraged musicians (of all colours) he unwittingly made the situation worse by further insulting black artists and staging a black only 'Africa Calling' concert 250 miles away in Cornwall performed at the same time as the Live 8 concert in London.

This book demonstrates throughout that SCIF, RAR and LMHR's focus has been on participation *and* activity, with the hope that this activity would engage youth into the wider political world and ultimately socialist politics. The contrast of this emphasis with Band Aid is stark. For Geldolf, money was the object of the exercise; going to gigs was important yes, but as passive consumers, not active organisers and participants. Selling records to raise money and ameliorate the suffering in Africa was Band Aid's only concern.[60] Likewise, the priority in Red Wedge was to garner support among young people and persuade them to vote for the Labour Party in the next election. For both Live Aid and Red Wedge, change inside society came from the 'top down'. For RAR it was 'change from below'. The point here is not to offer these examples as a discussion in correct or incorrect tactics and strategies, rather to demonstrate the differences in how they operated. Nor is the purpose to gauge the success of these organisations, for in any case how does one define success?

In terms of profile, money raised and audience, the Band Aid/Live Aid project dwarfs any other musical/political movement in history. It was universal, secured over £150 million in donations and record/gig sales and Live Aid was watched by over 1.5 billion people; yet poverty and famine remain in Africa, so by this criteria Band Aid cannot be deemed a success. If the litmus test of Red Wedge's activities was to secure a Labour victory in the 1987 General Election, then it too was an abject failure. Likewise, between 1976 and 1981, 31 black people were murdered by racists and the far right are still alive and kicking in 2021, so does that also negate RAR or the efforts of LMHR today?[61]

To draw conclusions over 'success or failure' is not helpful in understanding the dynamic of how and why people, especially young people, engage with politics. Nor does it enlighten us in the complicated process of how prevailing ideology is challenged and changed by personal experience.

Ultimately the question that needs to be asked is a simple one—is the changing of political consciousness an event or a process? If we see it as a process then, at the very least, we should be able to claim all of the above campaigns as *partly* successful. Failure isn't the fact that racism is still present or that neo-fascist organisations still exist. A different question should be asked—how successful would neo-Nazi groups be without the anti-fascist opposition? The answer to that question is impossible to qualify or quantify in any accepted academic way.

Subcultures

Lastly, what of youth subcultures so important throughout the last 70 years of British cultural history and in this book? Where have they gone? One attempt to explain this comes from Steve Redhead in his work *Rave Off: Politics and Deviance in Contemporary Youth Culture*. In his study of the rave scene he noted that subcultural divisions had been broken down as the style, musical taste and identity had been weakened and the rave scene was 'notorious for mixing all kinds of styles on the same dance floor', although this sartorial tolerance could possibly have been aided by the industrial amounts of acid and MDMA consumed at most 1980s raves.[62]

Similarly, 'retro-culture' and the nostalgia industry which began in the 1970s offers historic subcultures in ready-made formats to take away and assemble when one gets home. For the more adventurous or the less imaginative, combinations of different subcultural styles can be mixed and mis-matched if desired. But, is such frivolity the product of a society not versed in subcultural parlance? This book argues against this idea as to dismiss all youth in 2021 as being cryogenically frozen in some sort of postmodernist nightmare and unable to develop new subcultural forms is an insult to those teenagers to whom music and clothes are the very essence of their being. To wear the wrong trainers in grime circles would be a crime just as heinous as the wrong jacket for a teddy boy or the wrong collar on a shirt for a mod.

Furthermore, youth fashion remains important in the wider world, both politically and economically, outside the confines of subcultures. As Naomi Klein observed in her ground-breaking book *No Logo*, multinational clothing giants Nike regularly employed 'Cool Hunters' who were operatives sent out to the projects in New York City to spy on young black kids and steal their ideas to refashion Nike's own brand, a practice that continues to this day. In September 2020, Fred Perry, a clothing company steeped in British subcultural history, issued a statement in response to the 'Proud Boys', a group of American neo-Nazis active in opposition to the Black Lives Matter movement who wear Black and Gold-tipped Fred Perry polo shirts as their unofficial uniform:

> The Fred Perry shirt is a piece of British subcultural uniform, adopted by various groups of people who recognise their own values in what it stands for. We are proud of its lineage and what the laurel wreath has represented for over 65 years: inclusivity, diversity and independence. The black/yellow/yellow twin tipped shirt has been an important part of that uniform since its introduction in the late 70s, and has been adopted generation after generation by various subcultures, without prejudice.[63]

Fred Perry has now withdrawn that particular shirt in clear opposition to its use by fascists. Nevertheless, for many young people, lifestyle and identity politics have replaced the familiar environment of subculture. For others the homogenous British high street has nullified any sartorial creativity or directed it toward a uniform appearance emanating from the ubiquitous sportswear warehouse/shops on the outskirts of every town and city. The closure of youth clubs and lack of social spaces for young people to assemble combined with the isolation that tablets and iPhones have heralded does not make for communal activities.[64] Punishment for miscreant youth in 2021 is no longer being 'sent to your bedroom'.

In 1959 the average age of marriage was 28.4 for men and 25.4 for women. In 2016 it was 37.9 for men and 35.5 for women, and the age at which people are having children is also rising.[65] If youth ended with marriage and children and the responsibilities that brings, does this mean that youth is now older?[66] Has the 'generation gap' been deferred or has it disappeared completely as the people who are now parents, even grandparents, could have been involved with subcultures themselves when they were young and personally understand the need for youthful self-expression. If the oppressive parent does not exist, then has the need to rebel against them diminished too?

Furthermore, we have also seen the development of what Alan Watkins of *The Spectator* referred to as the 'young fogey'. Over 27 percent of young people aged 16-24 do not drink or take drugs compared with the 19 percent who refrained in 2005.[67] Combined with this, the Association of Licensed Multiple Retailers (ALMR), which represents nightclubs and music venues, says that in the last ten years, over 50 percent of all UK clubs have closed down.[68] Fragmented lifestyles and identities, as described by post-subcultural scholars such as Harris and Straw,[69] may be occurring, but young people are being young people together somewhere, and irrespective of what is described above, 'scenes' do exist for young people whether they are shrouded in a subcultural veneer or not.[70]

Legacy

So, what is the result of this work? What has been achieved? What did people get out of their involvement in SCIF, RAR and LMHR? There was no financial motive for any bands or individuals to be involved in any of these organisations. Indeed, in the case of SCIF some performers risked their careers by publicly endorsing SCIF's political campaign which was out of step with popular opinion. Frank Sinatra, with his support for the American civil rights movement and his involvement in SCIF, risked the McCarthyite blacklist in the US and being shunned in the UK. Lonnie Donegan, Tommy Steele and Marty Wilde did not further their careers by joining SCIF and expressing solidarity with black immigrants when racism was running rampant in the 1950s. Punk bands not only opposed their managers' reticence to be involved in overtly political campaigns like RAR, arguing it would be detrimental to the bands' careers, but risked the very real possibility of violence at their gigs.[71] There is little media glare, career enhancement or financial gain in Stormzy or Ed Sheeran being involved in LMHR today.

Artists subscribed to all these campaigns because they believed in the causes, they were against racism. For the people on the other side of the stage, the audience, they were able to go to gigs to see great bands and singers, enjoy themselves and feel part of a community that was not poisoned with racism, and maybe become active against racism themselves. The principled stance of anti-racists and anti-fascists involved in SCIF, RAR and LMHR was, and is, extremely important in the ongoing battle against racism and fascism. None of the organisations professed to stop fascism or eradicate racism, but they made and make a difference.

When David Widgery reflected that RAR was: "...temporary, we didn't stop racial attacks, far less racism",[72] he could also have been discussing SCIF and LMHR. There are inherent difficulties with proving a negative, so we will never know how many people's racist ideas were challenged and resulted in them travelling down a different road to becoming a racist or a fascist.

However, we do have testimony from those that were involved and whose ideas did change as a result of all three organisations. This then is the point: the newsletters from SCIF, their Christmas show, the clubs, the gigs, the *Panorama* programme, the RAR concerts, carnivals, stickers, badges and posters, LMHR's stadia events, the Facebook groups, internet broadcasts and grime concerts all have, and all will, leave indelible marks on the people involved. The individual contributions to anti-racism are small, but the collective profile is massive. Many people's lives were irrevocably changed by their participation or attendance at some of the gigs I have discussed.

Activist Geoff Martin, a fan at the first Victoria Park carnival in 1978, went on to organise the 30th anniversary one in 2008:

I was a 15-year-old kid very much into The Clash when I went to RAR. It completely changed my outlook. From that moment, I got involved in RAR and became a political activist. For many like me, it was the first political event we had been to. I remember the imagery and the Anti Nazi League arrows, the ANL lollipops. I was interested, but the big pull for me was getting to see The Clash for nothing. But from that I came away with a hell of a lot more than just Joe Strummer bashing out a few things. It's been with me ever since.[73]

Richard Boon who, as manager of the Buzzcocks, attended the Northern Rock Against Racism Carnival, summed up the effects of the event:

Rock Against Racism was an attempt to focus these young kids out there who were almost a lost generation. There hadn't been anything like it. There was an enthused atmosphere. You saw a big sea change where it was cool to be an anti-racist whereas before it was cool to be racist.[74]

Examples such as this make it possible to gauge what impact RAR had on young people and how it changed the minds of thousands of white and black youth. Former Labour Party leader Neil Kinnock sums up RAR's philosophy:

The fundamental significance of Rock Against Racism, like all cultural engagements in politics, was to do three things: one, to manifest the freedom that you're seeking to uphold and expand, and nothing does that better than music; secondly, to secure the interest and attendance of an audience that otherwise would almost certainly say they were not interested in politics; and thirdly, having done that, to convey to them you've got to be interested in politics because politics will otherwise control you.[75]

SCIF's tiny anti-racist nights in Soho and Notting Hill basements did not attract thousands but were a beacon of progressive politics that remains bright even now for those few left alive that took part. Right until her death in 2019, founding member of SCIF, Hylda Sims, glowed with pride over her role in the formation of Britain's first musical anti-fascist organisation. LMHR performs the same task as SCIF and RAR today and shows that anti-racists are not alone and a connection, even if it is online, can be made with others. Ultimately the success of SCIF, RAR and LMHR cannot be measured in any scientific way. All three groups impacted emotionally on the people involved and inspired them politically. The music, the meetings, the demonstrations and gigs live with them to this day. Inspiration, like the music that produces it, floats in the air and lives in the soul, it cannot be seen, it can only be felt.

It is befitting then that the end of this book ends where it began, in Notting Hill, west London. SCIF member Claudia Jones fought so hard to establish carnival in 1959 as a stance against the racism and violence of the 1958 riots and as a celebration of the music and culture in the world around her. Sixty years on, the Notting Hill Carnival in 2019 had a new permanent fixture that also celebrates the music and culture of today, a float hosted by Love Music Hate Racism. The racism still exists, but so does the fight against it.

Glossary of Musical & Subcultural Terms

Babylon's Burning: The title of this book comes from the title of a song recorded in 1979 by punk rock band The Ruts who were heavily involved in the musical anti-fascist organisation, Rock Against Racism.

Bassline house: Music related to UK Garage that originated in Sheffield in the early 2000s. Rhythmically, it is four-to-the-floor, fast and with a heavy emphasis on the bass.

Bhangra: Initially a traditional Indian music from the Punjab in the north of India, it became very popular with second generation Asian youth in Britain in the 1980s. It evolved to incorporate elements of British rock and pop.

Bright Young Things: Hedonistic middle to upper class coterie in 1920s Britain that revelled in flamboyant/fancy dress clothing, excessive drinking/drug taking and sex, gay, straight or otherwise.

Calypso/Mento: Calypso originated in Trinidad sometime in the 1940s. It was a music with syncopated African rhythms. Lyrically it was very topical, discussing political issues of the day, but also used double entendres to discuss matters of a sexual nature. Mento is more or less the Jamaican equivalent.

Casuals: Originated from elements of the mod revival (1978-85) and most importantly football fans. As Liverpool were the ascendant football club in Europe during the 1980s, fans attending away games in a variety of European countries discovered sportswear in city centres and duty-free shops unavailable in the UK at the time. Not identifiable to one specific musical form, as the subculture developed football and in particular, football violence became their raison d'être. As the name suggests, clothes whilst being smart are informally smart or 'smart-casual'. Much emphasis is placed on designer brands such as Stone Island, Burberry and Aquascutum, trainers are the preferred footwear.

Dandies: A pejorative term that emanates from the early 18th century to describe men 'overly concerned' with their appearance. It entered into popular usage again in the 1920s to describe affluent, fashionable young men of the jazz age who often accompanied their female counterparts, flappers.

Drill: Drill music originates from the south side of Chicago and is a form of Hip Hop. UK drill is a subgenre of this music from south London. UK drill artists often rap about violent and hedonistic criminal lifestyles but are fiercely defensive of this saying it is a true and representative expression of their lives.

Dubstep: A genre of electronic dance music that originated in South London in the late 1990s. Evolving from UK garage and dub reggae.

Emos: A rock music and fashion genre with an emphasis on 'emotional and confessional lyrics' originating on the northwest coast of America.

Folkies: Lovers of the folk music idiom. Styles ranged from old English and American folk music to the [then] modern-day folk of: Woody Guthrie, Pete Seeger, Phil Ochs and Bob Dylan from the USA, Davey Graham, Wiz Jones and Bert Jansch from the U.K. Clothes (as in an identifiable uniform) not central to the group.

Flappers: Young fashionable women in the 1920s, who flouted the conventional mores of western society and wore short skirts, excessive makeup, cut their hair short into 'bobs' and flaunted their disdain for [then] modern society. Flappers listened to jazz, they smoked and had sex outside of marriage.

Goths: Musical genre that evolved from post-punk in the late 1970s. Dark and introspective lyrics accompany angular music and fashion-wise has adapted a classic 'horror movie' look, velvet clothes and copious use of makeup for both males and females.

Greasers: British motorbike enthusiasts, given their nomenclature due to the constant maintenance of their notoriously unreliable motorbikes. The residue of this maintenance was engine grease which adorned both them and pretty much all their clothes, which were: t-shirts, Jeans and leather jackets. Listened to rock 'n' roll.

Grime: Is a type of music that emerged in east London in the early 2000s. It developed from earlier UK electronic music styles, garage and jungle but has Jamaican influences as well, especially dancehall. Musically, grime is relatively simple as the concentration of the genre is on the lyrics which are socio-realistic depictions of urban life.

Grunge: Rock music from the northwest coast of America, popular in the 1990s, part of the 'slacker' generation, sartorially influenced by the 'skater' look which was popularised especially by Seattle band Nirvana.

Hip-hop: Musical and cultural artform that emanates from New York in the 1970s. Musical samples form the backdrop to spoken or 'rapped' lyrics.

Hippies: Originally an American phenomena, becomes a subculture that grows out of the British psychedelic and counterculture scenes in the late 1960s. Simultaneously political and hedonistic, the clothes were even more free-flowing than its psychedelic precursor. Musically they vacillated between hard rock and acoustic singer-songwriters.

Hard Mods: Retrospective name used by some cultural historians to describe mid 1960s mods who began to drift away from the original mod ethos and adopt a more localised and gang/street fighting outlook.

House: House music is a genre of electronic dance music created by club DJs and music producers in Chicago in the early 1980s

Indie: A type of rock music that was popular in the 1970s-2000s that is outside the mainstream. Its name comes from the independent records labels who signed the bands.

Jump & Jive: Sometimes referred to as jump blues, an up-tempo African American jazz/blues, played by small groups and popular in the 1940s, primarily a dance music. It was the precursor to 1950s R&B.

Jungle: A style of music popular in the 1990s characterised by fast tempos, breakbeats and dub reggae basslines.

Lovers Rock: A black British adaptation of reggae popular in the 1970s focusing on love songs, as distinct from the political 'roots reggae' also popular at the time.

Modernists or Mods: Taking their name and clothing from American modern jazz musicians, mods are initially a London based subculture. There are four phases of mod: 1: The modernists that Colin MacInnes talks about in *Absolute Beginners*, lovers of jazz and Ivy League clothing from 1957-1960. 2: The R&B mods of Soho clubs like the Scene and the Flamingo wearing Italian clothes 1960-1963. 3: The Fred Perry & Levi mods, lovers of The Who and Small Faces and Brighton scooter runs 1963-1965. 4: The 1978-84 mod revival.

Modern Jazz: Is a catch-all definition that encompasses a variety of post WWII Jazz forms: bebop, hard-bop, cool jazz and soul jazz. It placed the musician and the musicianship at the forefront of the genre and pushed the limits of technical ability. It was also a political art form articulating a desire for civil rights in America. It is also associated with a particular style of dressing, Ivy League clothing.

Northern Soul: A northern England musical phenomena whose adherents were white but were obsessive about black American soul music. Evolving out of late 1960s mod clubs in northern towns and cities, obscure 1960s Tamla Motown type songs were played in 'all-nighters' i.e. clubs that opened on Saturday nights at 2300 and closed at 0800 the following morning. Speed was the drug of choice to accommodate the frenetic dancing.

Punk: Music and subculture that sought originality and simplicity in both its style and its music. Rejected wholesale (or at least pretended to) the prevailing musical orthodoxy and musical history. Sought to shock, musically, sartorially and politically. Similar in some respects to Dadaism.

Psychobilly: A musical and sartorial fusion popular in the 1980s. The rawness and attitude of Punk was combined with melodic sensibilities and rhythms of rockabilly.

Psychedelia: Short-lived musical and sartorial subculture that grows out of the mod underground club scene and subsequently forms the basis of the later hippy scene. LSD is at the root of this movement. The freer flowing brightly coloured clothing and musical experimentation that forms the basis of the movement is suggested by the drug.

Rave: Takes its name from the warehouse parties or 'raves' that were popular in the 1980s. The music played was electronic, mainly techno and house. A fashion evolved around the scene of loose-fitting casual sportswear clothes. MDMA was the drug of choice and the rave scene was fuelled by it.

Reggae: A synthesis of many disparate musical forms: Calypso, ska. rocksteady and American R&B. Like ska and rocksteady, reggae's emphasis is on the offbeat. Reggae's rise to popularity was concomitant with the rise of Rastafarianism in Jamaica and consequently the influence of the latter is profound. Rastafarianism was part of the current of black liberation or black-nationalist thought that swept the world in the late 1960s and early 1970s. Alongside the music, there were hairstyles and clothes that were identifiable reggae.

R&B: This was an African American music developed in the 1950s and 1960s. R&B was a 12-bar based dance music made by small groups, that was adopted by British groups in the 1960s.

Rockabilly: A 1950s American musical fusion of bluegrass and R&B. Considered by some to be the first and authentic rock 'n' roll.

Rocksteady: Rocksteady, is a development from ska, again with emphasis on the offbeat, but considerably slower in tempo and with emphasis on vocal harmonies. Rocksteady uses more major and minor seventh chords. Influenced by African American soul singers like Curtis Mayfield, rocksteady was more melodic and melancholic than ska.

Roots Reggae: A subgenre of reggae with lyrical content that specifically deals with Rastafarianism, politics, oppression, spirituality and liberation.

Scuttlers: A subculture from Manchester in the late 19th century. They were working-class members of street fighting gangs who adopted a distinctive dress code.

Ska/Blue Beat: Jamaican music form that accentuates the offbeat in 4/4 time using guitar or piano. Walking basslines are common. Tempo is quick and was primarily a dance music. Also known as Blue Beat in the UK as this was the main record label that Jamaican music was released on.

Skiffle: Music and sub-culture pre-dating rock 'n' roll. Emanating from the Trad scene, its proponents played a fast and furious acoustic British take on African American blues and American folk music. Central to its ethos was a DIY element, anyone could be in a band, you did not have to be a master of your instrument. Very similar to Punk in this respect some twenty years later. An unofficial uniform of Royal Navy surplus jumpers and duffle coats were prevalent as were the styles of the Parisian left bank and avant-garde, especially for women.

Stax-Volt: A white-owned R&B/soul music record label of black musicians and singers from Memphis, Tennessee formed in 1957.

Steampunks: More of a literary subculture than a musical one, although a wide variety of music is listened to. Steampunks have late Victorian literature and clothing as the basis of their movement and science fiction from that period.

Suedeheads: An offshoot of skinheads, wore their hair, slightly longer, shoes were preferred to boots and clothes became more important than the fighting that skinheads primarily were involved with. Musically, Jamaican rocksteady and reggae were their preferred genres.

Swing: A form of Jazz that was popular between the 1930s and 1940s. Swing is often framed as the most debated word in jazz, loose instrumental improvised solos weaved around the more formulaic structures of songs primarily played by big bands.

Tamla Motown: Music label from Detroit, Michigan that produced dance music throughout the 1960s and 1970s.

Teddy Boys & Girls: Subculture based on clothes/image initially taken from 'Edwardian style' jackets. Also wore 'drainpipe trousers, bootlace ties and 'brothel creeper' shoes.

Wore greased-back 'ducks arse' haircuts. Girls dressed in similar styles. Originates in late 1949 early 1950, adopts rock 'n' roll as its' music in 1956. Had revival in mid 1970s.

Traditional or Trad Jazz: Interpretive style of music and subculture originating in London in the late 1940s. The music is based on Dixieland Jazz from New Orleans in the first two decades of the twentieth century. British musicians wore clothes similar to African American 'minstrel' clothing. Trad fans mimicked musician's sartorial style but had little of their own.

Two-Tone: Record label and co-operative of punk and ska-infused bands originating in Coventry in 1979. Combining black and white members and original mod and skinhead clothing. Vocally anti-racist.

Glossary of Political Terms

AL: Africa League

AAC: The African-Asian Congress

AACP: Association of Advancement of Coloured People

ACTT: Association of Cinematograph, Television & Allied Technicians

AEU: Amalgamated Engineering Union

AFA: Anti-Fascist Action

ALARAFCC: All London Anti-Racist Anti-Fascist Co-ordinating Committee

ANL: Anti Nazi League:

ASLEF: Associated Society of Locomotive Engineers and Firemen

ASTMS: Association of Scientific, Technical and Managerial Staffs

BF: British Fascists/Fascisti

BF: Britain First

BM: British Movement

BNP: British National Party

BUF: British Union of Fascists

CPGB: Communist Party of Great Britain

CPSA: Civil & Public Services Association

DFLA: Democratic Football Lads Alliance

ED: English Democrats

FBU: Fire Brigades Union

FLA: Football Lads Alliance

FL: Fascist league

Frankfurt School: A school of social theory and critical philosophy associated with the Institute for Social Research in Germany (1918–33). It comprised intellectuals, academics, and political dissidents dissatisfied with the contemporary socio-economic systems. The Frankfurt theorists argued that Social Theory was inadequate for explaining the politics of 20th century liberal capitalist societies.

IFL: Imperial Fascist League

IMG: International Marxist Group

IS: International Socialists

IWA: Indian Workers Association

KPD: German Communist Party

LEL: League of Empire Loyalists

Leninism: A political ideology developed by Vladimir Lenin that takes Marxism as its philosophical and political base, but crucially, states that there is a need for a revolutionary political party to lead the struggle. This vanguard party, Lenin argued, comes from the most politically advanced sections of the working class and gives direction in a revolutionary situation and is essential in the transition from capitalism into socialism.

LMHR: Love Music Hate Racism

Marxism: A philosophy and method of analysing society using historical materialism as the means to understand its present and its past. Marxism places the economic system of a given society at its root and argues that this economic base conditions all other aspects of life, be it social, cultural, legal or political. It simultaneously sees class as the thing that inhibits humanity from reaching its potential and also as the vehicle for changing it. Marxism seeks to replace a society based on profit with one based on need.

Maoism: A political philosophy associated with Chinese Communist Party leader Chairman Mao, which usually describes itself as Marxist-Leninist, but which sees the peasantry (as opposed to the urban proletariat) as the key revolutionary class, following the example of the Chinese Revolution of 1949. Maoism had a major influence on many anti-colonial and guerrilla struggles in the Global South. Maoism also enjoyed a brief period of popularity in the 1960s and 1970s in some Western countries, especially among some student radicals, who viewed guerrilla struggle and the Chinese Cultural Revolution as a more radical expression of socialism than the stale, bureaucratic regimes of Russia and the Eastern Bloc. In fact, Maoism was at its heart a continuation of Stalinism.

NAAR: National Assembly Against Racism

NF: National Front

NP: National Party

NLP: National Labour Party

NSM: National Socialist Movement

NSDWP: National Socialist Workers Party of Germany (Nazis)

NUHKW: National Union of Hosiery & Knitwear Workers

NUJ: National Union of Journalists

NUM: National Union of Mineworkers

NUPE: National Union of Public Employees

NUR: National Union of Rail-workers

NUT: National Union of Teachers

PCI: Partito Comunista Italiano (Italian Communist Party)

PCE: Partido Comunista de España (Spanish Communist Party)

PNM: Peoples National Movement

Popular Front: An alliance of reformist, centrist and conservative parties or organisations,- and on occasions the revolutionary left- usually to oppose a specific reactionary or far-right threat. Such formations tend to be defined by what the most conservative sections are prepared to agree to and therefore tend towards caution, passivity and a compromising approach from the reformist wing in a continual search for respectability.

Prolekult: A Russian initiative, whose intention was to develop a 'laboratory of pure proletarian ideology' that would augment the October Revolution. Advocated the development of a distinct 'proletarian art' in opposition to the products of 'bourgeois art'.

RAR: Rock Against Racism

RCP: Revolutionary Communist Party

RPS: Racial Preservation Society

RMT: National Union of Rail, Maritime and Transport Workers

SCIF: Stars Campaign for Interracial Friendship

SCPG: St Peters Coloured Peoples Group

SKAN: School Kids Against the Nazis

SOGAT: Society of Graphical and Allied Trades

Stalinism: The political idea that the bureaucratic rule established under Joseph Stalin's leadership in the Soviet Union, was the continuation of the ideals and political aims of the 1917 Russian Revolution, and that the Eastern Bloc, China and other similar countries represented the 'socialist' third of the world. Associated with a tendency to subordinate the policies of communist and socialist parties internationally to the interests and dictates of the Soviet or Chinese leadership and towards a top-down bureaucratic approach to campaigns, movements and class struggle.

SWP: Socialist Workers Party

TASS: Technical, Administrative and Supervisory Section of the Amalgamated Engineering Union (AEU)

TGWU: Transport & General Workers Union (now part of UNITE)

Trotskyism: Political philosophy, associated with Leon Trotsky, one of the key leaders of the 1917 Russian Revolution, which asserted that the ideals and political gains of the revolution had been betrayed or overturned by the repressive, undemocratic Stalinist bureaucracy which came to dominate the Soviet Union from the mid- to late 1920s, and shaped the Eastern Bloc, China and elsewhere after WWII. Generally associated with an orientation on radical movements and working class struggle, and the attempt to keep alive the key tenets of Marxism and Leninism and the potential for socialist revolution to establish democratic workers' states internationally. As Hitler rose to power Trotsky advocated with increasing urgency for a united front of workers parties to confront the Nazis, a view in stark contrast to the various positions dictated from Moscow by Stalin.

UKIP: United Kingdom Independence Party

UM: Union Movement

United Front: An alliance of revolutionary, radical and reformist parties or organisations, around a temporary set of demands or to oppose a specific right-wing threat, based around the idea of unity in action around a limited set of aims, without demanding agreement in advance on other political questions.

WDL: White Defence League
WIG: West Indian Gazette
WRP: Workers Revolutionary Party
YSM: Yellow Star Movement

Interviews

Abbott, Diane, 11 July 2019
Billingham, Lee, 4 August 2019.
Bragg, Billy, 27 February 2019.
Brown, Geoff, 14 September 2020
Cochrane, Zak, 10 July 2019.
Dallas, Karl, 6 July 2015.
Dexter, Jeff, 9 March 2018.
Douglas, Jo 17 January 2017.
Goodyer, Ian, 18 February 2019.
Hain, Peter, 23 July 2018.
Huddle, Roger 27 June 2017.
Humphreys, Amber Vivienne, 8 March 2018.
Laine, Cleo, 28 September 2015.
Merrill, Derek and Judith, 21 April 2019.
Rana, Balwinder, 26 May 2019.
Samuels, Paul, 8 May 2019.
Saunders, Red, 10 July 2019.
Sillett, Paul, 25 May 2019.
Simons, Mike, 23 July 2018.
Sims, Hylda, 2 September 2015.
Squires, Rosemary, 19 August 2015.
Weyman Bennet, 10 July 2019.
Wilde, Marty, 16 December 2016.
Woodburn , Beverley, 6 October 2020
Young, Lewis, 11 October 2018.

Bibliography

Addison, Paul, *The Road to 1945: British Politics and the Second World War* (London,1994).

Adorno, Theodore, *Essays on Jazz* (Oxford, 2001).

Alessio, Dominic & Meredith, Kristen, *Blackshirts for the Twenty–First Century? Fascism and the English Defence League. Social Identities* (London, 2014).

Allen, Richard, *Skinhead* (London, 1973).

Anderson, Paul, *Mods: The New Religion* (London, 2013).

Barnes, Richard, *Mods* (London, 1979).

Baxter, Mark, Brummell, Jason, Snowball, Ian, *Ready, Steady, Girls: The Other Half of the Mod Equation* (London, 2016).

Beckman, Maurice, *The 43 Group* (London, 1993).

Beesley, Tony, *Sawdust Caesars: Original Mod Voices* (Peterborough, 2014).

Benn, Tony, *The Benn Diaries, 1940-1990* (Harmondsworth, 2005).

Bennett, Tony & Frith, Simon, *Rock and Popular Music: Politics, Policies, Institutions* (London, 1993).

Bosworth, Richard, *Mussolini* (London, 2002).

Bourne, Jenny, *The Beatification of Enoch Powell* (London, 2008).

Bradley, Lloyd, *Bass Culture, When Reggae Was King* (London, 2001).

Bradley. Lloyd, *Sounds Like London: 100 Years of Black Music in the Capital* (London, 2013).

Bragg, Billy, *Roots, Radicals & Rockers: How Skiffle Changed the World* (London, 2017).

Branson, Noreen, *The History of the Communist Party of Great Britain 1941-1951* (London, 1997)

Braun, Aurel, *The Extreme Right* (London, 1997).

Brocken, Mike, *The British Folk Revival: 1944-2002* (Aldershot, 2003).

Brown, Timothy, *Subcultures, Pop Music and Politics: Skinheads and 'Nazi Rock' in England and Germany* (London, 2004).

Burnett, Archie, *The Complete Poems of Phillip Larkin* (New York, 2012).

Callaghan, John, *Cold War, Crisis & Conflict: The CPGB 1951-1968* (London, 2003).

Callinicos, Alex & Simons,

Mike, *The Great Strike: The Miners' Strike of 1984-5 and its Lessons* (London,1985).

Callinicos, Alex, *The Revolutionary Ideas of Karl Marx* (London, 1987).

Cane-Honeysett, Lawrence, *The Story of Trojan Records* (Shropshire, 2018).

Carr, E H, *Socialism in One Country* (London, 1972).

Clayson, Alan, *Beat Merchants* (London, 1995).

Cliff, Tony & Gluckstein, Donny, *The Labour Party: A Marxist History* (London, 1996).

Cloonan, Martin, *Banned! Censorship of Popular Music in Britain, 1967-92* (London, 1996).

Cloonan, Martin, *Policing Pop* (New York, 2009).

Cloonan, Martin, *Popular Music and the State in the UK: Culture, Trade or Industry?* (New York, 2006).

Coates, David, Augustine, Peter & Lawler, Peter, *New Labour in Power* (Manchester, 2000).

Cohen, Sara, *Ethnography and Popular Music Studies* (Cambridge, 1993).

Cohen, Sarah, *Sounding Out the City: Music and the Sensuous Production of Place* (Cambridge, 1995).

Cohen, Stanley, *Folk Devils and Moral Panics, The Creation of the Mods and Rockers* (London, 2009).

Copsey, Nigel, *British Fascism and the Labour Movement* (London, 2005).

Copsey, Nigel, *Contemporary British Fascism: The British National Party and the Quest for Legitimacy* (London, 2009).

Copsey, Nigel, *Anti-Fascism in Britain* (Oxford, 2016).

Copsey, Nigel & Macklin, Graham, *The British National Party* (Oxford, 2011).

Corner, Paul, *Fascism in Ferrara, 1915-1925,* (Oxford, 1975).

Cronin, Mike, *The Failure of British Fascism* (Basingstoke, 1996).

Denselow, Robin, *When the Music's Over: The Story of Political Pop* (London, 1989).

Deverson, Jane & Hamblett, Charles, *Generation X* (London, 1965).

Dicks, Ted, *A Decade of The Who* (London, 1977).

Dorril, Stephen, *Blackshirt: Sir Oswald Mosley & British Fascism* (Manchester, 2006).

Dresser, Madge, *Black and White on the Buses; The 1963 Colour Bar Dispute in Bristol* (London, 2013).

Duncombe, S & Tremblay, M, *White Riot: Punk Rock and the Politics of Race*

(London, 2011).

Durham, Martin, *Women and Fascism* (London, 1998).

Eaden, James & Renton, David, *The Communist Party of Great Britain Since 1920* (London, 2002).

Eatwell, Roger, *Fascism: A History* (London, 2003).

Eatwell, Roger, *Fascism and the Extreme Right* (London, 2008).

Eatwell, Roger, *The New Extremism in 21st Century Britain* (London, 2014).

Eatwell, Roger & Wright, Anthony, *Contemporary Political Ideologies* (London, 1999).

Elms, Robert, *The Way We Wore: A Life in Threads* (Basingstoke, 2005).

Ensminger, David, *The Politics of Punk: Protest and Revolt from the Streets* (London, 2016).

Ferris, Ray & Lord, Julian, *Teddy Boys* (London, 2012).

Fielding, Nigel, *National Front* (Oxford, 1981).

Fingers, Al, *Clarks in Jamaica* (London, 2012).

Foot, Paul, *Immigration and Race in British Politics* (Harmondsworth, 1965).

Foot, Paul, *The Rise of Enoch Powell: An Examination of Enoch Powell's Attitude to Immigration and Race* (London, 1969).

Ford, Robert & Goodwin, Matthew, *Revolt on the Right: Explaining Support for the Radical Right in Britain* (London, 2014).

Fowler, David, *Youth Culture in Modern Britain, c.1920–c.1970: From Ivory Tower to Global Movement—A New History* (Basingstoke, 2008).

Frame, Pete, *The Restless Generation* (London, 2007).

Frith, Simon, *Performing Rites: On the Value of Popular Music* (Oxford 1996).

Frith, Simon & Street, John, *Rockin' the Boat: Mass Music and Mass Movements* (Boston, 1992).

Fryer, Paul, *Staying Power*: *The History of Black People in Britain* (London, 2010).

Gable, Gerry & Hepple, Tim, *At War with Society* (London, 1993).

Gelder, Ken & Thornton, Sarah, *The Subculture Reader* (London, 1997).

Giller, Don & Lozano, Ed, *The Definitive Bob Dylan Songbook* (New York, 2003).

Gilroy, Paul, *There Ain't No Black in The Union Jack* (London, 1987).

Glass, Ruth, *Newcomers: The West Indians in London* (London, 1960).

Goodwin, Matthew, *New

British Fascism (Oxford, 2011).

Goodyer, Ian, *Crisis Music: The Cultural Politics of Rock Against Racism* (Manchester, 2009).

Gordon, Sarah Ann, *Hitler, Germans and the 'Jewish question'* (Princeton, 1984).

Gould, Tony, *Inside Outsider: The Life & Times of Colin MacInnes* (Harmondsworth, 1986).

Gramsci, Antonio, *Selections from the Prison Notebooks of Antonio Gramsci* (London, 2018).

Green, Jonathon, *Days in the Life: Voices from the English Underground, 1961–1971* (London, 1994).

Griffin, Roger, *A Fascist Century* (Basingstoke, 2008).

Griffin, Roger, *Fascism* (Oxford, USA, 1995).

Griffin, Roger, *International Fascism: Theories, Causes and the New Consensus* (Oxford, USA, 2003).

Griffin, Roger, *Modernism and Fascism* (Basingstoke, 2007).

Griffin, Roger, *The Nature of Fascism* (London, 1993).

Grundy, Trevor, *Memoirs of A Fascist Childhood* (London, 1999).

Hall, Evelyn Beatrice, *The Life of Voltaire* (South Carolina, 2012).

Hall, Stuart & Jefferson, Tony, *Resistance Through Rituals: Youth Sub-Cultures in Post-war Britain* (London, 2006).

Hall, Stuart, *Centre for Contemporary Cultural Studies: Encoding and Decoding in the Television Discourse* (Birmingham, 1973).

Harris, Trevor, *Windrush (1948) and Rivers of Blood (1968): Legacy and Assessment* (London, 2019)

Hebdige, Dick, *Subculture, The Meaning of Style* (London, 2009).

Heffer, Simon, *Like the Roman: The Life of Enoch Powell* (London, 1999).

Hewitt, Paolo, *The Soul Stylists, Forty years of Modernism* (Edinburgh, 2000).

Hill, C P, *A History of the United States* (London, 1979).

Hobsbawm, Eric, *The Jazz Scene* (London, 1989).

Hobsbawm, Eric, *Uncommon People, Resistance, Rebellion and Jazz* (London, 1998).

Hobsbawm, Eric, *Interesting Times: A Twentieth-Century Life* (London, 2003).

Huddle, Roger & Saunders, Red, *Reminiscences of RAR* (London, 2016).

Jackson, Ben & Saunders,

Robert, *Making Thatcher's Britain* (Cambridge, 2012).

Johnson, Bruce & Cloonan, Martin, *Dark Side of the Tune: Popular Music and Violence* (Farnham, 2009).

Jones, Nigel, *Mosley: Life & Times* (London, 2005).

Kaufman, Will, *Woody Guthrie, American Radical (Music in American Life)* (Illinois, 2011).

Kershaw, Ian, *Hitler* (London, 2010),

King, Martin Luther Jr, *Letter from Birmingham Jail* (Harmondsworth, 2018).

Klein, Naomi, *No Logo* (New York, 2010).

Knight, Nick, *Skinhead* (London, 1982).

Kynaston, David, *Modernity Britain 1957-1962* (London, 2015).

Leach, Robert, *Theatre Workshop, Joan Littlewood and the Making of Modern British Theatre* (Gateshead, 2006).

Lewis, Brian, *Wolfenden's Witnesses: Homosexuality in Post-war Britain* (London, 2016).

Longhurst, Brian, *Popular Music & Society* (Cambridge, 2009).

Macilwee, Michael, *Teddy Boy Wars: The Youth Cult that Shocked Britain* (London, 2015).

MacInnes, Colin, *Absolute Beginners* (London, 1994).

MacInnes, Colin, *City of Spades* (London, 1968).

MacInnes, Colin, *Mr Love & Justice* (London, 1997).

Macklin, Graham, *Very Deeply Dyed in Black: Sir Oswald Mosley and the Resurrection of British Fascism after 1945* (New York, 2007).

Mailer, Hans & Schafer, Michael, *Totalitarianism Movements and Political Religions* (London, 2005).

Marable, Manning, *Race, Reform and Rebellion: The Second Reconstruction in Black America 1945-2006* (New York, 2007)

Marsh, Graham & Callingham, Glyn, *The Cover Art of Blue Note Records* (London, 2002).

Marshall, George, *Spirit of '69: A Skinhead Bible* (Manchester, 1994).

Martin, Jay, *The Dialectical Imagination: A History of the Frankfurt School and the Institute for Social Research* (Oakland, 1996).

Marx, Karl, *The German Ideology* (London, 1985).

Mathieson, David, *Radical London in the 1950s* (Oxford, 2017)..

McDevitt, Chas, *Skiffle: The Definitive Story* (Leeds, 2013)

McKenzie, Paul, *India: A History* (Harmondsworth, 1951).

McRobbie, Angela, *The Aftermath of Feminism: Gender, Culture and Social Change (Culture, Representation and Identity series)* (London, 2008).

Melly, George, *Revolt into Style* (London, 2013).

Miles, Barry, *Hippie* (London, 2005).

Miles, Robert, & Phizacklea, Annie, *White Man's Country: Racism in British Politics* (London, 1984).

Millward, Robert, *The Political Economy of Nationalisation in Britain, 1920-1950* (Cambridge, 2002).

Moore, Charles, *Margaret Thatcher: The Authorized Biography, Volume Two* (London, 2015).

Mosley, Nicholas, *Beyond the Pale: Sir Oswald Mosley and Family, 1933-80* (Oxford, 1983).

Moulton, Lorri, *The Atlantic Charter: Political and Economic Goals of Roosevelt and Churchill* (London, 2017).

Mussolini, Benito, *The Doctrine of Fascism* (1932) www.gutenberg.org/ ebooks/14058

Nayak, Anoop & Kehily, Mary Jane, *Gender, Youth and Culture* (London, 2008).

Newsinger, John, *The Blood Never Dried: A Peoples History of the British Empire* (London, 2003).

Okiji, Fumi, *Jazz as Critique: Adorno and Black Expression Revisited* (Redwood, 2018).

Olden, Mark, *Murder in Notting Hill* (Washington, 2011)

Olusoga, David, *Black and British: A Forgotten History* (London, 2016).

Payne, Stanley, *A History of Fascism* (University of Wisconsin Press, 2003).

Paxton O, Robert, *The Anatomy of Fascism* (Harmondsworth, 2004).

Peddie, Ian (ed), *Popular Music and Human Rights: British and American Music* (Farnham, 2011)

Perks, Robert & Thomson, Alistair, *The Oral History Reader* (New York, 2006).

Pilkington, Edward, *Beyond the Mother Country: West Indians and the Notting Hill White Riots* (London, 1988).

Preston, Paul, *Franco* (Illinois, 2011).

Pugh, Martin, *Hurrah for The Blackshirts* (London, 2006).

Rachel, Daniel, *Walls Come*

Tumbling Down: *The music and politics of Rock Against Racism, 2 Tone and Red Wedge 1976–1992* (London, 2016).

Ramdin Ron, *Reimaging Britain: 500 Years of Black and Asian History* (London 1999).

Ramdin, Ron, *The Making of the Black Working Class in Britain* (London, 2017).

Randall, Dave, *Sound Systems, The Political Power of Music* (London 2017)

Rawlings, Terry, *Mod: A Very British Phenomena* (London, 1999).

Redhead, Steve, *Rave Off: Politics and Deviance in Contemporary Youth Culture* (Manchester, 1993).

Redd, Mel & Simpson, Alan, *Against A Rising Tide: Racism, Europe and 1992* (Nottingham, 1991).

Renton, David, *Fascism: Theory and Practice* (London, 1999).

Renton, David, *Never Again: Rock Against Racism and the Anti-Nazi League 1976-1982* (London, 2019).

Renton, David, *When We Touched the Sky: The Anti-Nazi League 1977-1981* (Cheltenham, 2006).

Rice, Jonathan, *Guinness Book of British Hit Singles* (London, 2010).

Richardson, John, *(Mis) Representing Islam: The Racism and Rhetoric of British Broadsheet Newspapers* (London 2004).

Robb, Jon, *Punk Rock: An Oral History* (London, 2012).

Rubin, Bret, 'The Rise and Fall of British Fascism: Sir Oswald Mosley and the British Union of Fascists', *Intersections 11, no 2: 323-380* (London, 2010).

Sabin, Roger, *Punk Rock, So What* (Routledge 1999).

Savage, Jon, *England's Dreaming* (London, 2005).

Savage, Jon, *The Kinks: The Official Biography* (Frome, 1984).

Sherwood, Marika, *Claudia Jones, A Life in Exile* (London, 1999).

Shuker, Roy, *Popular Music: the Key Concepts* (Abingdon, 2005).

Skidelsky, Robert, *Oswald Mosley* (New York, 1975).

Smith, Andrew, *I Was a Soviet Worker* (New York, 2007).

Smith, Evan, *British Communism and the Politics of Race* (Chicago, 2017).

Smith, Evan, '"Class before Race": British Communism and the Place of Empire in Post-war Race Relations', *Science and Society* 72:4 (October 2008) pp.455-481.

Street, John, *Mass Media, Politics and Democracy*

(Basingstoke, 2001).

Street, John, *Music and Politics* (London, 2011).

Street, John, *Politics and Popular Culture (London, 1997).*

Street, John, *Rebel Rock: The Politics of Popular Music* (Oxford, 1986).

Tagg, Phillip, *Introductory Notes to the Semiotics of Music* (photocopied document, Liverpool Hope University, 1999).

Taylor, Stan, *The National Front in English Politics* (London, 1982)

Testa, M, *Militant Anti-Fascism: 100 Years of Resistance* (Edinburgh, 2015).

Thane, Pat, *Divided Kingdom, A History of Britain,1900 to the Present* (Cambridge, 2018).

Thurlow, Richard, *Fascism in Britain* (London, 2009).

Trilling, Daniel, *Bloody Nasty People, The Rise of Britain's Far Right* (London 2013).

Trotsky, Leon, *Fascism, What It Is & How to Fight It* (New York, 1972).

Vague, Tom, *Getting It Straight in Notting Hill Gate: A West London Psycho-Geography Report* (London, 2003).

Vahasalo, Minna, *They've Got the Bomb, We've Got the Records, The Roles of Music in The Making of Social Movements: The Case of the British Nuclear Disarmament Movement, 1958-1963* (Tampere, 2016).

Van Maanen, John, *Tales of The Field* (London, 1988).

Vansttart, Peter, *In the Fifties* (London, 1995).

Walker, Martin, *The National Front* (London, 1977).

Walker, Sean, *The Long Hangover: Putin's New Russia and the Ghosts of the Past* (New York, 2018).

Waters, Anita, *Race, Class and Political Symbols* (New Brunswick, 1985),

Weight, Richard, *Mod: A Very British Style* (London, 2013).

Widgery, David, *Beating Time* (London, 1986).

Wildeblood, Peter, *Against the Law* (London, 1959).

Wilkinson, Paul, *The New Fascists* (London, 1981).

Winlow, Simon, *The Rise of the Right: English Nationalism and the Transformation of Working-Class Politics* (Bristol, 2017).

Zetkin, Clara, *Fighting Fascism: How to Struggle and How to Win* (Haymarket Books, 2017).

References

Introduction

1 This was true in the 1950s and the 1970s. However, from the early 1980s onwards the skinhead Nazi look has been adopted all over Europe, Australia and most noticeably in America. Ironically, this fashion has been completely dropped by the far right in the United Kingdom and during the 1990s was used by gay men as a fashion *and* political statement.

2 Griffin, 1993, p.146.

3 Mussolini, 1932.

4 Zetkin, 2017, p.71.

Ch1 **The Origins of the Notting Hill Riots of 1958**

1 India had provided the largest volunteer army in history, the British Indian Army, some 2.5 million strong. They had also suffered the Bengal famine which killed around the same amount in 1943. McKenzie, 1951, p.1.

2 Notably Ghana on the 6 March 1957. The fate of Sudan achieving independence a year earlier was inextricably intertwined with the history of Egypt, formally independent in 1922 and politically in 1956. Jamaica and Trinidad became independent in 1962, Guyana and Barbados in 1966, the other Caribbean islands had to wait until the 1970s or 1980s. There are still four Caribbean islands controlled by Britain today.

3 Moulton, 2017.

4 Foot, 1965, p.117.

5 Fryer, 2010, p.349.

6 Fryer, 2010, pp.358-362.

7 Fryer, 2010, p.373.

8 *Office of National Statistics* (ONS), Population by Country of Birth and Nationality Report (August 2015) www.ons.gov.uk/peoplepopulationandcommu-nity/populationandmigration/internationalmigration/articles/populationbycountryofbirthandna-tionalityreport/2015-09-27.

9 Ibid.

10 Jump & Jive and R&B with their rhythmic off-beats floated across the airwaves from the southern states of America into the West Indies and were crucial to the formation of Ska, Rocksteady and subsequently Reggae. Also, the oil drums that enabled that uniquely Trinidadian sound, the steel band, were left on the island by the American Navy at WWII's end. Randall, 2017.

11 Fryer, 2010, p.374.

12 Fryer, 2010, p376. See also Dresser, 2013.

13 Fryer, 2010, p.376.

14 Glass, 1960, p.76.

15 Cabinet Papers: 1954:1; *The Times*, 2 January 1985, cited in Ramdin, 1999, p.175.

16 Fryer, 2010, p.375.

17 Fryer, 2010, p.374.

18 Paul Stephenson, a British born black man would later organise the Bristol bus boycott in 1963, achieved national prominence when he organised a boycott of pubs in Bristol that refused to serve black people. His campaigns paved the way for the Race Relations Act of 1965. *The Guardian*, 1 October 2020, https://bit.ly/3qowrKp.

19 BBC Documentary: *A Very British History, The First Black Brummies* broadcast 23/02/2019.

20 Booth used the colour yellow to describe the middle to upper class and wealthy and the colour black for the lowest class which he called 'vicious and semi-criminal'. 'What were the poverty maps', *Charles Booth's London*, The London School of Economics, 2016. booth.lse.ac.uk/static/a/4.html

21 Ibid.

22 According to the *Daily Mail* of 26 May

2012, 22 Portland Road, a five-bedroom semi-detached house with a 'Bulthaup kitchen' and a private cinema, sold for £6m. At the other end of the road, Flat 14 at Winterbourne House fetched a more modest £244,000.

23 Thurlow, 2009, p.67.

24 Amongst who were the National Fascisti, the New Party and the Imperial Fascist League. Thurlow, 2009, pp.87-91.

25 In the 1920s, two organisations, the People's Defence League and the National Union for Combatting Fascism were set up. The Communist Party of Great Britain (CPGB) also set up the Workers' Defence Corps, initially to protect pickets against strike breakers in the 1926 General Strike, but this group morphed into the Labour League of Ex-Servicemen, a specifically anti-fascist organisation. In the 1930s opposition to Mosley centered around the CPGB but in 1934 a Co-Ordinating Committee for Anti-Fascist Activities was formed. Copsey, 2016, p.10.

26 This was open support for Mosley. Whether there was assistance behind closed doors is a matter of conjecture. Rothermere remained an enthusiastic advocate of both Hitler and Mussolini throughout the 1930s. Even congratulating Hitler on the annexation of Czechoslovakia in 1938.

27 Thurlow, 2009. p.105.

28 Thurlow, 2009.p.234.

29 Thurlow, 2009, p.234.

30 Beckman, 1993, p.40.

31 Leese lived in Notting Hill Gate at 74 Princedale Road, London W11, more of which later.

32 Beckman, 1993, p.60.

33 Some of these new groups were the British Peoples Party, the League of Ex-Servicemen and Women, the Union for British Freedom and the Imperial Defence League.

34 Beckman, 1993, p.73.

35 Beckman, 1993, pp.83-84.

36 For reasons of space, there is no discussion here of the Nottingham riots, although they impacted upon British society as well. The same underlying causes were behind the riots in both Nottingham and Notting Hill. However, as SCIF operated mainly in London it is here that is the focus of this section.

37 *The Kensington Post,* 8 August 1958. The men were arrested just around the corner in The Goldhawk Club in Shepherds Bush which went on to become the home for pop band The Who only six years later.

38 *The Kensington News,* 19 September 1958.

39 Foot, 1965, p.132.

40 Foot, 1965, p162.

41 Cohen, 2009, p.28.

42 See edwardianteddyboy.com.

43 Hebdige, cited in Longhurst, 2009, p.97.

44 *Brighton Herald,* 20 November 1954.

45 Cohen, 2009, p.7.

46 *The Daily Worker,* 23 October 1958.

47 *The Daily Worker,* 9 January 1959.

48 Ibid.

49 Cohen, 2009, p7.

50 *The Times,* 5 September 1958.

51 Cohen, 2009, p.20.

52 Cohen, 2009, p.7.

53 Melly, 2013.

54 Thurlow, 2009, p263.

55 See interview with Colin Jordan outside White Defence League Headquarters. 74 Princedale Road, London W11 in 1958. See https://vimeo.com/425007028

56 *BBC Panorama,* The White Defence League, 13 April 1959. See: www.youtube.com/watch?v=0ljl2PMUf-wY&t=9s.

57 See Renton, 1999, Dorril, 2006 and Griffin, 2008.

58 Beckman, 1993, pp.56-60.

59 It is important to add however, that not all teddy boys were enticed by the racism and violence surrounding Mosley. As working-class men, they would have worked in industries where there was a high level of trade union organisation. Consequently, they would have been open to the range of political arguments that existed inside the trade union movement at the time. Some were in the Labour Party and there are even examples of teddy boys in the Communist party, so-called Red Teds.

60 Fryer, 2010, pp.376-381.

61 Glass, 1960, p.134.

62   Count Suckle was a Jamaican-born sound system operator and club owner who was influential in the development of ska, reggae and Afro-Caribbean culture in the United Kingdom. We shall meet him again in Chapter Three.

63   *The Kensington Post,* 4 September 1958.

64   *The Guardian.* 24 August 2002: www.theguardian.com/uk/2002/aug/24/artsandhumanities.nottinghillcarnival2002

65   Ibid.

66   Ibid.

67   Glass, 1960, p.140.

68   Benn, 2005, p.233.

69   Mervyn Jones, cited in Fryer, 2010, p.380.

70   Ibid.

71   *Daily Mail,* 8 June 2013.

72   Fryer, 2010, p.377.

73   The Labour Party later issued a statement unambiguously rejecting immigration controls and promising the next Labour government would 'introduce legislation making illegal the public practice of discrimination'. Fryer, 2010, p.380.

74   Vague, 2003, p.37.

75   Kynaston, 2015, p177.

76   Vague, 2003, pp.35-37.

77   *Daily Mail,* 8 June 2013.

78   See Racist Riots of 1958, Notting Hill, London, England at www.youtube.com/watch?v=LvhkOokRm-I.

79   Vague, 2003, p.37.

80   John Bean formed The National Labour Party, yet another neo-fascist party in 1957, merged it with the WDL in 1960 and he eventually ended up in the National Front and then became a leading member of The British National Party.

81   *The Kensington News & West London Times,* 26 September 1958.

Ch2 **The Stars Campaign for Interracial Friendship**

1   *Melody Maker,* 6 September 1958.

2   Ibid. Founding SCIF member Karl Dallas told this writer that without Preston SCIF would never have happened. Interview with Karl Dallas, 6 July 2015.

3   *Melody Maker,* 6 September 1958.

4   *Melody Maker,* 13 September 1958.

5   Interview with Karl Dallas, 6 July 2015.

6   Hobsbawm, cited in Harris, 2019, p.39 There were also sports personalities who signed a similar statement of support in response to the riots. They were- Danny Blanchflower, Jimmy Hill, Jack Crump, Joe Erskine, Thelma Hopkins, Derek Ibbotson, George Knight, Stanley Matthews, Ken Norris, Frank Sando, David Sheppard, and Alan Wharton.

7   Glass, 1960., p.198.

8   *Kensington Post,* 3 October 1958.

9   Interview Hylda Sims, 2 September 2015. Historian Eric Hobsbawm was a modern jazz lover and wrote about the music under the *nom de plume* of Francis Newton.

10   Interview with Karl Dallas, 6 July 2015.

11   Interview with Hylda Sims, 2 September 2015.

12   The English Folk-Dance Society had collected thousands of quintessentially English folk tunes and dances in order to save them from extinction. Coincidently, Alan Lomax an American ethnomusicologist undertook a similar project in America in the 1930s, which led, in part, to the folk revival of the 1950s and 1960s.

13   At its founding conference was 'a festival of Labour Choral Union and Co-operative Musical Associations, embracing some 44 choirs and five orchestras.' They came together to 'co-ordinate workers' musical activity' and 'instead of 'ordinary' music being brought to the workers, it is the music of workers' struggle, of workers' battles and of their triumphs which is brought to the musical arena'. www.workers-music-association.co.uk/434833096.

14   Although confusingly, the CPGB had set up the Challenge Jazz Club to listen to and discuss the aesthetic and political merits of the music in the 1940s.

15   This was to have implications on the few black American musicians who did manage to gig in the UK in the 1950s. They were discouraged in playing their electric guitars lest they

offend the sensibilities of the folk puritans. Later, this reached infamous heights at the Bob Dylan gig at the Manchester Free Trade Hall in 1966, where a member of the audience shouted 'Judas' as Dylan donned his Fender Telecaster and proceeded to perform an electrified set.

16 The term Prolekult comes from the Russian 'proletarskaya kultura' or proletarian culture. This was an experimental Soviet artistic institution that arose in conjunction with the October revolution. It involved local cultural societies and avant-garde artists and was most prominent in the visual, literary, and dramatic fields. It sought to replace existing bourgeois culture with a new revolutionary working-class one.

17 It is no surprise then, given this dichotomy, that the Trotskyist Socialist Workers Party masthead at the top of their newspaper declared: *Neither Washington Nor Moscow, But International Socialism.*

18 Musicians Union: www.muhistory.com/contact-us/1951-1960/

19 *Kensington News,* 26 December 1958.

20 Ibid.

21 *Melody Maker,* 20 December 1958.

22 Interview with Rosemary Squires, 19 August 2015.

23 *The Kensington Post,* 23 January 1959.

24 Ibid.

25 *The Kensington Post,* 16 January 1959.

26 Ibid.

27 Ibid.

28 *The Kensington News & West London Times*, December 1959.

29 Grundy, 1999, p.199.

30 Sherwood, 1999, p.116.

31 Cohen, 1995, p.434.

32 Cited in Longhurst, 2009, p.252.

33 Hobsbawm, 2003, p.68.

34 Victor Musgrove, cited in Gould, 1986, p.176,

35 *The Kensington Post,* 30 January 1959.

36 Hobsbawm, 2003, p.68.

37 Smith, 2008, p.78.

38 Ibid.

39 Kynaston, 2015, p.180.

40 Smith, 2008, p.84.

41 Sherwood, 1999, p.70.

42 Smith, 2017, p.9.

43 Smith, 2017, p.462.

44 Smith, 2017, p.463.

45 Sherwood, 1999, p.65.

46 Sherwood, 1999, p.83.

47 Ibid.

48 *The Kensington Post*, 14 March 1958.

49 Ibid.

50 Ibid.

51 Ibid.

52 Foot, 1965, p.224.

53 Glass, 1960, p.198.

54 Hobsbawm, cited in Harris, 2019, p.39

55 Hobsbawm, 2003, p.68.

56 *Melody Maker,* 28 March 1959.

57 David Olusoga, 'The Unwanted', *BBC documentary*, broadcast 24 June 2019, www.bbc.co.uk/iplayer/episode/m00068sk/the-unwanted-the-secret-windrush-files.

58 Examples of this included, secret and illegal information gathering at labour exchanges, so-called 'race surveys' specifically targeted at black people seeking work. David Olugosa, *The Unwanted,* BBC documentary, 24 June 2019.

59 These characteristics were the racist stereotypes we are now very familiar with — propensity to violence, over-sexed, preponderance of disease, laziness, drug taking and uncleanliness. *Youtube,* 'Britain's Racist Immigration Laws in 1968', December 2008, www.youtube.com/watch?v=X-LIXo-8_7g

60 This was achieved by re-categorising immigrants into skilled and unskilled labour. Government documents recently released demonstrate the explicit intention of this policy was to discriminate against black and Asian workers. David Olugosa, *The Unwanted,* BBC documentary, 24 June 2019.

61 *BBC Panorama,*The White Defence League, 13 April 1959, http://news.bbc.co.uk/panorama/hi/front_page/newsid_8320000/8320142.stm

62 Ibid.

63 Ibid.

64 Ibid.

65 Ibid.

66 Tise Vahimagi, 'TV in the 1950s', *BFI Screenonline*, www.screenonline.org.uk/tv/id/1321302/

67 Interview with Marty Wilde, 16

December 2016.

68   *The Kensington Post*, 24 September 1958.

69   See Mark Olden's *Murder in Notting Hill* for a full account of this murder. Olden, 2011.

70   One of the reasons SCIF used free broadsheets to carry their message was in reply to the *North Kensington Leader*, a neo-fascist broadsheet circulated by Mosley's Union Movement around the Notting Hill area.

71   *The Daily Worker*, 27 May 1959

72   Ibid.

73   *Melody Maker* 28 May 1958.

74   Ibid.

75   Interview with Fred Dallas, 6 July 2015.

76   Grundy, 1999, p.180.

77   *Lassie* was a popular dog food at the time, *Kit-e-Kat* was a cat food. Ibid.

78   Grundy, 1999, p.180.

79   Opposition to a perceived decadence in society, the rebirth of nation, ultra-nationalism and the subsumption of the individual, only the reference to anti-communism is missing. This definition can be found on p.7 of this book and is taken from Griffin, 1993, p.146.

80   Griffin, 1993, p.189. This definition can be found on page 7 of this book.

81   *The Guardian:* britishguardian. blogspot.com/2017/10/sir-oswald-mosleys-election-leaflet-for.html.

82   Interview with Hylda Sims, 2 September 2015.

83   *Melody Maker,* 14 November 1959.

84   Of course, there are always exceptions to the rule as evidenced by Eric Clapton's racist tirade in Birmingham in 1976 supporting Enoch Powell's 'Rivers of Blood speech. We shall examine this outburst in Chapter Four.

85   Sherwood, 1999, p.89.

86   *BBC News*, 20 July 1957, news.bbc. co.uk/onthisday/hi/dates/stories/july/20/newsid_3728000/3728225.stm

87   *The Guardian*, 19 Sepember 2013. See: www.theguardian.com/science/political-science/2013/sep/19/harold-wilson-white-heat-technology-speech

88   Glass, 1960, p.173.

Ch3 **1960 - 1976, Society and Culture**

1   Addison, 1994, pp.89-93.

2   Aside from the NHS, The Bank of England in 1946, The National Coal Board in 1947, The Railways in 1948 and Iron and Steel in 1950. The process of nationalisation in many other industries would continue up until the 1970s. Millward, 2002, pp.85-87.

3   Ministerial statement 'Defense Policy Approved: Conscription to End With 1939 Class', reported in *The Times*, 18 April 1957, p.4.

4   AKA the Montagu Trial. The case brought against Lord Montagu, Peter Wildeblood and Michael Pitt-Rivers was 'conspiracy to incite certain male persons to commit serious offences with male persons' i.e. gay sex. Wildeblood, 1957, pp.1-15.

5   Lewis, 2016, pp.29.

6   Derek Bentley was hanged for the murder of a policeman in the course of a burglary. His conviction was quashed in 1998. Ruth Ellis shot her boyfriend David Blakely dead outside a pub in London. At her trial in June 1955, she was found guilty of murder and was sentenced to death. Evidence—withheld at the trial—demonstrates that Ellis was a victim of repeated domestic violence and weeks before the murder had miscarried her child after another violent attack by Blakely. Mathieson, 2017, pp.287-292.

7   *The Telegraph*, 21 October 1960, www.telegraph.co.uk/culture/books/8066784/Lady-Chatterley-trial-50-years-on.-The-filthy-book-that-set-us-free-and-fettered-us-forever.html.

8   Burnett, 2012, p.387.

9   *The Telegraph*. 21 October 1960.

10   *ONS*, UK Labour Market, 2016. See: www.ons.gov.uk/employmentandlabourmarket/peoplenotinwork.

11   Ibid.

12   Elms, 2005, p.57.

13   Infamously, trad jazz fanatic and trumpeter Ken Colyer and his 1951 pilgrimage to New Orleans which saw him incarcerated in a Louisiana state penitentiary for repeatedly breaking the colour bar and playing on stage

with African American musicians. He was finally deported home on the luxury liner the SS United States. Bragg, 2017, pp.67-69.

14   There are numerous quotes from contemporary jazz musicians and fans to support this statement. Hewitt, 2000, pp.17-29. The instruments the musicians played were also different. Trad musicians played clarinets, banjos, acoustic guitars, harmonicas, trombones and trumpets and although modern jazz players also used trumpets, they were played in a different style. Saxophones, electric guitars vibraphones and pianos were all utilised in modern jazz, instruments that traditional jazz could not countenance.

15   Anderson, 2013. p.12.

16   Marsh & Callingham, 2002.

17   John Simons, interview cited in Hewitt, 2003, p.32.

18   Principally, Harvard, Princeton and Yale.

19   Marsh & Callingham, 2002, p.8.

20   King, 2018, p27.

21   Barnes, 1979, p.6.

22   Ibid. p.12.

23   Mailer's controversial 1957 essay was an observation of white American 'hipsters' or 'beats', who were highly influenced by jazz and black culture in general. It received plaudits and critics in equal measure from both the black and white literati.

24   Deverson & Hamblett, 1965, p.124.

25   Whilst racist terms such as 'spades' may be unacceptable to 21st century eyes and hackneyed clichés about black peoples 'natural ability' to sing and dance is now a racist stereotype that is rejected, the battle for a descriptive vocabulary that black people could take ownership of was only just beginning in the 1960s—the war is not yet won. The point however remains that these young white people, whatever language they used, were progressive in their adoption of black culture and the mod subculture was radically different to any that had happened before.

26   Ska was also colloquially known as Blue Beat in the UK. This was the name of a London based record label initially set up to cater for the West Indian community in London and it became increasingly popular with mods. Blue Beat was an imprint of Emil E Shalit's Melodisc Records which had been in operation since 1947. Anderson, 1979, p.91.

27   Interview with Amber Vivienne F. Humphreys, 8 March 2018.

28   Barnes, 1979, p.13. The Flamingo was a night club in Wardour Street, Soho that opened its doors in 1952. It specialised in jazz, R&B and soul and was very popular with mods from the late fifties onwards. It was also popular with black GI's on weekend leave from the proliferation of American military bases in the UK at the time, as well as the Caribbean community. At weekends, when the Flamingo closed at midnight, the premises became 'The All-nighter' which as the name suggests ran until 6.00am Sunday morning.

29   Quoted in Carl Gayle, The Reggae Underground, *Black Music,* Vol. 1, Issue 8 (July 1974), forum.speakerplans.com/reggae-sound-system-list-back-in-the-real-days_topic17036_page3.html.

30   Interview with Jeff Dexter, 21 March 2018.

31   *Daily Mirror,* 27 October 1963: www.nationalarchives.gov.uk/education/resources/sixties-britain/.

32   Thurlow, 2009p.320.

33   Walker, 1977, p.164.

34   Fountaine had been publicly disowned by the Tories, after a series of openly antisemitic rants, he also described the Labour party as semi-alien mongrels and hermaphrodite communists. His other fascist credentials included, fighting for Franco in the Spanish Civil War.

35   Walker, 1977, p.34.

36   Thurlow, 2009, p.23.

37   Ibid, p.233.

38   Copsey, 2016, p.105.

39   Ibid, p.107

40   Bishopsgate Institution Library, *The 62 Group* (Tony Hall Collection), p.13.

41   Copsey, 2016, p.169.

42   Ibid, p.168.

43   Testa, 2015, p.172.

44   Matthew Wright, 'Britain Racist

Election': Channel 4, *The Arts Desk*, 16 March 2015: https://theartsdesk.com/tv/britains-racist-election-channel-4

45   Bob Pitt, "If you desire a coloured for your neighbour vote Labour' — the origins of a racist leaflet', *Medium*, 22 May 2017, https://bit.ly/35RxhWr. This leaflet was later to reappear in the south London ward of Clapham in the 1970 general election.

46   *The Guardian*, 15 October 2014, www.theguardian.com/world/oct/15/britains-most-racist-election-smethwick-50-years-on.

47   Cliff & Gluckstein, 1996, p.294.

48   Foot, 1965, p.124.

49   Colin Jordan became the leader—or to call him by his official sobriquet *World Fuhrer*—of the paradoxically named World Organisation of National Socialists in the mid 1960s. He was involved in an increasingly bizarre collection of openly Nazi groups until he lost what credibility he had in fascist circles when he was arrested for stealing three pairs of red women's knickers from Tesco's in Leamington Spa.

50   This political fissure was no doubt aided by Tyndall's fianceé Christine Dior. Although engaged to Tyndall, she married Colin Jordan whilst Tyndall languished in prison for the arson attacks.

51   'Rational', that is, in relative terms.

52   *The Guardian*, 31 October 2016, www.theguardian.com/stage/2016/oct/31/enoch-powell-rivers-of-blood-play-what-shadows-ian-mcdiarmid.

53   Heffer, 1999, p.500.

54   Fryer, 2010, p.385.

55   'My father and Enoch Powell', *The Shropshire Star* (Weekend supplement), 8 October 2016. p.3. Article by Nicholas Jones, condensed from the book *What Do We Mean By Local? The Rise, Fall—and Possible Rise Again—of Local Journalism* (Bury St Edmonds, 2013).

56   Bourne, 2008. journals.sagepub.com/doi/abs/10.1177/0306396808089290.

57   Heffer, op.cit., p.467.

58   Fryer, cited in Smith, 2017, pp.106-107.

59   The Asian community was in Kenya at the behest of the British empire. Some were the descendants of indentured labourers shipped to Africa to build the Ugandan-Kenyan railway at the turn of the 20th century. The rest had been purposely installed as an educated 'buffer' of middle-class administrators and shopkeepers, specifically designed to deflect African anger away from British imperial exploitation and toward the Asian community.

60   Foot, 1969, p.111.

61   Thurlow, 2009, p.246.

62   Ibid. p.241.

63   Martin Walker, 1979, p.67.

64   Ibid. p.189.

65   Again, 'reasoned' in fascist terms.

66   Some of Colin Jordan's ex-followers also realised the implications of the act, went underground and formed Column 88, a clandestine neo-Nazi and extremely violent paramilitary group.

67   See glossary.

68   Hewitt, 2000, p.76.

69   The term 'hard mods' has been adopted retrospectively by cultural historians. There is no contemporary use of the phrase.

70   Marshall, 1994, p.9.

71   Knight, 1982, p.30.

72   Hall & Jefferson, 2006, p.167.

73   Hewitt, 2000, p.88.

74   Ibid. p.89.

75   Fryer, 2010, p.372.

76   Ibid.

77   Britain's visible minorities: A demographic overview. Census on Ethnic Groups. *Notes on Census*. See: crossasia-repository.ub.uni-heidelberg.de/286/1/demography.pdf.

78   Census on Ethnic Groups. *Notes on Census*. See: crossasia-repository.ub.uni-heidelberg.de/286/1/demography.pdf.

79   Fryer, 2010, p.374.

80   Ferris, 2012, p.63.

81   Hewitt, 2000, p.90.

82   Knight discusses this and concludes: "Many blacks were skinheads or formed their own crews, such as the Kilburn Blacks". Knight, 1982, p.20.

83   Rocksteady had accented guitar riffs, heavier basslines, three-part vocal harmonies, and was very much influenced by American soul singer Curtis Mayfield. Many rocksteady

artists who had recorded ska music in the early 60's, for example: Derrick Morgan, Toots & the Maytals and Desmond Dekker went on to become some of the finest exponents of this important, but short-lived musical genre. Cane-Honeysett, 2018, p.21.

84   The clubs such as: The Ska Bar, The Ram Jam Club, The Golden Star and The Cue Club all had live Jamaican acts appearing for the Caribbean community, so the up to date Jamaican styles could be copied from the likes of Desmond Dekker and Prince Buster et al. Knight, 1982, p.14 and Marshall, 1994, p.28.

85   Knight, 1982, p.12.

86   Hewitt, 2000, p.92.

87   Marshall, 1994, p.9.

88   Allen, 1973, p.20. Allen went on to write a series of novellas about youth culture in England, each one graphically detailing the trials and tribulations of young people and their subcultures. They feature racism (sympathetically) as a central component in many of them.

89   Marshall, 1994, p.59.

90   Ibid. p.60.

91   Paul Anderson's forensic investigation into skinheads found no middle-class involvement in the skinhead movement at all. Similarly, I have found no other reference to middle class skinheads in any other material I have sourced. Anderson's book *Scorcha* is due to be published in August 2021.

92   Dick Hebdige (somewhat unfairly) created the following equation to delineate between mods and hippies: Working Class + Mod + Speed = Action, Middle Class + Hippy + Marijuana = Passivity. Hebdige, cited in Hall & Jefferson, 2006, p.79.

93   The term counterculture is used to delineate from subculture. Whereas subcultures in the 1950s/1960s were generally based around music and clothes and (on occasion) had a political expression. The counterculture of the 1960s was based around political expressions which had a musical and sartorial expression.

94   The Beatles performed *All You Need Is Love* on *Our World,* the first live global television link, on 25 June 1967. It was watched by 400 million people in 26 countries. The programme was broadcast via satellite. *The Beatles. com:* www.thebeatles.com/song/all-you-need-love. Similarly, the Apollo 11 Moon landing in 1969 was watched by some 600 million worldwide. *NASA. com:* www.nasa.gov/audience/forstu-dents/k-4/home/F_Apollo_11.html.

95   Universities grew from twenty-two to forty-five in the mid- to late 60s after the Robbins Report was published in 1963. www.educationengland.org. uk/documents/robbins/robbins1963. html.

96   Communist Party, *Britain's Road to Socialism,* available at https://www. communistparty.org.uk/programme/

97   Smith, 2017, p.104.

98   Ibid.

99   Timothy J Hatton & George R Boyer, 'Unemployment and the UK labour market, before, during and after the Golden Age', *European Review of Economic History*, Vol. 9, No. 1 (April 2005), pp. 35-60 https://www.jstor. org/stable/41378412

100 *BBC News*, 'UK unemployment tops one million', 20 January 1972, http://news.bbc.co.uk/onthisday/ hi/dates/stories/january/20/ newsid_2506000/2506897.sto

101 *ONS*, Consumer Price Inflation Time Series https://www.ons.gov.uk/ economy/inflationandpriceindices/ datasets/consumerpriceindices

102 *BBC News*, 4 October 2017, www.bbc. co.uk/news/uk-politics-33772016.

103 Cliff & Gluckstein, 1996, p.323.

104 Ibid.

105 The Social Contract was a deal proposed by the Wilson government, and supported by the trade union leadership, to end national pay bargaining for public employees and enable negotiations on a sector by sector basis. To sell the deal the Labour government promised a repeal of the Tories' 1971 Industrial Relations Act in exchange for what were effectively, wage restraints.

106 These broad guidelines are set out by Griffin in the introduction.

107 Ugandan Asians, like the Kenyans, had been encouraged to work in

Africa by the British for the empire.

108 These were those that had British passports, of the other 30,000, they left Africa to settle in other Commonwealth countries.

109 Cliff & Gluckstein, 1996, p.323.

110 Fryer, 2010, p.385.

111 House of Commons speech, 6 July 1976, www.parliament.uk/business/publications/parliamentary-archives/.

112 *BBC News,* 7 August 1972, news.bbc.co.uk/onthisday/hi/dates/stories/august/7/newsid_2492000/2492333.stm.

113 Cliff & Gluckstein, 1996, p.333.

114 Ibid.

115 Testa, 2015, p.186.

116 Renton, 2019, p.35.

117 Copsey, 2016, pp.141-143.

118 Ibid.

119 Testa, 2015, p.188.

120 This group were formerly known as the Movement for Colonial Freedom, and were briefly discussed in Chapter Two. They were an anti-racist and anti-imperialist group formed by Labour MP Fenner Brockway. See Copsey, 2016, p.119.

121 Which in turn prompted an ad hoc oppositional group called Trade Unionists Against Fascism. Copsey, 2016, p.118.

122 Read gained notoriety at the time for his response to the murder of Asian teenager Gurdip Singh Chaggar in Southall in June 1976, when he said: "One down, one million to go". *The Guardian,* 10 January 2010, www.theguardian.com/stage/2008/jan/10/theatre1.

123 As with Kenya and Uganda so with Malawi. Malawi had been a British colony, where Asian labour had been imported by the British to administer colonial rule and deflect anger away from the Britain and onto the small middle-class Asian population.

124 Rachel, 2016, p.117.

125 Walker, 1977, p.196. This 44 percent vote for the NF and NP (combined) in Lewisham is estimated at over 50 percent of the entire white vote in the election. See Cliff & Gluckstein, 1996, p.333.

126 Renton, 2019, p.52.

Ch4 **Rock Against Racism**

1 Street, 1997, pp.74-75.

2 Huddle, 2017, p.195.

3 Dankworth and Preston's letter to *Melody Maker*: 'At a time when reason has given way to violence in parts of Britain, we, the people of all races in the world of entertainment, appeal to the public to reject racial discrimination in any shape of form. Violence will settle nothing: it will only cause suffering to innocent people and create fresh grievances. We appeal to our audiences everywhere to join us in opposing any and every aspect of colour prejudice wherever it may appear.' *Melody Maker,* 6 September 1958.

4 *Melody Maker,* 4 September 1976.

5 Saunders cited in Huddle, 2017, p197. This again was similar to the response to the first SCIF appeal: "Letters, telephone messages, even telegrams and personal callers offering support have come into this office". *Melody Maker* 13 September 1958.

6 *BBC News,* 20 January 1972, http://news.bbc.co.uk/onthisday/hi/dates/stories/january/20/newsid_2506000/2506897.stm

7 Saunders cited in Huddle, 2017, p.197.

8 Amongst the countless pub-rock bands were Ian Dury & The Blockheads, Eggs over Easy, Eddie & The Hot Rods, The Steve Gibbons Band and the future Clash frontman Joe Strummer in his first band of note, The 101ers.

9 The Sex Pistols first album released in 1977 was called *Never Mind the Bollocks, Here's the Sex Pistols.*

10 Dadaism was an early 20th century art movement wholly in opposition to the logic, reason and aesthetic of capitalism and it emerged in protest to WWI. Dadaism rejected bourgeois art and intended to offend people with art of its own. The Situationists were a loose anti-authoritarian organisation (1957-1972), which stated alienation and commodity fetishism as the essential reasons why late twentieth century capitalism degraded people's lives. They rejected the 'system' using any appropriate form of spectacle they

could create and adopted the tactic of 'détournement' which took the slogans and logos of advertising and the expressions of capitalist production, usurped them and used them against the system itself.

11   Joe Strummer from The Clash draped the German flag behind his amp and stencils of terrorist organisations were festooned all over The Clash's stage wear. Clash guitarist Mick Jones was initially in a punk band with Tony James—later to be in Generation X—called London SS.

12   Huddle, 2017, p.198.

13   Only Mark Perry's punk fanzine *Sniffin' Glue* (July 1976—August 1977) outsold *Temporary Hoarding*. Huddle, 2017, p.198.

14   Huddle, 2017, p.111.

15   Goodyer, 2009, p.12. For example, there were articles on Ireland, women's oppression and British history.

16   Huddle, 2017, p.248.

17   The 'skank' is the up (and sometimes down) stroke performed on the guitar, on the off-beat, that provides the rhythmic essence of ska and rocksteady and whilst it is also there in reggae, it is the bass that becomes of central importance.

18   Waters, 1985, p.9.

19   These are just five examples of British reggae acts from the many that we could use.

20   Fryer, 2010, p.388.

21   Ibid, p.386.

22   Black households were five times as likely to live in shared dwellings than their white counterparts. 40 percent of black people lived in overcrowded accommodation compared to 11 percent of whites. Over 50 percent of Asians compared to 17 percent of whites had neither their own hot water nor an inside toilet. Fryer, 2010, pp.388-389.

23   Paul Gilroy points out that these figures can be read in a variety of ways. Gilroy, 1987, p.111. Stuart Hall also discusses this in his theory of 'encoding and decoding' especially regarding black crime and its reportage. Hall, 1973.

24   This well-documented police racism

is discussed elsewhere. See Fryer, 2010, Gilroy, 1987, and not least, The Scarman Report commissioned by the government after the 1981 riots, see 'The Struggle for Race Equality: An Oral History of the Runnymede Trust, 1968-1988', www.runnymedetrust.org/histories/1980s.html.

25   Bradley, 2001, p.82.

26   Fryer, 2010, p.387.

27   Interview with Beverley Woodburn, 6 October 2020.

28   A musical and political statement not lost on punk band The Clash who covered the song on their first album, *The Clash*.

29   www.bobmarley.com.

30   Huddle, cited in Goodyer, 2009, p.85.

31   Ibid.

32   *Today* was a Thames Television current affairs magazine program broadcast live at 6pm on weekdays. The particular episode featuring the Sex Pistols was broadcast on 1 December 1976 and was Britain's first glimpse into the emerging punk rock subculture.

33   Huddle, cited in Goodyer, 2009, p.87.

34   Gilroy, cited in Goodyer, 2009, p.85.

35   Bushell, cited in Goodyer, 2009, p.85. Bushell later became spokesman of the profoundly reactionary Oi! movement and his drift to the right-wing of politics was as rapid as the tempo of the punk singles he initially championed.

36   Widgery, 1986, p.66.

37   Rachel, 2016, p.204.

38   Numerous examples could be given of which Elvis Costello, Squeeze, The Undertones and The Jam are just four.

39   Kate Webb, cited in Widgery, 1986, p.95.

40   Rachel, 2016, p.205.

41   The Labour Party or the CPGB had not mustered the same level of popular support on a cultural level, at any point. This includes the variety of initiatives they were both involved with such as the avowedly anti-fascist Theatre Workshop or the folk revival clubs of the 1950s.

42   Cliff & Gluckstein, 1996, pp.333-336.

43   This amounted to some 12.5 percent of the vote in areas like Hackney and Tower Hamlets. Ibid.

44   *Socialist Worker,* 5 June 2007, socialistworker.co.uk/art/11584/ Stop+and+search+++racist,+then+and+now.
45   This demonstration was on 13 August 1977.
46   The SWP was formed out of the International Socialists as they grew in size and stature.
47   For instance, Labour deputy Prime Minister Michael Foot and General Secretary of the Labour Party Ron Haywood directly compared antifascists (i.e. the SWP) to fascists. The Labour Party West Midlands organiser went further and described the SWP as: 'Red fascists...who besmirch the name of democratic socialism'. Cliff & Gluckstein, 1996, p.334.
48   Ibid, p.335. See glossary of political terms for union definitions.
49   See Smith, 2017, for a discussion on the CPGB attitude to racism throughout this whole period.
50   Rachel, 2016, p.129.
51   Ibid, p.142.
52   Ibid, pp.136-137.
53   Ibid, p.142.
54   Ibid, p.145.
55   Huddle, 2017, pp.44-45.
56   Rachel, 2016., p.148.
57   David Renton, 2006, pp.145-146.
58   Rachel, 2016, p.149.
59   Ibid, p.162.
60   Ibid.
61   *Manchester Evening News,* 8 July 2018, www.manchestereveningnews.co.uk/ news/greater-manchester-news/ rock-against-racism-day-manchester-14877439.
62   Ibid.
63   Rachel, 2016, p.170.
64   Renton, 2019, p.136.
65   Huddle, 2017, p.247.
66   Interview with Mike Simons, 23 July 2018.
67   Huddle, 2017, p.174.
68   Listings and adverts for RAR gigs are featured throughout the period 1977-1981 in the music papers, *NME, Sounds, Record Mirror* and *Melody Maker.*
69   Such as Adam and the Ants, 'I Won't Let That Dago By', The Stranglers, "I Feel Like A Wog' and Siouxsie and the

Banshees 'Love in a Void'. Sabin, 1999, pp.201-205.
70   Ibid, p.200.
71   Ibid, pp.205-206.
72   Widgery, 1986, p.89.
73   Interview with Mike Simons, 23 July 2018.
74   Cliff & Gluckstein, 1996, pp.333-336.
75   Although attributed to Voltaire, he did not actually say this. The quote is from Evelyn Beatrice Hall paraphrasing Voltaire in her biography, *The Life of Voltaire. See* Hall, 2012.
76   Cliff & Gluckstein, 1996, pp.333-336.
77   Fryer, 2010, p.397.
78   Goodyer, 2009, p.112.
79   *Calypso* was the first album in history to sell a million copies and was inducted into the Library of Congress National Recording Registry in 2018. It is one of 25 audio recordings marked for preservation as a representative of America's artistic, cultural and historic treasures. See: www.cbsnews. com/news/harry-belafonte-explains-the-story-behind-calypso/.
80   This Beatles link to Calypso is rarely mentioned. Lord Woodbine aka Harold Adolphus Philips, aside from his role as a musician and club owner, was a promoter/manager for the (pre) Beatles before Brian Epstein and Alan Williams. Such was his involvement with the young Lennon and McCartney that the two were often called 'Woodbine's Boys'. Woodbine also drove the band from Liverpool to their first residency in Hamburg in 1960. According to Beatles expert Mark Lewisohn, John Lennon's first composition was a song called 'Calypso Rock'.
81   See Bradley, 2013.
82   Interview with Balwinder Rana, 26 May 2019.
83   Goodyer, 2009, p.82.
84   Syd Shelton, cited in Goodyer, 2009, p.94.
85   Widgery, 1986, p.61.
86   Gilroy, 1987, p.103.
87   The Open University. Indian Workers Association. www.open.ac.uk/ researchprojects/makingbritain/ content/indian-workers-association.
88   Interview with Balwinder Rana, 26 May 2019.

89 Due to 'logistics' i.e. a traffic jam, this did not happen.

90 Balwinder Rana, cited in Huddle, 2017, p184.

91 Interview with Geoff Brown, 14 September 2020.

92 *Manchester Evening News*, 8 July 2018, www.manchestereveningnews.co.uk/news/greater-manchester-news/rock-against-racism-day-manchester-14877439.

93 Interview with Balwinder Rana, 26 May 2019.

94 Alien Kulture were an Asian band, apart from the self-confessed 'token white' guitarist, Huw Jones. See www.alienkulture.co.uk.

95 Frith, 1996, p.69.

96 Although it was resisted at all times. For a discussion on this see Randall, 2017, pp.27-35.

97 *Runnymeade Trust*, 'Margaret Thatcher Claims Britons Fear Being 'Swamped'', https://www.runnymedetrust.org/histories/race-equality/59/margaret-thatcher-claims-britons-fear-being-swamped.html

98 Daniel Trilling, 'Thatcher: The PM who brought racism in from the cold', *Verso Blog*, 10 April 2013, www.versobooks.com/blogs/1282-thatcher-the-pm-who-brought-racism-in-from-the-cold.

99 *The Times*, 29 October 2014, www.thetimes.co.uk/article/as-maggies-clerk-i-was-swamped-by-racist-bilge-6vh8dvbfm2g.

100 *The Spectator*, 29 October 2014, blogs.spectator.co.uk/2014/10/how-maggies-swamped-comment-crushed-the-national-front/.

101 *The Daily Telegraph,* 30 December 2009, www.telegraph.co.uk/news/politics/margaret-thatcher/6906503/Margaret-Thatcher-complained-about-Asian-immigration-to-Britain.html.

102 *The Guardian,* 30 December 2009, https://www.theguardian.com/uk/2009/dec/30/thatcher-snub-vietnamese-boat-people

103 David Widgery, 1986, p.14.

104 Rachel, 2016, p.224.

105 Interview with Lewis Young, Southall school student, 11 October 2018.

106 Leeds Museums, 'Rock Against Rac-

ism Racism, 15 August 2017, www.youtube.com/watch?v=DR01x9waNql

107 Huddle, 2017, p.248.

108 Rachel, 2016, p.227.

109 Ibid.

Ch5 **Thatcher to Blair: 1980s & 1990s**

1 The Specials, *Ghost Town.* genius.com/The-specials-ghost-town-lyrics.

2 Nearly three million people were unemployed. *ONS,* Unemployment Rates 1971-2021, www.ons.gov.uk/employmentandlabourmarket/peoplenotinwork/unemployment/timeseries/mgsx/lms

3 The deaths were commemorated in many reggae songs of the period three examples of which are: Benjamin Zephaniahs *13 Dead,* Linton Kwesi Johnson's *New Cross Massakah* and Johnny Osbourne's *13 Dead and Nothing Said.*

4 *BBC News Magazine,* 17 June 2011: www.bbc.co.uk/news/magazine-13780074.

5 Fryer, 2010, p.399.

6 Olusoga, 2016, p.187.

7 Thane, 2018, p.346.

8 Camilla Schofield cited in Jackson & Saunders, 2012, p.100.

9 Office of National Statistics: *Ethnicity Facts and Figures,* www.ethnicity-facts-figures.service.gov.uk/crime-justice-and-the-law/policing/stop-and-search.

10 Yaojun Li, 'Ethnic unemployment in Britain (1972-2012)', *Race Matters,* 15 January 2014, https://www.runnymedetrust.org/blog/ethnic-unemployment-in-britain

11 Kevin Jones, 'A National Social Care Service beyond COVID-19: Lessons from the History of Mental Health Social Work and the Origins of the NHS', *History & Policy,* 14 June 2021, www.historyandpolicy.org/policy-papers/papers/immigration-and-the-national-health-service-putting-history-to-the-forefront.

12 Immigration Acts that affected black commonwealth citizens occurred in each of the following years: 1962, 1968, 1971, 1981 and 1993.

13 House of Commons Library: *Migra-*

tion Statistics, Briefing Paper: Number SN06077, 11 December 2018.

14   *ONS*, 1991 Census: www.ons.gov.uk/census/1999census/1999censusdata. The 2011 census reports that these figures are now, 3 percent and 4.9 percent respectively. www.ons.gov.uk/census/2011census/2011censusdata.

15   Cabinet Office: *Ethnic Minorities & the Labour Market: Interim Analytical Report* 2002, Chapter 1, p63. Naylor, M & Purdie, E, 'Results of the 1991 Labour Force Survey' *Employment Gazette*, April 1992, table 20.

16   Hassan Mahamdallie, 'Racism: Myths and Realities', *International Socialism Journal* 95 (Summer, 2002), p.25

17   Ibid.

18   Deborah Garvie, The Black and Minority Ethnic Housing Crisis, *Shelter*, September 2004, https://england.shelter.org.uk/professional_resources/policy_and_research/policy_library/the_black_and_minority_ethnic_housing_crisis

19   Miles & Phizacklea, 1984, pp.148-149.

20   *The Daily Express*,18 January 2015.

21   On 4 May 1979, on the steps of 10 Downing Street, Thatcher quoted from St Francis of Assisi: 'Where there is discord, may we bring harmony. Where there is error, may we bring truth. Where there is doubt, may we bring faith. And where there is despair, may we bring hope'. These words were not, in fact, by St. Francis of Assisi but by a 19ᵗʰ century follower.

22   In fact, it was a staggering victory. Thatcher's party secured an overall majority of 144 seats, the largest for either party since the Labour Party landslide of 1945. The result left Thatcher as the first leader of any party in the 20th century to serve a full term and then increase their majority. Not only that, she was the first Conservative Party prime minister in the twentieth century to win two general elections in a row. See Moore, 2015, pp.63-64.

23   Thane stresses that Thatcher's priority was to 'crush the unions'. Thane, 2018, p.350.

24   Amongst those performing at concerts in support of the miners were, Wham! The Style Council, The Redskins, The Housemartins, Bronski Beat and Billy Bragg. There was also a single released called *Soul Deep*, organised by Paul Weller and released in December 1984 with the proceeds going to the Miners Support Group and the widow of a scab miner killed on his way to work.

25   Bragg cited in Rachel, 2016, p.361.

26   Denselow, 1989, p.252.

27   The gig was in Madison Square Garden and featured, Bob Dylan, Eric Clapton, Leon Russell, Ringo Starr and Ali Akbar Khan. According to UNICEF the concert raised over $250,000. www.unicef.org.

28   *BBC News*, 13 July 1985, http://news.bbc.co.uk/onthisday/hi/dates/stories/july/13/newsid_2502000/2502735.stm

29   *History.com*, 13 July 1985, https://www.history.com/this-day-in-history/live-aid-concert

30   Neil Nehring, 'The Evolution of the Political Benefit Rock Album' in Peddie, 2011, p.96

31   *BBC News*, 13 July 1985, news.bbc.co.uk/onthisday/hi/dates/stories/july/13/newsid_2502000/2502735.stm.

32   Interview with Billy Bragg, 27 February 2019.

33   Rachel, 2016 p.386.

34   Some of the artists supporting Red Wedge included: Jimmy Somerville, Jerry Dammers, The Style Council, The Communards, Junior Giscombe, Madness, Tracy Ullman, The The, Heaven 17, Bananarama, Prefab Sprout, Elvis Costello, Gary Kemp, Tom Robinson, Sade, The Beat, Lloyd Cole, The Blow Monkeys and The Smiths. There was also an 'Alternative Comedy' tour which was very successful.

35   Although the Musicians Union had attempted to recruit rock stars to campaign for the Labour Party once before in the 1974 general election but received only two replies to their appeal. One From ex-Animal Alan Price saying yes, the other from Kinks frontman Ray Davies, saying no, he was voting Tory. Simon Frith & John Street, *Marxism Today*, 28 June 1986. banmarchive.org.uk/collections/mt/pdf/86_06_28.pdf.

36   Tracey Ullman's single *My Guy,* cwww.youtube.com/watch?v=Mn7_qoWDzmY.

37   Three bands that did not support Red Wedge were, The Redskins, The Housemartins and Easterhouse.

38   Artists Against Apartheid, *Sun City,* See: www.youtube.com/watch?v=a-opKk56jM-I.

39   There were over seventy-five performers, amongst whom were: George Michael, Al Green, Hugh Masekela, Whitney Houston, Stevie Wonder, The Bee Gees and Simple Minds.

40   Denselow, 1989, p.276.

41   Twenty-four Conservative MP's had put forward a House of Commons motion criticising the BBC for giving 'publicity to terrorists' i.e. Mandela and the ANC. Much of the concert was censored, especially by Fox Television in America, who even refused to refer to the concert by name and billed the show 'Freedomfest'.

42   Deneslow, 1989, p.143.

43   This is a conservative estimate as there are many more that did not enter into popular media. *The Telegraph,* 7 December 2011, www.telegraph.co.uk/culture/music/8941575/Charity-single-hits-list.html.

44   Elms, 2005, p.184.

45   John Galliano became a world-famous fashion designer, Dylan Jones became the editor of *GQ* magazine in Britain and Kim Bowen became a costume designer and editor of Australian *Vogue.*

46   *The Guardian,* 4 October 2009: www.theguardian.com/music/2009/oct/04/spandau-ballet-new-romantics.

47   *Birmingham Mail*, 27 July 2017, www.birminghammail.co.uk/whats-on/music-nightlife-news/birmingham-rave-scene-nightclubs-1990s-9517423.

48   Also contained within the act was legislation overturning provision for traveller sites, increased police powers to take and retain intimate body samples and the criminalisation of previous civil offences such as the right to protest for environmental issues and hunt saboteurs.

49   UK Government, *Criminal Justice and Public Order Act 1994*, www.legislation.gov.uk/ukpga/1994/33/part/V/crossheading/powers-in-relation-to-raves.

50   This campaign incorporated a variety of disparate groups all affected by the proposed legislation: Advance Party, Reclaim the Streets, Hunt Saboteurs, the Free Party, Squatters Rights groups and many others. *Datacide Magazine:* datacide-magazine.com/revolt-of-the-ravers-the-movement-against-the-criminal-justice-act-in-britain-1993-95/.

51   The Union flag was used throughout this period in the popular arts. Actress Patsy Kensit, reclined on a bed of Union flags, Geri Halliwell from the Spice Girls had a Union flag dress, Oasis guitarist Noel Gallagher had a union flag painted on his guitar.

52   Whatever the validity of these multicultural claims, one thing is certain, Britpop was a wholly white affair.

53   Blur even had the former Greater London Council leader and Labour politician Ken Livingstone appear on their 1995 album *The Great Escape.*

54   George Marshall, 1994, p.73.

55   The Angelic Upstarts, The Business and The Oppressed as three examples.

56   *Punk77*: www.punk77.co.uk.

57   Renton, 2019, p.111.

58   Durham, 1998, p.110.

59   Ibid.

60   *Bulldog,* March 1979.

61   Sham 69 gigs were the focal point for the BM in particular and frequent violence, orchestrated by the BM and NF, occurred at their gigs, culminating in 'Shams Last Stand' at the Rainbow venue in north London, where an organised pitched battle wrecked the concert. Interview Paul Sillett, 26 May 2019.

62   Much of this fighting was not played out 'ideologically' as many were simply *against* skinhead violence and racism rather than being *for* a particular left-wing political position.

63   Interview with Paul Sillett, 26 May 2019.

64   Matthew Worley, 'Shot By Both Sides: Punk, Politics and the

End of 'Consensus'," *Contemporary British History*, 26:3, (September 2012). www.researchgate. net/publication/262904506_Shot_By_ Both_Sides_Punk_Politics_and_the_ End_of_'Consensus'.

65   The leading white power band playing at these concerts was Skrewdriver who were open supporters of the NF, the BM and the BNP. Other neo-Nazi bands included, Skullhead and No Remorse.

66   These gigs would invariably end in violence. The links forged at these concerts and rallies in the 1980s can still be seen in 2021 as many leading far right activists throughout Europe today served their apprenticeships during these years and at these gigs. Blood & Honour is now an organisation operating in over twenty countries.

67   Brown, 2004.

68   *International Business Times*, 21 December 2013, www.ibtimes. com/memories-former-british-far right-extremist-transformation-jo- seph-pearce-1517666.

69   See *Music and the Holocaust*: holocaustmusic.ort.org/politics- and-propaganda/third-reich/ reichskulturkammer/

70   *History.Com:* www.history. com/this-day-in-history/ mussolini-re-establishes-a-fascist-re- gime-in-northern-italy.

71   Widgery, 1986, p.53.

72   African American music had been described as 'race music' from the 1920s onwards.

73   *The Economist*, 16 August 2011, www.economist.com/bage- hots-notebook/2011/08/16/ we-have-been-here-before.

74   Brown, 2004.

75   Cohen, 2009, p.35.

76   Taylor, 1982, p.165.

77   Copsey, 2009, p.19.

78   Thurlow, 2009, p.292.

79   Eatwell, 2003, p.108.

80   Gilroy, 1987, p.171.

81   Goodyer, 2009, p.197.

82   Strasserism is a form of Nazism based on two German brothers in the NSDAP who were opposed to Hitler's strategies and tactics.

They argued for a concentration on anti-capitalist, working-class mass activism rather than the racial purism and antisemitism of Hitler, but fascists they remained.

83   Copsey, 2009, p.23.

84   Ibid.

85   Walker, 1977, p.107.

86   Ibid.

87   Thurlow, 2009, p.252.

88   The British Movement changed its name to the British Nationalist and Socialist Movement in 1985 and changed it back again in 1995. The BM exists only online today.

89   The Front National renamed and rebranded themselves as Rassemblement National in 2018.

90   Benoist's often contradictory political statements do not disguise the fact that he is, as Roger Griffin described, 'an ideal type definition' of a fascist. Griffin, 2008, p.35.

91   Eatwell, 2014, p.108.

92   *The Guardian.* 18 October 2009. www. theguardian.com/politics/2009/ oct/18/nick-griffin-question-time-bbc.

93   Eatwell, 2014, p.118.

94   Thurlow, 2009, p.275.

95   Eatwell, 2014, p.109.

96   See *Times of Israel*, 24 January 2019: https://www.timesofisrael.com/why- are-us-pro-israel-groups-boosting-a- far-right-anti-muslim-uk-extremist/

97   Griffin, 2003, p.118.

98   Ibid, p.119.

99   Ibid.

100 On a leaflet for the BNP candidate Derek Beackon said: 'I am only going to represent the white people [in Millwall ward]. I will not represent Asians. I will not do anything for them. They have no right to be in my great country'. Youth Against Racism in Europe, *A Brief History of the BNP*, www.yre.org.uk/history.html.

101 *The Telegraph*, 10 January 2006, www.telegraph.co.uk/news/ uknews/1399666/Factbox-British-Na- tional-Party.html.

102 Much of this information was exposed by ex-hooligan and neo-Nazi turned mole Tim Hepple who worked undercover for anti-fascist magazine *Searchlight* in the 1980s. Gable & Hepple, 1993.

103 *BBC Panorama*, BNP: Under The Skin, 2011, news.bbc.co.uk/hi/english/static/in_depth/programmes/2001/bnp_special/roots/1992.stm.

104 Marcia Cox, 'Welling 1993', *Socialist Review*, (October 2013) socialistreview.org.uk/395/welling-1993.

105 Anti-Racist Alliance was formed in November 1991. It was an organisation of local anti-racist groups and black political activists, many of whom had spent the 1980s campaigning inside the Labour Party for black sections to become part of its federal structure. ARA argued that black self-organisation and robust legislation was the key to fighting racism and fascism. The difference in political priorities and strategies between ARA and ANL are demonstrated by the response to the BNP threat and the increase in racist murders. On 15 October 1993 two competing demonstrations were held in London. ARA called a 'Speak Out Against Racism' in Trafalgar Square (14 miles from the BNP HQ) and the ANL organised a demonstration which intended to march on the BNP HQ in Welling and close it down.

106 See www.gov.uk/government/publications/the-stephen-lawrence-inquiry,

107 See House of Common Home Affairs Committee, 'The Macpherson Report: 10 Years On', July 2009, www.parliament.uk: publications. parliament.uk/pa/cm200809/cmselect/cmhaff/427/42703.htm.

108 Palmar cited in Coates, Augustine & Lawler, 2000, p213. See also, Home Office, 'The Stephen Lawrence Inquiry: Report', February 1999, https://www.gov.uk/government/publications/the-stephen-lawrence-inquiry

109 'Balwinder Rana at an anti-BNP march in 1993', *The Guardian*, 29 January 2016, https://www.theguardian.com/artanddesign/2016/jan/29/balwinder-rana-anti-bnp-march-welling-1993

110 Ford & Goodwin, 2014, p.188.

111 Thane, 2018, p.440.

112 Ibid, p.141.

113 Griffin, 2003, p.125.

114 Ibid, p.127.

115 Ibid.

116 See *BBC News*, 24 February 1999, news.bbc.co.uk/1/hi/uk/285535.stm.

117 *The Independent*, 17 April 2018, www.independent.co.uk/news/uk/home-news/stephen-lawrence-murder-25-years-changed-a-nation-police-institutional-racism-macpherson-anniversary-a8307871.html.

118 Solomon Hughes, 'Immigration: Labour Puts Asylum in Focus', *Socialist Review*, July/August 2002, socialistreview.org.uk/265/immigration-labour-puts-asylum-focus.

119 Ibid.

120 Griffin, 2003, p.125

Ch6 **Love Music Hate Racism**

1   House of Commons Library. Electoral performance of the British National Party in the UK. See: researchbriefings.files.parliament.uk/documents/SN01982/SN01982.pdf.

2   Ibid.

3   Nick Griffin, North West Region and Andrew Brons, Yorkshire and Humber Region.

4   These included: Paul Samuels (Head of Atlantic Records), musician Pandit G (Asian Dub Foundation), Jay Strongman (Kiss FM DJ), grime artists Flowdan (Roll Deep) and DJ Target. A grime artist manager, Jamie Morris-Ley, a member of reggae band Misty in Roots (name unknown), Peter Jenner and Jerry Dammers.

5   Interview with Weyman Bennett, 10 July 2019.

6   Ibid

7   Interview with Lee Billingham, 4 August 2019.

8   Interview with Weyman Bennett, 10 July 2019.

9   Huddle, 2017, p.111.

10   See *BBC News Magazine:* news.bbc.co.uk/1/hi/magazine/7351610.stm

11   Ibid.

12   See: LMHR: www.lovemusichateracism.com.

13   *NME* (27 August 2002), www.nme.com/news/music/doves-73-1380536

14   Also playing were Mick Jones, The Stands, Billy Bragg, D Double E + Footsie Dirrty Doogz, 15 Family, N.A.S.T.Y.

Crew Red, Alert 80s, Matchbox B-Line Disaster, Goldie Lookin' Chain, Corey Johnson, Blade & Naydean Hardkaur, Bigga Fish plus a dance tent.

15   On the bill was Jerry Dammers, formerly of The Specials and indie bands Last Gang and Snap!

16   According to organisers the carnival: 'Cost nearly £400,000 to put on... Every band played for free and every penny raised came either from trade unions or donations from artists and individuals'. *Socialist Review:* socialistreview.org.uk/326/new-challenges-anti-fascism.

17   *Socialist Review*: socialistreview.org. uk/371/ten-years-loving-music-and-hating-racism.

18   See *BBC*: news.bbc.co.uk/1/hi/ magazine/7351610.stm [retrieved, 20/05/2019].

19   The *New Statesman*: www.newstatesman.com/arts-and-culture/2008/05/ love-music-festival-racism.

20   Ibid.

21   Melanie Baddeley, Stephen Batkin, Michael Coleman, Mark Leat, David Marfleet, Phillip Sandland, Tony Simmonds, Alby Walker, Ellie Walker.

22   LMHR: www.lovemusichateracism. com/local-groups/. [retrieved, 20/05/2019].

23   Ibid.

24   These included: Lee Jasper (Ken Livingstone's race relations advisor), Labour MP Diane Abbott, Labour councillor Kumar Murshid and NAAR's Sabby Dhalu, also left organisations Socialist Action and Students Assembly Against Racism.

25   Affiliation came from the TUC and many individual unions: FBU, UNISON, NUT, UNITE, CWU and PCS. Support also came from the Muslim Council of Britain and the Jewish Council for Racial Equality. The steering committee consisted of Labour Party members, Lee Jasper and Sabby Dhalu and the SWP's Weyman Bennett.

26   *NME* (27 August 2002), www.nme. com/news/music/doves-73-1380536. 558

27   *Socialist Review* (November 2013), socialistreview.org.uk/385/anti-fascism-and-spirit-united-front.

28   Ibid.

29   See Richardson, 2004 and also *Get Shot of the Lot of Them: Election Reporting of Muslims in British Newspapers, Patterns of Prejudice,* Volume 43 (London, 2009).

30   *The Guardian:* www.theguardian. com/commentisfree/2018/apr/27/ islamophobia-not-british-press-issue-got-to-be-kidding, See also National Union of Journalists: www.nuj.org.uk/ islamophobia.

31   Of the popular vote the Labour Party won: 43 percent in 1997, 40 percent in 2001 and 35 percent in 2005. See House of Commons Information Office: www.parliament.uk.

32   Cyprus, Czech Republic, Estonia, Hungary, Latvia, Lithuania, Malta, Poland, Slovakia and Slovinia. The admission of these countries into the EU meant citizens of these countries, could now travel to, and work in, all EU nations.

33   Trilling, 2013, p.120.

34   Thane, 2018, pp.440-442.

35   Questions such as: 'When did British film studios flourish'? 'Was Anne of Cleves a Spanish princess'? and 'How long does it take to give blood'? See: www.test-questions.com/life-in-the-uk-test-39.php.

36   A clear example of this tactic has been the campaign over Asian grooming gangs in the Yorkshire area. See Novara Media: novaramedia.com/2019/06/12/ child-sexual-exploitation-asian-grooming-gangs-and-the-left/. Also, Counterfire: www.counterfire.org/ articles/opinion/19930-the-far right-grooming-gangs-and-racist-lies.

37   European Election Results 2004 available at data.gov.uk/dataset/ d912d859-ad28-46cf-891f-f1762c8c24ff/ european-election-results-2004.

38   Trilling, 2013,, p.131.

39   Ibid.

40   researchbriefings.files.parliament. uk/documents.

41   Even, the leader of the opposition David Cameron was moved to say this slogan sounded like the National Front. See BBC: news.bbc.co.uk/1/hi/ uk_politics/7097837.stm.

42   This tactic was part of the BNP 'Activist Handbook'. Trilling, 2013, p.134.

43   Ibid.

44   Andrew Brons history of fascist involvement goes all the way back to Colin Jordan and the National Socialist Movement in the 1960s and has been involved in every manifestation of it ever since.

45   House of Commons Library. Electoral performance of the British National Party in the UK. See: researchbriefings.files.parliament.uk/documents.

46   Although overall, they still secured over 500,000 votes nationwide. researchbriefings.files.parliament.uk/documents.

47   See *Socialist Worker:* socialistworker.co.uk/art/20507/BNPs+Barking+housing+myths+demolished.

48   Ibid.

49   The *Independent:* www.independent.co.uk/news/uk/politics/how-the-bnp-is-gaining-ground-in-barking-with-a-campaign-of-lies-and-distortions-474853.htm.

50   www.24housing.co.uk/news/uk-social-housing-crisis-is-fuelling-bnp-progress/

51   Trilling, 2013, p.177.

52   Ibid.

53   See p.41 of this book for Jeffery Hamms quote.

54   The Labour Party 2010 general election manifesto also carried a section entitled: 'Crime and Immigration' implying the two are linked, another favourite far right association. Trilling, 2013, p.179.

55   Hodge had also stated that 8/10 local people intended to vote for the BNP for which she was again reprimanded by the Labour party. UAF canvassing returns showed 60 percent of voters said they were anti-BNP. See: uaf.org.uk.

56   UAF: uaf.org.uk/2010/05/hodge-unite-against-fascism-'vital'-to-beating-bnp's-griffin-in-barking/.

57   Ibid.

58   *The Guardian*, 4 May 2012: www.theguardian.com/commentisfree/2012/may/04/bnp-local-elections-electoral-force-finished.

59   All of whom have since dissolved.

60   *The Guardian,* 20 October 2009: www.theguardian.com/politics/2009/oct/20/bnp-membership-list-wikileaks.

61   Spreadsheet obtained from LMHR organiser Lee Billingham. Interview 4 August 2019.

62   *The Guardian*, 4 May 2012, www.theguardian.com/commentisfree/2012/may/04/bnp-local-elections-electoral-force-finished,

63   Ibid.

64   *Socialist Review*, June 2007, socialistreview.org.uk/315/aint-music-nazis-ears

65   *Socialist Review*, November 2013, socialistreview.org.uk/385/anti-fascism-and-spirit-united-front.

66   Trilling, 2013, pp.183-184.

67   This 'multi-culturalism' will be discussed later.

68   Tommy Robinson was a one-time leader of notorious Luton casual hooligan firm MIGs (Men In Gear) who were involved in sustained acts of football related violence across the country and in particular against the local Asian community in Luton in the early 2000's.

69   He also would later on became vice-chairman of the neo-fascist British Freedom Party after they split from Griffin and the BNP in 2010. Yaxley-Lennon's 'right-hand' man and co-founder of the EDL was Kevin Carroll, also an ex-member of the BNP.

70   Notably 'Casuals United' closely affiliated to the EDL whose motto was 'One Nation, One Enemy, One Firm'. They attempted to organise warring football firms into a national 'army' to oppose the 'Islamification of Britain'.

71   Hewitt, 2004 p.154.

72   See Weight, 2013; Elms, 2005; Nayak, & Kehily, 2008 and Hewitt, 2004.

73   The EDL had over 90,000 members on its Facebook page. See Alessio & Meredith, 2014, p.104.

74   *Socialist Review*, May 2010, socialistreview.org.uk/347/edl-divisions-develop. *Socialist Review* is the monthly magazine of the SWP.

75   Corner, 1975.

76   *Socialist Review*, May 2010, socialistreview.org.uk/347/edl-divisions-develop.

77   Trotsky, 1972, p.27.

78   Opposition to a perceived decadence in society, palingenesis, the rebirth

of nation, ultra-nationalism, the sub-sumption of the individual to a highly centralised state and anti-commu-nism.

79 See Gordon, 1984. Also, the *Jew-ish Chronical*, 29 December 2017: www.thejc.com/news/world/when-jews-backed-a-fascist-mussoli-ni-king-victor-emmanel-1.451099.

80 edlreview.blogspot.com/2012/04/edl-leader-threatens-whole-british.html.

81 The Quilliam Foundation was a think tank set up by Maajid Nawaz in 2008 which claimed to counter 'Islamic extremism'. It dissolved in 2021. *The Guardian*, 12 October 2013: https://www.theguardian.com/uk-news/2013/oct/12/tommy-robinson-quilliam-founda-tion-questions-motivation

82 *The Sun:* www.thesun.co.uk/news/8493245/tommy-robinson-pro-testers-gather-outside-bbc-as-anti-fascists-shout-racist-scum/, .

83 *Socialist Review:* socialistreview.org.uk/362/fighting-fascism-cable-street-1936-tower-hamlets-2011.

84 *Socialist Review:* socialistreview.org.uk/326/new-challenges-anti-fascism. .

85 Although in the north west of England UAF/LMHR with trade unions, faith groups and local activists were at the centre of the 'Griffin Must Go 'campaign conducted over several years. Nick Griffin and Andrew Brons both lost their seats in the 2014 EU election.

86 Interview with Mike Simons, 26 July 2018.

87 See www.europarl.europa.eu/elections2014-results/en/election-re-sults-2014.html.

88 *The Guardian*, 26 May 2014: www.theguardian.com/politics/2014/may/26/ukip-european-elections-po-litical-earthquake.

89 Farage is of course no such thing. Public school educated, ex-merchant banker and now career politician, Farage is the opposite of what he pro-fesses.

90 *The Guardian*, 28 November 2017, www.theguardian.com/uk-news/2017/nov/28/hostile-en-vironment-the-hardline-home-of-fice-policy-tearing-families-apart.

91 *The Guardian*, 22 April 2018: www.theguardian.com/uk-news/2018/apr/22/hostile-environment-land-lords-check-immigration-status-un-der-coalition-government.

92 LMHR spokesperson Zak Cochrane interview in *Voice* magazine, 28 January 2019: www.voicemag.uk/interview/4978/interview-love-mu-sic-hate-racism

93 Interview with Paul Samuels, 8 April 2019.

94 Ibid.

95 *New York Times*, 22 January 2011, www.nytimes.com/2016/01/22/opin-ion/the-eight-second-attention-span.html.

96 *Socialist Review*: socialistreview.org.uk/444/love-music-hate-racism.

97 Paul Samuels interview, 8 April 2019.

98 This link had already happened organically as rapper and Ivor Novello award winner 'Dave' had already featured footballer Raheem Sterling in his video 'Black'. An attempt is being made to get Chelsea footballer Callum Hudson Odoi and rapper Tinie Tem-per and have a conversation about race and their sporting and musical journeys.

99 Paul Samuels interview, 8 April 2019

100 Conversely, there are some 'metal bands' who have expressed interest in getting involved. Paul Samuels inter-view, 8 April 2019.

101 Interview with Mike Simons, 18 August 2020.

102 Government statistics show that for BAME groups, there are still higher levels of unemployment, overcrowd-ing in housing and you are nine times as likely to be stopped and searched by the police if you are black than white. www.ethnicity-facts-figures.service.gov.uk.

103 Specifically, music with a backing track, rather than a live band.

104 *Daily Mail*: www.dailymail.co.uk/news/article-6365489/Harriet-Harman-attacked-claiming-drill-music-knife-crime.html.

105 *Music Culture:* musicculturenews.com/2019/02/05/skengdo-and-am-the-uk-drill-rappers-sentenced-for-performing-their-music/.

106 The injunction remained in place

for two years until January 2021, after which they returned to making music. *DJ Mag*, 15 January 2021: https://djmag.com/news/injunction-banning-skengdo-am-lifted-after-two-years

107   *New Statesman:* www.newstatesman.com/culture/music-theatre/2018/06/treating-drill-rappers-terrorists-colossal-mistake.

108   *Statistica* website: www.statista.com/statistics/519308/eu-referendum-voting-intention-in-uk-by-age/.

109   Interview with Mike Simons, 18 August 2020.

110   Nevertheless, it is true that around the country there were local LMHR groups who did support Corbyns campaign and were involved in gigs and fund raisers for the Labour Party.

111   Amongst those performing at the festival were: headliners, Clean Bandit, Glen Matlock, Declan McKenna, DVTN, Feminist Jukebox, Hookworms, Jermain Jackman, Rae Morris, Potent Whisper, Nia Wyn, Reverend and The Makers, Sam Fender, She Drew The Gun, and The Magic Numbers.

112   *The Guardian*, 16 June 2018, https://www.theguardian.com/politics/2018/jun/16/labour-live-for-the-few-not-the-many

113   *Total Politics*, 25 February 2020, https://www.totalpolitics.com/articles/diary/richard-burgon-praises-labour-live-event-he-calls-more-party-backed-festivals

114   *The Jewish Chronical,* 12 September 2019, www.thejccom/news/uk/tuc-congress-votes-overwhelmingly-for-israel-boycott-jeremy-corbyn-palestine-palestinians-bds-1.488509

115   *The Guardian,* 20 May 2019, www.theguardian.com/world/2019/may/20/racism-on-the-rise-since-brexit-vote-nationwide-study-reveals,.

116   *The Times*, 30 march 2018, https://www.thetimes.co.uk/article/premier-league-clubs-warned-over-far-right-football-lads-alliance-0mgq2lppv

117   One such post argued for Dianne Abbott to be deported in order to spend more time with her 'primates'. *Socialist Review* (May 2018) socialistreview.org.uk/435/all-out-stop-racists-organising.

118   *The Guardian*, 17 march 2017, www.theguardian.com/world/2018/mar/17/football-lads-alliance-secret-facebook-page-racism-violence-sexism.

119   Anne Marie Waters is an ex-UKIP member who formed Britain First 'to fill the space left by the BNP'. The organisation contains a collection of Holocaust deniers, rabid Islamophobes and ex-BNP members.

120   Paxton, 2009.

121   Trilling, 2013, p.129.

122   *The Independent*, 22 May 2019, www.independent.co.uk/news/uk/home-news/un-poverty-austerity-uk-universal-credit-report-philip-alston-a8924576.html,

123   *Manchester Evening News*, 26 May 2019, www.manchestereveningnews.co.uk/news/greater-manchester-news/tommy-robinson-concedes-defeat-european-16335733.

124   Ibid.

Conclusion

1   Widgery, 1986, p.53.

2   *BBC Panorama*, 'White Defence League', 13 April 1959, youtube: www.youtube.com/watch?v=olJl2PMUfwY.

3   Andy Dangerfield, 'Did music fight racism?' *BBC News Magazine,* 24 April 2008, news.bbc.co.uk/1/hi/magazine/7351610.stm.

4   Griffin, 2008, p.103.

5   Ibid.

6   Thurlow, 2009, p.105.

7   Copsey, 2016, p.101.

8   Beckman, 1993, p.70.

9   Copsey, 2009, p.108.

10   Ibid.

11   Ibid.

12   Copsey, 2016, p.115.

13   Lizzie Dearden, 'The Sun and Daily Mail accused of 'fuelling prejudice' in report on rising racist violence and hate speech in UK', *Independent*, 8 October 2016, https://bit.ly/3hTjKoq

14   Fraser Nelson, 'How Maggie's 'swammped' comment crushed the National Front', *The Spectator*, 29 October 2014, blogs.spectator.co.uk/2014/10/

how-maggies-swamped-comment-crushed-the-national-front/

15   Thurlow. 2009, p.256.

16   Interview with Peter Hain, 23 July 2018. See also Goodyer, 2009 and Renton, 2009.

17   Gilroy, 1987 p.131.

18   Interviews with Peter Hain, 23 July 2018 and then shadow home secretary Diane Abbott, 13 July 2019.

19   The term has also been used loosely and erroneously to describe political leaders including Saddam Hussein, Margaret Thatcher, Donald Trump and Nigel Farage.

20   In April 2018 the Campaign Against Antisemitism's Joseph Glasman implicitly compared Corbyn's leadership of the Labour Party to the rise of Adolf Hitler. Labour MP Ruth George compared Tory MP Amber Rudd to Hitler in 2016. Veteran MP Ken Livingstone was suspended from the Labour party for claiming that Hitler had supported Zionism.

21   Gilroy, 1987, p.118.

22   See *Temporary Hoarding* issues 5, 6, and 9. Ironically, an opposite criticism levelled at ANL/RAR at the time was there were too many articles about broader issues such as systemic racism.

23   Griffin, 2008, pp.121-122.

24   Thurlow, 2009, p.262.

25   Marx, 1985.

26   How political consciousness is changed is discussed at length by Gramsci, 2018.

27   Although Hain had joined the Labour Party in the autumn of 1977.

28   Goodyer, 2009, p.24.

29   Evan Smith's work has begun to explore this relationship as well. See Smith, 2017 and Smith, 2008.

30   Sherwood, 1999.

31   Goodyer, 2009, p.26.

32   Copsey, 2009, p.124.

33   Street, cited in Goodyer. 2009, p.89.

34   Goodyer, 2009, p.89.

35   Street, 1997, p.280.

36   Frith & Street, 1992.

37   Frith & Street cited in Goodyer, 2009, p.29.

38   Matthew Worley, 'Shot by Both Sides: Punk, Politics and the End of 'Consensus'', *Contemporary British History*, 26:3 (September 2012) p.345, www.researchgate.net/publication/262904506_Shot_By_Both_Sides_Punk_Politics_and_the_End_of_'Consensus'.

39   Ibid.

40   Goodyer, 2009, p.63.

41   Renton, 2019, p.76.

42   Goodyer, 2009, p.28.

43   Street, 2011, p.88.

44   'Arguments certainly did arise between the different participants within RAR, but it is hard to find any compelling evidence of systematic interference from the SWP'. Goodyer, 2009, p.63.

45   This quote has also been attributed to poet Vladimir Mayakovsky and playwright Bertolt Brecht.

46   Fumi Okiji, 2018, p.72.

47   Adorno, 2001, p.77. Italian Marxist Antonio Gramsci also wrote extensively on culture and 'cultural hegemony' arguing that no prevailing culture can ever be completely hegemonic, even under the most brutal dictatorships. 'Counter-hegemonic' cultures exist and alternate ways of 'thinking and doing' have revolutionary potential because they run counter to the dominant power. For Gramsci, these cultures could be, for instance, trade unions or folk groups. See Gramsci, 2018. Stuart Hall developed Gramsci's ideas further and suggested that counter-hegemonic cultures may be found in youth subcultures, for instance, punk or Rastafarianism. See Hall & Jefferson, 2006.

48   Brocken, 2003, p.92.

49   Vahasalo, 2016.

50   Widgery, 1986, p.55.

51   Worley, op.cit., p7. See also Benjamin Piekut, 'Music for Socialism, London 1977', *Twentieth Century Music*, 16:1 (February 2019) pp.67-93, https://www.researchgate.net/publication/331781347_Music_for_Socialism_London_1977.

52   Ibid.

53   Ibid.

54   Widgery, 1986, p.87.

55   The Clash: www.theclash.com

56   The most obvious case in point being Jimmy Pursey and New Wave band

Sham 69. Not a skinhead band, but a band with a skinhead following; not a 'political' band but a band with a (right-wing) political following. The endless speculation over Pursey's participation in the first ANL carnival was ended when he appeared onstage with The Clash to perform their encore of White Riot. Whilst Pursey's lyrics may have dealt with the angst of teenage working-class life—boredom, unemployment, violence and crime—they lacked the relative political sophistication of Joe Strummer, Tom Robinson, Elvis Costello and later Paul Weller.

57   Smith, 2017, p.11.

58   See Kaufmann, 2011.

59   *Evening Standard,* 16 June 2005, www.standard.co.uk/showbiz/geldof-u-turn-over-live8-7173120.html.

60   Margaret Thatcher supported Band Aid because its emphasis was on individuals giving money. "'What fascinated me was this' she told *Smash Hits,* 'it was not why doesn't the government give more? but 'what can I do as a person'?" *Channel 4 News,* 11 April 2013, www.channel4.com/news/margaret-thatcher-pop-music-band-aid-geldof-protest-songs.

61   Figures for black deaths from, Peter Fryer, 2010, p.395.

62   Redhead, 1993, p.3.

63   *Fred Perry,* 'Proud Boy's Statement', 24 September 2020, https://help.fredperry.com/hc/en-us/articles/360013674918-Proud-Boys-Statement

64   Angela McRobbie discusses this in her work *The Aftermath of Feminism.* See McRobbie, 2008.

65   *Office of National Statistics,* Marriages in England and Wales 2016, https://bit.ly/3r1TACR.

66   In their 2006 work *Resistance through Rituals,* Stuart Hall and Tony Jefferson identified youth as between the age of 16 to 21. Hall & Jefferson, 2006.

67   See *Office of National Statistics*, Drug Use, Alcohol and Smoking, www.ons.gov.uk/peoplepopulationandcommunity/healthandsocialcare/drugusealcoholandsmoking/.

68   *BBC News*, 'UK nightclubs closing at alarming rate', 10 August 2015, https://www.bbc.co.uk/news/newsbeat-33713015.

69   J. Patrick Williams, 'Authentic Identities: Straightedge Subculture, Music and the Internet', *Journal of Contemporary Ethnography*, 35:2 (April 2006) https://doi.org/10.1177/0891241605285100

70   Coffee shop culture, shopping centres, goths, emos, steampunks, drill and grime all co-exist in 2021 as communal activities whether they are subcultural or not.

71   Goodyer, 2009, p.89.

72   Widgery, 1986, p.8.

73   *The Independen*t, 25 April 2008, www.independent.ie/entertainment/music/rock-against-racism-remembering-that-gig-that-started-it-all-26441221.html

74   Rachel, 2016, p.170.

75   Ibid, p.226.

Index